CLASSIC RESEARCHES IN GENERAL CHEMISTRY

Series Editor · HAROLD HART, MICHIGAN STATE UNIVERSITY

LIQUIDS

CLASSIC RESEARCHES IN GENERAL CHEMISTRY

DALE DREISBACH · HIRAM COLLEGE

AND

SOLUTIONS

HOUGHTON MIFFLIN COMPANY · BOSTON

NEW YORK · ATLANTA · GENEVA, ILL. · DALLAS · PALO ALTO

To Frank Hovorka

Cover Photo: Liquids, being intermediate between the highly ordered solids and the randomly dispersed gases, are in continual turmoil. Liquid molecules are driven first this way, then that, torn between the attracting forces of cohesion and the separating actions of repulsion and kinetic activity, in addition to being thwarted at every turn by spatial requirements. The illustration on the cover portrays this turmoil. The particles remain in the condensed state but there is no indication of an ordered structure. Pictured is a viscoelastic liquid being stirred and exhibiting the unexpected property of perpendicular stresses forcing the liquid up the stirring rod. An example of such a liquid is a solution of a linear polymer in a liquid hydrocarbon. Another unexpected property of this solution is that it has an elongation many times greater than that of ordinary rubber. (Courtesy Esso Research and Engineering Company.)

EDITOR'S INTRODUCTION

The accelerated pace of scientific discovery which characterizes our time has necessarily eliminated the historical approach to the study of science. Elementary texts in chemistry and physics cannot detail the often tortuous arguments, hypotheses, and experiments upon which currently accepted theories and facts are built. The result is often simply an outline of where we stand today, with only a few cogent arguments or supporting experiments enumerated. During the continuous distillation and condensation (which, indeed, are necessary to prevent elementary texts from becoming encyclopedic), many discoveries, when described in textbook fashion, lose their freshness.

But scientific discovery is a thrilling and exciting process, and a zest for it should be imparted to the beginning student. This series of paperbacks was initiated with the view that much might be done toward this end if the beginner could read about key discoveries in science in the words of the men who wrote of them. The research worker who contributes to the advancing front of science must read of discoveries as they appear in the scientific journals; he cannot wait until they become the subject matter of textbooks. It would seem advisable, then, to introduce the neophyte to the original literature as early in his scientific career as possible. The difficulty encountered in doing this lies in the student's lack of a suitable background necessary for him to profit from being turned loose amongst the journals with a list of references to read. Indeed, he may be dissuaded altogether from the sciences if subjected to such a "trial by fire" procedure. It was therefore decided that original papers, or portions thereof, be selected and presented with sufficient editorial comment to set the stage for each paper and to clarify passages which might be troublesome to the beginner. For the most part, the great scientists are allowed to speak for themselves.

The non-science major who takes a year of college chemistry or physics as part of his liberal education will find that this little book makes fascinating reading not only because the scientists come alive on its pages, but also because he can learn much about the use of logic and scientific method. But foremost, this book will make excellent supplementary reading for the professional student of chemistry or physics who wants to understand in greater detail the basis for our modern theories of the structure of liquids and solutions.

HAROLD HART

v

PREFACE

Early textbooks of physical chemistry as well as those of general chemistry and physics of the same era had adequate descriptions of the liquid state of matter. Discussions centered around physical properties and their correlations, but little was done about a theory of structure for liquids. Through the years, more and more attention was given to the relatively simpler solids and gases and less to liquids so that recent texts have very little coverage of this complex state of matter. Ironically, important developments during the last three decades have pushed liquid research to the forefront at a time when students are relatively unaware of the opportunities in the field. An important objective of this book is to introduce the reader to some of the original papers in order to renew interest in liquids.

The first important equation of state for liquids and gases was derived by van der Waals in 1873 and much effort has been expended in attempts to describe liquids in terms of the known makeup of gases. The first major break from this approach came with the publication by Debye and Menke (1930) of a classic article on liquid structure which established by experiment and theory the need for a closer look at liquid-solid relationships. Their findings set the stage for a flurry of papers on proposed structures for liquids. Among these were the cluster concepts of J. E. Mayer, the model structures of Frenkel, Eyring, and Lennard-Jones and Devonshire, and the molecular distribution functions of groups of molecules developed by Kirkwood, Bogolyubov (he calls them correlation functions), and Born and Green.

According to Abel, the most effective route to understanding in any field is "by studying the masters, not their pupils." An outstanding confirmation of this contention may be seen in the translated article of Debye and Menke cited above. Also reproduced are original writings by leading researchers as Eyring, Lennard-Jones and Devonshire, Kirkwood (in the Appendix), Bernal, Metropolis and collaborators, Alder and Wainwright, and Hildebrand, among others. By having access to these papers, it is hoped that the readers will gain a greater insight into the subject and that they in turn will want to undertake original investigations.

Because of the general neglect of liquids in recent years greater emphasis is placed on this state of matter than on solutions. The fascinating history of solutions of electrolytes is sketched briefly, climaxing in the Debye-Hückel interionic attraction theory. The student is referred to the cluster theory, such as described in H. L. Friedman's *Ionic Solution Theory*, for recent developments in electrolytes. There is little in the way of a spectacular breakthrough in the field of solutions of non-electrolytes. Reasonably steady progress has been made since the pioneering work of Gibbs, Raoult, van't Hoff, and Ostwald in the last quarter of the nineteenth century. Professor Van Ness in his *Classical Thermodynamics of Non-Electrolyte Solutions* presents a systematic treatment of these mixtures.

The author has received immeasurable help from the many books and articles that have been consulted in his writing. It is a pleasure to mention Professor Barker's *Lattice Theories of the Liquid State*, J. I. Frenkel's *Kinetic Theory of Liquids*, Born and Green's *A General Kinetic Theory of Liquids*, Professor Green's *The Molecular Theory of Fluids*, Professor Rowlinson's *Liquids and Liquid Mixtures*, I. Z. Fisher's *Statistical Theory of Liquids* with a supplement by Rice and Gray, Hildebrand and Scott's *Regular Solutions*, Professor Dole's *Introduction to Statistical Thermodynamics*, Lewis and Randall's *Thermodynamics*, revised by Pitzer and Brewer, Professor Moore's *History of Chemistry*, Professor Partington's *A Short History of Chemistry*, and Professor Findlay's *A Hundred Years of Chemistry*.

I wish to express my gratitude to many associates, friends, and students, to Charlene McAfee and John and Paul Dreisbach, in particular, for the assistance they have given in writing this book. Of especial help were L. E. Balch and D. B. Moss who read the manuscript and gave many valuable suggestions during its preparation. I am deeply indebted for the untiring and skillful help given me by Karen Weltzien Oliver and Martha Orcutt Hugus who helped search the literature, typed the manuscript, prepared the drawings, and reread the final copy. I am happy to express my appreciation to the editorial staff of Houghton Mifflin for their help and for their understanding of the problems encountered in writing.

Dale Dreisbach
Hiram, Ohio

CONTENTS

▪ PART ONE

Theories and Concepts
of the Liquid State

It is difficult to overemphasize the importance of the liquid state, since life as we know it cannot exist without liquids. Although men have studied the liquid state for centuries, surprisingly, the first published theory on liquid structure did not appear until the early 1930's. Unfortunately, in recent years publications in general physical science have largely neglected the liquid state at the very time of a great upsurge in research in this field. The most pressing need at present is for a suitable theory based on sound assumptions covering all aspects of the liquid state. Logically, uncomplicated substances such as liquid argon would be described first, after which any resulting theory could presumably be modified to handle more complex liquids. Considerable effort has already been expended in the direction of a formal mathematical analysis leading to simple liquid theory, and it is probable that an acceptable, rigorous theory will result from such an approach.

Other less formal approaches based on models have been developed to the point of considerable usefulness in that they may be applied to many types of liquids with reasonable success. Moreover, it is possible to modify these model theories to fit experimental facts. This method of attack is both interesting and rewarding, even though the expectation of developing a strict theory in this way is quite limited. Studies are centered around the spatial arrangement of molecules, the investigation of which gives rise to many and varied possibilities. Nevertheless, it is difficult to determine the exact pattern of the most probable molecular distribution. Models will be discussed in considerable detail since the greatest effort toward a solution to the problem of liquid structure has been in this direction.

It will be instructive to turn our attention first to the various ideas that have been advanced during the last several decades to explain the behavior of liquids.

Many different theories of liquid structure can be found in the literature, some with occasional points in common, yet none of these theories provides an acceptable answer to the characterization of the liquid state. Since there is insufficient agreement among investigators to permit discarding any of the concepts which have been proposed, most of these theories will be included in this work, although particular attention will be focused on several better-known ideas.

CHAPTER 1

The States of Matter

THE THREE STATES OF MATTER

Matter in its many forms has been the subject of inquiry from the very beginning of human curiosity. Observation and investigation through the years have led to the present system of classifying matter as gas, liquid, or solid, according to various physical characteristics.

The general apportionment of molecules in each of the three physical states should be considered when investigating liquid structure. Figure 1 indicates roughly the relative volumes occupied by a given number of molecules in each state. It also illustrates the lack of order in gases and the definite order found in crystalline solids. Intuitively, it might be assumed that it is possible to analyze the crystalline state theoretically, a task that has met with reasonable success. At the other extreme, in ideal gases essentially complete disorder or randomness is found, but here, too, a satisfactory analysis is possible. Non-ideal gases and vapors are somewhat more difficult to describe and dense gases and liquids have not yet been satisfactorily characterized.

The Gaseous State

In the gaseous state the discrete particles or molecules of matter are spatially separated from one another. The molecules possess freedom of motion and their movement is essentially continuous and random in nature. Since each molecule is a separate entity with considerable space around it, the behavior of any given particle is reasonably independent of other particles. The distances of separation are great enough so that the frequency of collision is low even though the average speed of air particles is about 500 meters per second. All

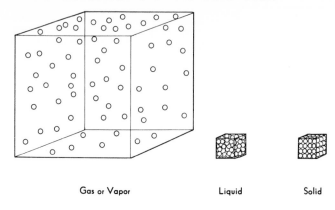

Gas or Vapor   Liquid   Solid

FIGURE 1

An indication of the distribution of molecules and the relative volumes occupied by matter in its three states.

particles in nature are mutually attracted to each other, but usually these attractive forces play only a minor role in the behavior of molecules in a gas. Being free from these interactions, all gases respond in essentially the same manner to any small impressed force. For example, Boyle's Law depicting the effect of pressure on the volume of a gas applies to all gases regardless of their chemical nature.

Equation of State

The gaseous state is satisfactorily characterized by the kinetic theory, which culminated from an extensive array of experimental and theoretical studies in this field. The development of this theory requires certain assumptions such as the stipulation of continual motion of the molecules. Ordinarily, little is said about the origin of this motion, even though it is certainly an intriguing problem. This basic kinetic theory makes it possible to correlate the laws of Boyle, Charles, Gay-Lussac, Dalton, Avogadro, and Graham.

By combining the laws of Boyle and Charles the well-known equation of state

$$PV = RT \tag{1}$$

is obtained. This equation successfully relates the three quantities, pressure, volume, and temperature, for an ideal gas. Deviations from the idealized relations embodied in the kinetic theory and in Equation (1) increase as the temperature of a gas is lowered. Many proposals have been made to alter the equation in order to allow for these deviations. The resulting relations are also equations of state.[1] Bernoulli (1738) was the first to recognize the effect of the actual volume occupied by the molecules themselves. To account for this factor, Equation (1) can be altered to

$$P(V - b) = RT \quad \text{or} \quad PV = RT + Pb \tag{2}$$

where b is a constant representing the volume of the molecules. More terms may be added to increase the effectiveness of the equation. Thus, experimental data may be represented by a **virial equation** (Kamerlingh-Onnes, 1899) of the form

$$PV = RT\left(1 + \frac{B(T)}{V} + \frac{C(T)}{V^2} + \cdots\right) \tag{3}$$

The constants B, C, etc., are functions of temperature and are called, respectively, the second, third, etc., *virial coefficients*. These coefficients are important in interpreting data related to liquid and also gas structure. Although virial coefficients are determined by experiment, it is possible to correlate them with theory. Factors other than the volume of the molecules cause deviations from the ideal gas law; they, too, are allowed for in these constants.

There are two formal theoretical approaches to an equation of state for liquids and dense gases.[2] One is to consider all the attractions between the molecules in terms of their potential energies. The total potential energy may be obtained by summing all the values between pairs of molecules to provide a *configurational integral*, Q. The second method involves choosing a molecule as the central unit and determining the *radial distribution function*, $g(r)$, of the molecules around this central one. In each case equations are obtained which may be directly related to pressure and, hence, to the virial equation. Finally, the terms in the virial equation are identified with the functions in the theoretical equations in attempts to interpret the nature of gases and liquids. These theoretical equations form the bases for most of the developments related to liquid structure theory.

The most famous equation of state is

$$\left(P + \frac{a}{V^2}\right)(V - b) = RT \tag{4}$$

first derived on the basis of theory by van der Waals. The constants a and b are characteristic for each gas, and the term, a/V^2, is designed to take care of the attraction between molecules. The magnitude of this attractive force

[1] Over one hundred equations of state have been reported in the literature; most of them are modifications of van der Waals' equation. Dieterici proposed the equation $P(V - b) = RTe^{-a/RTV}$ which gives superior results at higher pressures. He intended that the exponential factor should allow for the effect of molecular attraction.

[2] E. U. Condon and H. Odishaw (eds.), *Handbook of Physics* (New York: McGraw-Hill Book Company, Inc., 1958), pp. 5–46.

has recently been measured experimentally by Boris Derjaguin and Irene Abrikossova.[3] This intermolecular force is not the chemical bond that causes atoms to combine into molecules, but is a general force which tends to draw all matter together.

The Liquid State

As a gas is cooled, a point is reached at which there is a transition from the gaseous to the liquid state. If the pressure is adjusted properly, the gas will condense to a liquid with very little discontinuity in the properties of the substance. It is not easy to distinguish between matter as a gas and as a liquid at this unique critical point. The combination of critical temperature, critical pressure, and critical volume specifies the critical point which is characteristic for each substance. Temperature, not pressure, is the controlling factor in this transformation, since it is possible to prevent liquid formation by simply holding the temperature of the substance slightly above the critical value.

A more complicated equation than van der Waals' will be needed for the critical region. Benedict, Webb, and Rubin[4] proposed the following relation for dense fluids:

$$P = RTd + (B_0RT - A_0 - C_0/T^2)d^2 + (bRT - a)d^3 + agd^6$$
$$+ \frac{cd^3(1 + hd^2) \, exp \, (-hd^2)}{T^2} \qquad (5)$$

where d is the density of the material. This lengthy equation has eight constants, A_0, B_0, C_0, a, b, c, g, and h, which must be determined for each substance. It is logical to depict the properties of a liquid from the standpoint of deviant gas behavior since a liquid forms when deviations from ideal gas behavior are great. Some degree of success has been achieved in this direction. Although kinetic activity is greatly restricted, it continues to play a significant role in determining the behavior of liquids. Lowering the temperature reduces kinetic action, and this in turn permits the existing cohesive forces to hold the liquid material together in a dynamic but condensed condition. Solidification occurs at sufficiently low temperatures, and the resulting solids possess little kinetic activity, the crystal forces being in control.

Behavior of Liquids

Although the boiling point of a liquid is not a unique physical property, it is widely used and represents the upper temperature for most experimental in-

[3] B. V. Derjaguin and I. I. Abrikossova, *Zhur. Eksptl. i. Teoret. Fiz.*, **21**, 945 (1951); *Soviet Phys.-JETP*, **3**, 819 (1956); and B. V. Derjaguin, *Sci. Am.*, **203**, 47 (July, 1960).
[4] M. Benedict, G. W. Webb, and L. C. Rubin, *J. Chem. Phys.*, **8**, 334 (1940); **10**, 747 (1942); *Chem. Eng. Progr.*, **47**, 419, 449 (1951).

vestigations of this state of matter. The boiling point is well below the critical point, and on the absolute temperature scale it is roughly two-thirds of the critical temperature. Most liquids are studied at room temperature, which is usually well below the boiling point and hence far removed from the critical temperature and the gaseous state. As an illustration, a liquid boiling at 127° Celsius (400°K) might have the following hypothetical values on the absolute temperature scale (°Kelvin):

Critical temperature . . . . . 600°K (upper limit for this liquid)

Boiling point . . . . 400°K

Room temperature . . . . . 300°K

Freezing point . . . . . . 250°K

This indicates that the data for substances which are liquid at room temperature will ordinarily be determined much nearer the freezing point than the critical point. For this and other reasons, known properties of liquids might be expected to resemble solids rather than gases.

The Solid State

The solid state lends itself most readily to investigation. As early as 1669, Niels Stensen (Steno) discovered an orderly pattern in crystalline solids. He established the rule that the angle between lines drawn perpendicularly to two given faces of a crystal is constant for a particular substance. X-ray and electron beam studies of solids have substantiated and expanded the ideas of an orderly arrangement of particles in crystals so that the structure of solids is now fairly well understood. The theory of gases, as indicated earlier, is in a satisfactory state at present. The "in-between" state of liquids, however, remains to be properly characterized with regard to structure.

During the transition from solid to liquid there is a change in the physical structure of a substance. This melting process is accompanied by a definite increase in **enthalpy** (heat of fusion) which shows that there is a greater amount of energy in matter in the liquid state than in the solid state. Another quantity, **entropy**, indicates in a certain way the amount of heat energy in a system and also is a measure of the degree of disorder or randomness of the molecular motion in a body. The molecules in a solid are arranged in fixed orderly positions and have low entropy, whereas the molecules in a gas are free to move randomly and their entropy is high. As first deduced by T. W. Richards, the increase in entropy on normal melting for many monatomic crystalline solids is approximately 2 calories per gram formula weight. The corresponding entropy increase for the liquid-to-vapor transition is about 21 calories according to the experimental discovery of Frederick Trouton. Although other factors are involved, the increases of entropy in these two transitions show that the entropy of a substance is considerably higher in the gaseous state than in the solid form.

This observation agrees with the fact that there is extensive random molecular motion in a gas, whereas the particles of a solid have an ordered structure, with essentially none of the free motion found in gases.

SYSTEMS OF CLASSIFYING MATTER

In addition to the gas, liquid, and solid system of grouping substances, other classifications such as crystalline and non-crystalline or gaseous and condensed might be used. Metallurgists and crystallographers often use the crystalline and non-crystalline system to include crystalline solids as a class distinct from the other forms of matter. The other system sets gases aside as the unique phase. Although there is merit to all of these systems of classification, the method used does not in itself solve the problem of liquid structure. Classifications might, however, indicate directions of approach to theories of liquids, and in this way emphasize the comparison of a liquid to only one of the other states at a given time. For example, at temperatures not far removed from the freezing point, it may be simpler to relate liquids to solids. This approach is the basis of much of the current X-ray and neutron-scattering work that is being done on liquids.

WANTED: A THEORY OF LIQUID STRUCTURE

Since the structure of liquids is one of the important unsolved problems, those who may be considering a career in science would do well to investigate this very fascinating field. The fact that the structure of liquids is elusive results not from a lack of information, but rather from the great complexity of matter in this in-between state.

In his comprehensive treatise, Partington attests to the extensive study of the behavior of liquids by citing 11,758 references through June, 1950. He states also that "it is very probable that some important recent papers have been missed."[5] The literature includes such properties as density, thermal expansion, compressibility, viscosity, thermal conductivity, surface tension, specific heat, vapor pressure, freezing and boiling point, latent heats of vaporization and fusion, and critical constants. Although Partington indicates many correlations among these properties, he discusses the theory of the structure of liquids only briefly, believing that "this subject was still in an undeveloped state." Of course, any proposed theory must satisfy the experimental information relating to the physical and chemical properties of liquids.

The behavior of liquids results chiefly from the interplay between kinetic energy and intermolecular forces. In ideal gases only kinetic activity need be

---

[5] J. R. Partington, *Advanced Treatise on Physical Chemistry*, Vol. II: *Properties of Liquids* (London: Longmans, Green and Company, Inc., 1951).

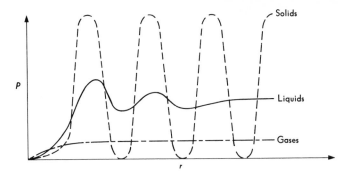

FIGURE 2

The extent of orderliness of molecular structure in the three states may be indicated by plotting the probability, P, of finding a second molecule at a distance, r, from a central molecule against the distance, r. Adapted from The International Dictionary of Applied Mathematics (Princeton: D. Van Nostrand Company, Inc., 1960), p. 610.

considered; in crystalline solids the intermolecular forces prevail; but in the case of liquids both factors must be taken into account. The expected kinetic activity of the molecules of liquids is constrained by the intermolecular forces which are in effect, but the latter are not sufficiently dominating to bring about the long-range order found in solids. There does not seem to be a suitable explanation for any postulated short-range order in liquids. The complex nature of liquids makes it necessary to introduce simplifying techniques in their analysis. In the majority of cases either mathematical approximations or structural models have been utilized in attempts to develop a theory for liquid structure.

The relative chaotic activity of molecules in the three physical states may be illustrated by considering the positions of molecules in space with respect to any given central molecule. If they are essentially rigid spherical units, the probability, P, of finding a second molecule at a distance, r, from the central one may be indicated by the distribution curves in Figure 2. The regularly spaced peaks for solids represent an orderly pattern of molecules. There is no indication of orderliness in dilute gases, but some vestige of it does appear in liquids. Information of this kind is applied in the kinetic theories of liquids which are discussed in Chapter 2.

CHAPTER 2

Clustering of Molecules

CLUSTER THEORY

A natural approach to depicting a liquid would be one which considers it to be derived from a gas, since the transition from the gaseous to the liquid state through the critical point is essentially continuous with little distinction between the two phases. J. S. Rowlinson discusses published material on critical phenomena at length and describes the lack of agreement on the actual positions of critical points in his book.[1] A gas or vapor below the critical temperature can be transformed to a liquid by merely raising the pressure to the proper value, less pressure being required at lower temperatures than at higher ones. The temperature at which the relatively low pressure of one atmosphere brings about condensation is a quantity of practical significance, since this is the normal boiling point. Regardless of pressure, liquids cannot be formed above the critical temperature because of the dominant kinetic activity. Since temperature is the critical factor and kinetic activity is dependent on temperature, an explanation of the behavior of liquids at and below their critical points might be expected to be related to their molecular motion as well as to their attraction.

A basic precept of the kinetic theory is the translational movement of molecules, which assigns the same average kinetic energy to all gases at a given temperature. This explains the similarities in the physical properties of various gases. The extensive space available and the motion of molecules in gases assure their separation except for the brief time of contact during collision. The chance of more than two molecules colliding simultaneously in a gas is very small because of their wide separation. The attractive force itself is rela-

---

[1] J. S. Rowlinson, *Liquids and Liquid Mixtures* (London: Butterworth and Company, 1959), Chap. 3.

tively insignificant, provided chemical reaction is ruled out and only simple van der Waals forces are considered. Since the average kinetic activity is the same for all molecules at a given temperature, it is necessary to look further for an explanation of the differences observed in the properties of various liquids. For a given substance, the mean speed of the molecules is the same in both the vapor and liquid states, but the mean energies of the molecules are different in the two states because there is a considerable negative potential of interaction between the liquid molecules. Intermolecular forces vary from substance to substance, so it would be logical to consider these forces as accounting for the differences in the physical properties of substances in the condensed states.

The tendency for gas molecules to remain together for a significant period of time after colliding becomes greater as the temperature is lowered. This results in the formation of clusters consisting of one, two, three, or more molecules. Following the work of Ursell (1927) and others, Mayer and his collaborators applied the cluster concept to the problems of condensation and the critical state.[2] The use of this concept made it possible to bypass the difficulties of computation encountered in the large number of possible configurations which would result if all the molecules were treated separately.

On the basis of chance, a certain number of molecules will be present in a given small region of a fluid at any specified time. It is possible to calculate this number for an ideal gas in random motion. For real gases, however, the normal attractive forces will tend to increase the number of neighbors around any one molecule within the region, thus producing clusters of molecules with restricted motions. As the temperature decreases, the size and number of clusters increase. Increased pressure also increases the number of clusters because the available space is decreased. Since kinetic action is rather violent in gases and vapors, these clusters are not permanently formed, but are continually losing and gaining molecules.

The mathematical development by Mayer led to a satisfactory description of the condensation of a saturated vapor into a liquid. Other investigators have added to his work, among them H. S. Green who has outlined the improved theory in his book on fluids.[3] The theory states that during condensation the individual clusters of a vapor coalesce and lose their identity. The liquid which results may be simply considered as one giant cluster: that is, many neighboring molecules about any given molecule. Unlike the behavior in gases, there is essentially no free interplay between individual clusters in liquids. This theory reasonably describes vapors and the process of condensation, but not liquids

---

[2] J. E. Mayer, *J. Chem. Phys.*, **5**, 67 (1937); J. E. Mayer and P. G. Ackermann, *ibid.*, **5**, 74 (1937).

[3] H. S. Green, *The Molecular Theory of Fluids* (Amsterdam: North-Holland Publishing Company, 1952), Chap. 4; (New York: Interscience Publishers, Inc., distributor). See also H. L. Friedman, *Ionic Solution Theory* (New York: Interscience Publishers, Inc., 1962), Part 1; I. Z. Fisher, *Statistical Theory of Liquids* (Chicago: University of Chicago Press, 1964), supplement by S. A. Rice and P. Gray.

or the mechanism of crystallization. It is evident that other modes of attack on the structure of liquids are needed. At this point, therefore, it is desirable to consider another proposed interpretation for the behavior of matter in the liquid state.

CYBOTACTIC STATE THEORY

Stewart and his co-workers studied the X-ray patterns of several different liquid alcohols consisting of rod-like or straight chain molecules and found evidence for two distinct intermolecular distances.[4] One value was essentially constant for all the different alcohol series; the other varied linearly with the length of the alcohol molecule. The constant quantity was interpreted as representing the perpendicular distance between more or less parallel, rod-like molecules. This idea suggested some degree of order in the way the alcohol molecules are arranged. The other quantity was related to the number of carbons in the chain, in that it showed a specific increase with each CH_2 group added to the molecule. There was little resemblance between the X-ray patterns of these liquids and those of the corresponding solids, however, which indicated that the scattering results for liquids do not arise from crystal fragments, but rather from temporary molecular space-array units. Stewart calls these units **cybotactic groups**. The remaining molecules between these groups are distributed in a random fashion. Since molecules randomly leave and re-enter the cybotactic groups, the over-all picture is one of essentially random structure. Because this behavior was found only in rod-like molecules and has not been observed in other types, it is not a general property of liquids. Considerable effort has been expended in attempts to develop the idea of the cybotactic state into a general theory for liquid structure, but these have met with little success.

Not only did X-ray scattering provide the essential information for the development of this theory, but X-rays in general have played an important role in many attempts to explain the nature of liquids. Since X-ray patterns of liquids exhibit features somewhat like those of crystalline solids, some investigators infer that there are solid-like aspects to liquids.

[4] G. W. Stewart and R. M. Morrow, *Phys. Rev.*, **30**, 232 (1927).

CHAPTER 3

X-Rays and the Solid-Like
Theory of Liquids

During the early experiments on the diffraction of X-rays by crystalline solids, investigators used amorphous materials for contrast to show the variation in X-ray patterns provided by different classes of materials. Liquids were among the amorphous substances they used, and although no distinct patterns were observed, the intensity of the scattered X-rays was not uniformly distributed as would be expected for substances devoid of structure. Both Debye and Ehrenfest thought this non-uniformity in X-ray patterns was the result of somewhat definite spacings of the molecules in liquids. Following this proposal, many suggestions were made in attempts to relate the structure of liquids to that of solids. Keesom and de Smedt appear to have been the first to suggest an incipient crystalline structure for liquids. At about the same time, Joffé published his concept of irregularities in crystalline solids, and shortly thereafter Frenkel considered the possibility of vacancies in liquids. Zernike and Prins (1927) assumed a statistically regular arrangement of molecules in the liquid state. These discoveries and suggestions all point to an ordered arrangement of molecules in a liquid.

In a container of volume, V, the chance of finding a particle in a small element of volume, dV, is dV/V. This element could be in the form of a spherical shell of thickness, dr, and at a distance, r, from a given particle. The element dV would then be given by $4\pi r^2 dr$. If the particle is an actual molecule, certain restrictions will be imposed. The molecule has significant dimensions and, since overlapping is prohibited for the most part, the centers of any two molecules will be separated by a distance of at least one diameter and repulsive forces may cause a greater separation. Simultaneously, attractive forces tend to cause grouping of the molecules. These restrictive factors may be lumped together into a quantity called the radial distribution function, W.[1] By using this quantity, the number of molecules in the above shell would be

$$\frac{N}{V} W 4\pi r^2 dr$$

where W, frequently denoted as $g(r)$, is a function of the distance, r, and N is the number of molecules in V.

Debye was among the first investigators to use X-rays in the elucidation of the structure of matter, and he and Menke carried out a classic study to provide experimental information about the nature of W. Their paper, which is presented below, was primarily responsible for the idea of order in liquids.

▼   "When radiating liquids by X-rays, one obtains a scattering picture representing the superposition of two different interference phenomena. If the intermolecular part can be separated from the intramolecular part, conclusions about the structure of the liquid can be drawn. Up to now the method used was first to find out by calculation something about the relative positions of the molecules, and to compare this theoretical result, even if only qualitatively, with the experimental results. Even with the simplest assumptions possible, namely, that the molecules behave like hard spheres, it has not been possible to carry out such calculations exactly. It therefore seemed indicated to us to carry out the procedure in the opposite direction, *i.e.*, to put the experimental results of the scattering first and to deduce from them, without any prejudice, the structure of the liquid. We reported about this procedure and gave some tentative results at the meeting (Gautagung) in Halle.

"Mercury, which, as a monatomic liquid, should give especially simple results, was first investigated.

"If a volume which contains N mercury atoms is irradiated and if the scattered radiation of the different single atoms did not interfere with one another, one would observe an intensity:

$$J = \frac{1 + \cos^2 \vartheta}{2} N\psi^2 \tag{1}$$

ψ^2 is a function of the angle ϑ between primary and secondary ray, which characterizes the scattering of the single atom (atom-form factor), while the factor $(1 + \cos^2 \vartheta)/2$ was introduced in order [to] account for the polarization occurring during scattering. The angular distribution of ψ^2 can either

---

[1] The nature of W is discussed by Morrell and Hildebrand on pp. 44–48.

be calculated according to Fermi or obtained from experimental data about the scattering of mercury vapor. It is, of course, assumed in the above equation that the correction due to the absorption in the irradiated volume has already been carried out. This correction becomes especially simple if one permits the primary ray to fall on a free surface of the liquid and investigates the radiation emitted by this surface. This is the reason why we have chosen this method of observation. The result of this experiment is not in agreement with Equation (1). As is well known, certain maxima and minima of intensity occur which should not occur according to Equation (1). The angle between primary and secondary ray was originally used as the variable; it is, however, more convenient to introduce not ϑ itself, but the quantity:

$$s = 2 \sin \frac{\vartheta}{2} \tag{2}$$

as the variable. One may then represent the result of the experiment in a purely experimental fashion by assuming:

$$J = \frac{1 + \cos^2 \vartheta}{2} N\psi^2 E(s) \tag{3}$$

in place of Equation (1). Here $E(s)$ is a function of s which can be determined purely by experiment. This function is represented in Figure 3 in accordance with our experiments; for higher values of s, E approaches unity. (That $E(s)$ could be represented for values which surpass $s = 2$ is based on the fact that the experiments, which were originally carried out with Cu-K_α-radiation, were later completed by experiments with Mo-K_α-radiation of shorter wave length.)

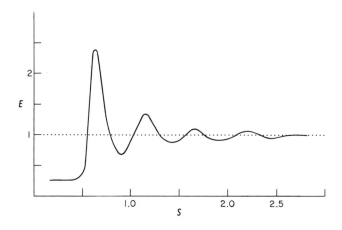

FIGURE 3

"The problem is to determine the structure of the liquid from the experimental curve $E(s)$. The structure can be characterized in the following manner. If two atoms within the liquid are marked and one thinks of oneself as moving along with one atom, which at the end of a distance r carries with it a volume element dS, the probability for the second atom being found with its center within dS can be written as:

$$W \frac{dS}{V} \qquad (4)$$

If V is the entire volume which may be used, $W = 1$ would mean that all distances (r) are of equal probability. In general, however, W will depend on r. If one succeeds in determining this probability function, the structure of the fluid will be determined. Let us first assume W as known. It can then be shown that the function $E(s)$ can be calculated according to the formula:

$$s[1 - E(s)] = 2 \frac{\lambda^3}{d^3} \int_0^\infty \rho[1 - W(\rho)] \sin 2\pi s\rho d\rho \qquad (5)$$

We have chosen for the variable not the distance r itself, but the ratio of distance to wave length:

$$\rho = \frac{r}{\lambda} \qquad (6)$$

The quantity d is defined by the equation:

$$Nd^3 = V \qquad (6')$$

d^3 therefore is the volume occupied on the average by one atom. However, matters are just reversed. W is not known as a function of ρ, but E is known as a function of s. Using Fourier's theorem, one can invert Equation (5) and one obtains:

$$\rho[1 - W(\rho)] = 2 \frac{d^3}{\lambda^3} \int_0^\infty s[1 - E(s)] \sin 2\pi\rho s ds \qquad (7)$$

In order to find the value of the probability function W from the observed curve $E(s)$ for any distance p measured in wave lengths, one only needs to carry through the integration suggested in Equation (7). Zernike and Prins have already suggested this possibility; they, however, had no intensity curves which they could have used. The result, obtained for W by actually carrying out the reversion in the case of mercury is shown in Figure 4, in which the distance from the central atom is given in Å. First, it is clear that certain distances, about 3 Å., 5.6 Å., 8.1 Å., etc., are preferred, and that in-between distances are avoided if possible by the atom. The curve thus shows that even in the liquid stage there exists a quasi-crystalline structure and defines this structure quantitatively, using the probability curve. Thus, for

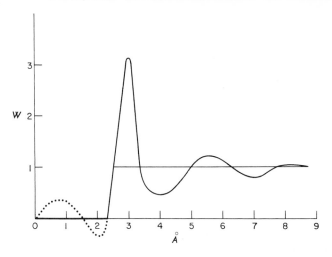

FIGURE 4

instance, one can read from the curve that the distance 3 Å. is about 6 times as probable as the distance 4 Å. For small distances one should expect $W = 0$. The integration, according to Equation (7), gave, instead, the dotted part of the curve. The deviation is explained by the fact that for the calculation of the W curve for small distances the shape of the E curve for high values of s is of importance. The intensity distribution in the maxima and minima of high orders, however, cannot be determined very accurately. In the meantime we are trying to improve the accuracy of the intensity curve as well as to extend the method to other liquids, especially those with molecules of a greater number of atoms."[2]   ▲

The rather convincing evidence presented by Debye and Menke encouraged investigators to try to develop a model for liquids which incorporates solid-like characteristics. Prior to the X-ray studies, the consensus was that liquids should more logically be related to gases. The X-ray diffraction halos, however, have given impetus to the study of the solid-like aspects of liquids, and interest in this approach remains to the present time. Recent theoretical discussions are more cautious with regard to the solid-like nature of liquids, a fact that will be evident in the following descriptions of theories of liquid structure.

[2] P. DEBYE and H. MENKE, *Physik. Z.*, **31,** 797 (1930); trans. in *Collected Papers of Peter J. W. Debye* (New York: Interscience Publishers, Inc., 1954), p. 133.

CHAPTER 4

Cell Concepts

HOLE THEORY

An interesting reversal of the cluster and group theories of Mayer and Stewart stems from the postulation of holes in a liquid. Such holes could logically arise if structure existed in the make-up of a liquid. One of the early suggestions involving such holes or vacancies in liquids was made by Frenkel.[1] The concept of interstices and vacant sites in crystalline solids (see Figure 5) had already been proposed by Joffé, but the situation in liquids is not strictly analogous to that in solids. The particles are arranged in rigidly ordered patterns in crystals, so that any missing unit results in a hole and any dislocation of the ordered pattern may cause a fault or crevice in the lattice.

A rigidity similar to that in solids does not exist in liquids, so definite interstices will not be formed. The lack of precise positions for the molecules in liquids precludes any real meaning for the idea of specific vacant sites. As a clearer picture of liquids developed, Frenkel shifted to less definite ideas about the nature of his vacancies. This is not to say that the equivalent of such holes is lacking in liquids, for density and other data indicate there should be even more space present in liquids than in the corresponding solids near the melting point. Water density, of course, represents an exception to normal behavior. Free space in liquids probably occurs as irregularly shaped gaps which continually change in number, size, and shape as the molecules translate and rotate into different positions. This model involving spaces in the structure of a liquid is somewhat indefinite, but the basic idea has been applied in several modifications and extensions of the hole theory.

---

[1] J. Frenkel, *Kinetic Theory of Liquids* (New York: Dover Publications, Inc., 1955), pp. 7, 106; (New York: Oxford University Press, 1946).

a   b

FIGURE 5

Vacancies (a) and interstices (b) are represented by solid units.

CELL THEORY AND FREE VOLUME THEORY

Developments of Henry Eyring

In order to put the hole concepts on a more quantitative basis, several attempts have been made to give the holes definite shapes and properties. In 1936 Eyring used the ideas of the hole theory to initiate the first liquid structure model that would make possible the calculation of various physical quantities.[2] In a continuing series of papers, he and his collaborators progressed from a hole structure to a "fluidized, cellular model." In his more recent publications Eyring considers the vacancies to be "smeared-out, fleeting, and fluidized" as a result of the conflict between the tendency to cell formation and the rapid motion of molecules as they jump into the holes and distort the cell. By determining the energy needed for a molecule to occupy a vacancy, it is possible to arrive at an evaluation of the physical properties and to relate these properties to the molecular behavior of the liquid.

In the cell theory, a single molecule is considered to be entrapped in each cell which consists of eight to twelve symmetrically arranged molecules. The number of molecules around the entrapped one in a cell is called the *coordination number*. In Figure 6 the entrapped molecule is centrally located, as can be seen in the shadow picture of the stick-and-ball model of a postulated cell. The distance between any two molecules of the cell is not greatly different from the diameter of the molecule itself for simple rare gas elements in the liquid state, a property which fixes the size of the cell. Certain restrictions, to be described later, are imposed on the movements of the molecules. The cohesion between molecules may be described in terms of the potential energy, and it is believed that this attractive potential varies inversely as the sixth power of the distance

[2] H. Eyring, *J. Chem. Phys.*, **4**, 283 (1936).

FIGURE 6

A postulated cell as depicted by a stick-and-ball model and its shadow picture.

of separation. Eyring postulates that the potential field is uniform within his cell and that a molecule therein may be considered to have the freedom of motion of an ideal gas molecule.

The space available for the movement of the entrapped molecule is called the *free volume*. This is not the same as the entire cell volume because the enclosed molecule can move only until it touches a cell molecule, and this leaves regions which cannot be occupied. Figure 6 depicts a certain degree of structure which produces small regions within the total cell volume that are not available for occupancy either by the entrapped molecule or by those comprising the rest of the cell. It is not possible to fill all space by arranging spheres about a central sphere! The imposed restrictions result in a lower entropy than would exist if the molecules had complete freedom of movement in the entire volume. The difference between the actual lower entropy and the value expected if all the space were available is called the *communal entropy*, a quantity which is used frequently in connection with liquid structure theory.

The need for a cell or other model theory arises from the fact that attempts are being made to explain the macroscopic nature of liquids on the basis of the constituent molecules. Thermodynamics deals with the macroscopic behavior of matter; one of the important thermodynamic quantities of a liquid is available energy, usually referred to as Helmholtz *free energy*, A. By definition $A = E - TS$, where E is internal energy, T is temperature, and S is entropy.

The energy of a system may be apportioned, or partitioned, between various parts such as translational, rotational, and vibrational energies. This provides a quantity called the partition function, f, which is related to A by the equation

$$A = -kT \ln f$$

where f is defined by

$$f = \sum_i e^{-E_i/kT}$$

where k is the Boltzmann constant, e is the base of natural logarithms, and $e^{-E_i/kT}$ is the Boltzmann factor, one of the key quantities of science. The evaluation of f permits the calculation of thermodynamic properties, such as S, E, and C_v, from standard relations as indicated below:

$$S = -\left(\frac{\partial A}{\partial T}\right)_v = k[\ln f + T(\partial \ln f/\partial T)_v]$$

$$E = A + TS = kT^2(\partial \ln f/\partial T)_v$$

$$C_v = (\partial E/\partial T)_v = k/T^2\left[\partial^2 \ln f/\partial \left(\frac{1}{T}\right)^2\right]_v$$

where E is internal energy, C_v is heat capacity at constant volume, and T is temperature on the absolute scale. Eyring uses the following equation in which the integral is the partition function:[3]

$$A = -kT \ln \frac{\int e^{-H/kT} dq_{si} \cdots dp_{3N}}{N! h^{3N}}$$

N is the number of molecules, h is Planck's constant, H represents the sum of potential and kinetic energies, and q and p are position and momentum terms, respectively. A major problem in the study of liquids concerns the evaluation of the integral. It can be determined for ideal gases in which the molecules are essentially independent and for solids with definite long-range order in the crystal lattice, but its value for liquids is difficult to ascertain. Molecules in the liquid state are close enough to be subject to strong cohesive forces which, along with the considerable kinetic activity, must be accounted for with greater precision than has yet been attained.

[3] H. Eyring, *Intern. Sci. and Technol.*, No. 15, 15 (March, 1963).

When Eyring considers the spaces in liquids as mobile, fluidized, smeared-out vacancies, he distinguishes between vacancies surrounded by molecules and vacancies surrounded by vacancies, as the latter have no dynamic properties. He attributes a solid-like character to the molecules of a cell surrounding a vacancy. Energy (E) is required for a molecule to get into a vacancy. This energy may be obtained from the relation $E = aE_s/n$, where E_s is the energy of sublimation of the substance as a solid, n is the number of vacancies, and a is a constant. Once E is evaluated, it is possible to obtain the partition function. In this way a knowledge of small scale molecular behavior provides information about the bulk properties of liquids.

In a recent article Eyring describes his model theory as it exists in its most advanced state and maintains that it may be applied in more ways and with better success than any other theory. This is a classic example of the use of a model with parameters which have been adjusted until they give results which agree with those from experimentation. EYRING uses existing gas and solid models as well as known properties of liquids to develop his theory which is described in the following excerpt from his and MARCHI'S article, "Significant Structure Theory of Liquids."

▼   "... From X-ray scattering experiments on liquids such as argon we gain information of a more detailed nature. As the temperature of a solid increases, the coordination number of nearest neighbors decreases from 12 in the solid to 10 or 11 in the liquid at the melting point. With rising temperature the coordination number, z, steadily decreases to approximately 4 at about five degrees below the critical temperature and then rises to 6 at the critical point. While the coordination number is decreasing to 4, the distance between nearest neighbors remains almost constant (3.8 Å for argon). Then as z rises to 6 the distance between neighbors increases (to 4.5 Å). Furthermore, the X-ray data indicates that those molecules immediately surrounding a given molecule (i.e., its nearest neighbors) are arranged in an orderly manner. The second and third nearest neighbors are arranged in a somewhat random fashion and beyond that chaos reigns. To say this in another way, a liquid possesses short range order, but a total lack of a long range order.

"Excess Volume — Fluidized Vacancies

"Now may we reconcile the fact that as the temperature increases the volume increases, yet the average distance between molecules remains fairly constant? A simple way of explaining this is to imagine that some of the molecules are replaced by vacancies. For example, argon expands 12% upon melting. This corresponds to removing about every eighth molecule. This would have two desirable effects. First, it would increase the volume simply by increasing the number of sites at the same time keeping the intermolecular distance more or less constant. And second, when two or more molecules share a vacancy, the lattice structure or orderly arrangement is destroyed so that we no longer have long range order.

"Since the introduction of vacancies into a liquid seems to be a simple and satisfactory way of accounting for expansion, constant intermolecular distance, and lack of long range order, we shall now proceed to formulate a partition function which skirts certain difficulties and yet expresses this concept.

"The key to the Pandora's box of liquids lies in elucidating the use a liquid makes of the *excess volume*, $V - V_s$, where V is the molar volume of the liquid and V_s is the molar volume of the solid. The liquid apparently utilizes this excess volume in two ways. First of all, if a molecule is rambunctious enough, that is to say if it has sufficient kinetic energy, it will take possession of some of this excess volume by pushing the neighboring molecules out of the way. By doing this it will gain entropy, or speaking in terms of a partition function, it will gain a degeneracy factor. The second use the liquid makes of the excess volume is to allow the molecule to possess translational degrees of freedom. Let us observe some particular molecule in the liquid. At some particular time it will be completely surrounded by other molecules, and so it will be vibrating about some point in space with about the same fundamental vibration frequency that it would have in the solid. When it is oscillating this way, we say that it is behaving in a *solid*-like manner. It then acquires some energy (by collisions with one or more of its neighbors) and transfers this energy into one of its vibrational modes of motion. The molecule then vibrates so hard in some direction that it pushes the neighboring molecules aside and takes possession of an additional position. In this process of moving to a new position external vibrational degrees of freedom are converted into translational degrees of freedom. When a liquid molecule possesses translational degrees of freedom, we say it is acting in a *gas*-like manner. One naturally asks, how are the total number of degrees of freedom to be partitioned between solid- and gas-like degrees of freedom?

"Before answering this question we should make a few comments about the excess volume. There are no stationary solid-like vacancies in a liquid. Light scattering experiments rule out such inhomogeneities in density. Furthermore, it is well known that liquids superheat when they are heated in vessels so clean that bubbles do not form on the walls. Thus it is clear that pure liquids have no 'holes' large enough to act as nuclei for bubble formation. Also the structure of a liquid is very unstable with molecules rapidly shifting their position. Due to this rapid and irregular motion of the molecules, care must be exercised in speaking of a lattice or empty lattice site. Nevertheless, there is an excess volume, $V - V_s$, in the liquid, and this excess volume can be acquired by a molecule by pushing out its competitors. Only when a molecule has enough energy to push the neighboring molecules aside, however, does it become appropriate to speak of a hole or empty lattice site coming into existence. We call these holes *fluidized vacancies* or sometimes simply holes or vacancies. We wish to make clear, however, that these holes are very different from the locked-in almost static vacancies found in solids. The analogy between holes in a liquid and positions in an electron sea is very good. It is immaterial whether we think of molecules or electrons moving in one direction or holes or positrons moving in the other. Now certainly a hole by itself has no properties; but when a hole is surrounded by molecules, it becomes convenient to think of the hole as possessing properties. By moving into the hole, the surrounding molecules confer gas-like properties on the hole. It is simply a question of convenience whether we speak of the molecules possessing translational degrees of freedom or of the holes behaving as gas-like molecules; both descriptions refer to the same phenomenon. Likewise the term solid-like molecules does not imply that there are microcrystalline regions in the liquid. We simply mean that for short periods of time the motion of a molecule will be oscillatory. During other periods of time the motion of a molecule is translational. It reduces to a question of semantics whether we refer to these motions as solid- and gas-like or vibrational and translational.

"Returning to the division of the total number of degrees of freedom, we assume that the excess in volume between the solid and liquid, to a sufficient degree of approximation, can be measured in terms of holes of molecular size. In one mole of liquid there are $(V - V_s)/V_s$ moles of vacancies per mole of molecules. The fraction of occupied positions adjacent to a vacancy is, assuming complete randomness, V_s/V. Now as we said before, a hole surrounded by vacancies has no properties; it is the molecules around a hole which confer properties on the vacancy. Thus if we multiply the number of holes, $(V - V_s)/V_s$, by the probability of molecules occupying positions around the hole, V_s/V, we obtain $(V - V_s)/V$ for the fraction of vacancies endowed with gas-like properties. The remaining fraction of a mole, V_s/V, may be thought of as associated with solid-like molecules.

"Accordingly, the heat capacity at constant volume, C_v, of a mole of argon should be given closely by the sum of the contributions from V_s/V moles of solid and $(V - V_s)/V$ moles of gas. Thus:

$$C_v = 6 \cdot \frac{V_s}{V} + 3 \cdot \frac{V - V_s}{V} \tag{1}$$

This expression was first suggested by Walter and Eyring. Its validity is tested in Figure 7. The results are sufficiently encouraging to cause us to develop the fluidized vacancy theory.

"The concept of fluidized vacancies has another advantage: it explains quite nicely the law of rectilinear diameters. This law states that the average density of a liquid and its vapor is nearly independent of temperature decreasing slowly in linear fashion as the temperature increases from the melting to the critical point. If a molecule is transferred from the liquid to the vapor without displacing the neighbors, i.e., leaving a vacancy, all bonds to neigh-

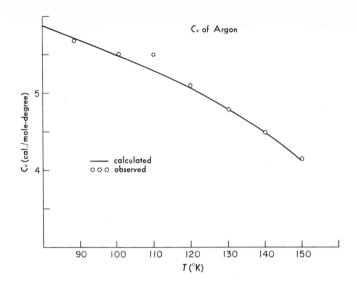

FIGURE 7

Heat capacity at constant volume for liquid argon. The solid curve represents Equation (1), and the circles represent the experimental data. Adapted from H. Eyring and R. P. Marchi, J. Chem. Educ., 40, 562 (1963).

bors are broken. In ordinary vaporization only half this energy is required since again all bonds to its neighbors are broken, but each bond joins two molecules and therefore only half the energy of a bond should be charged against each molecule. Thus the energy to make a vacancy just equals the heat of vaporization. Further, a vacancy in the liquid moves about as freely as does a molecule in the vapor. Thus the entropies of a hole and of a gas molecule should be about equal. Now since the vacancies and the vapor molecules have the same energy and entropy, it is to be expected that there will be as many vacancies per unit volume of liquid as there are molecules per unit volume of vapor. Thus the sum of the densities of the liquid and vapor will be constant except for the slight lattice expansion of the liquid causing the density of the liquid to decrease slightly with temperature. Consequently, the mean density of liquid and vapor should decrease slightly with temperature.

"A cardinal principle in significant structure theory is that molecular structures in the vapor are mirrored in the liquid as analogous structures made out of vacancies. Thus individual molecules translating in the vapor are mirrored as vacancies translating in the liquid. Rotating molecules are mirrored as rotating vacancies. Association of vapor molecules is matched in the liquid by association of the corresponding vacancies which translate and rotate like their molecular counterparts. This principle has been applied and verified for ordinary liquids, metals, and molten salts.

"Formulation of the Partition Function

"We return to the formulation of the partition function. If a molecule is to take possession of one of the fluid vacancies, it must push the neighboring molecules aside. When it does have the required energy, the additional sites become available to a molecule and there is a degeneracy factor equal to the number of sites available. The number of additional sites will be equal to the number of neighboring position[s], n_h, which a rambunctious molecule can occupy multiplied by the probability that the molecule has enough energy, ϵ, to move into one of these sites. Thus the number of additional sites is:

$$n_h e^{-\epsilon/kT}$$

Therefore, the total number of positions available to a given molecule is

$$1 + n_h e^{-\epsilon/kT} \tag{2}$$

If we now assume that the vibrational degrees of freedom, i.e., the solid-like molecules, are adequately represented by an Einstein oscillator (which for temperatures corresponding to the liquid region is a good approximation), we can write for the partition function, f, for a monatomic liquid such as argon the expression:

$$f = \left\{ \frac{e^{E_s/RT}}{(1 - e^{-\theta/T})^3} \cdot (1 + n_h e^{-\epsilon/kT}) \right\}^{N(V_s/V)}$$

$$\cdot \left\{ \frac{(2\pi mkT)^{3/2}}{h^3} (V - V_s) \right\}^{N(V-V_s)/V} \cdot \left\{ \left(\frac{N(V - V_s)}{V} \right)! \right\}^{-1} \tag{3}$$

The first set of brackets [i.e., braces] represents the solid-like portion of the partition function. The remaining portion is the gas-like part. In the partition function for a nonlocalized independent system the number of complexions is overcounted due to the indistinguishability of the particles. Thus we must divide by the number of particles factorial. This explains the factorial term, $[N(V - V_s)/V]!$, at the end of the equation (3). Using Sterling's approximation, $x! = (x/e)^x$, equation (3) becomes

$$f = \left\{ \frac{e^{E_s/RT}}{(1 - e^{-\theta/T})^3} (1 + n_h e^{-\epsilon/RT}) \right\}^{N(V_s/V)}$$

$$\cdot \left\{ \frac{(2\pi mkT)^{3/2}}{h^3} \cdot \frac{eV}{N} \right\}^{N(V-V_s/V)} \tag{4}$$

where θ is the Einstein characteristic temperature. Note that when $V = V_s$, the exponent of the second set of brackets goes to zero leaving the partition function of a solid since $n_h e^{-\epsilon/RT}$ also goes to zero. When V is much larger than V_s, the first set of brackets effectively becomes unity and we are left with the partition function of a gas. Accordingly, this partition function has the correct asymptotic behavior. Within the solid-like portion of the partition function the factor $e^{E_s/RT}/(1 - e^{-\theta/T})^3$ occurs. This is the Einstein partition function for the external vibrations of the atom. E_s is the sublimation energy, and so the reference energy in this theory is for the atoms in their lattice framework rather than the separated atoms.

"The quantity $(1 + n_h e^{-\epsilon/RT})$ is the geometrical degeneracy factor, and it is a direct result of a molecule appropriating excess volume. Accordingly, we expect n_h to be proportional to the excess volume,

$$n_h = n(V - V_s)/V_s \tag{5}$$

while ϵ should be inversely proportional to the excess volume and directly proportional to the energy of sublimation of the solid. Thus

$$\epsilon = \frac{aE_sV_s}{V - V_s} \tag{6}$$

We next require values for the proportionality factors n and a. These may be evaluated by calculating n_h and ϵ near the melting point where the liquid still approximates a solid lattice. Thus near the melting point the fraction of the neighboring positions, Z, which are empty and therefore available for occupancy is

$$Z \cdot \left(\frac{V - V_s}{V}\right) = \left(Z\frac{V_s}{V}\right) \cdot \frac{V - V_s}{V_s} = n\frac{V - V_s}{V_s} \tag{7}$$

Hence

$$n = \frac{ZV_s}{V} = 12 \cdot \frac{1}{1.12} = 10.7 \tag{8}$$

is to be compared with the value 10.8 required to fit experimental data. These added positions should be available without extra energy to a neighboring molecule. However, in melting, the other neighbors to the position have gained the kinetic energy of melting by spreading into the vacancies. According to the virial theorem the kinetic energy of melting is half the total energy of melting, E_m. Thus at, or very near the melting point

$$\frac{aE_s \cdot V_s}{V - V_s} = \frac{n - 1}{Z} \cdot \frac{1}{2} E_m \simeq \frac{n - 1}{Z} \cdot \frac{1}{2} \frac{V - V_s}{V} E_s \tag{9}$$

Hence

$$a = \frac{n - 1}{Z} \cdot \frac{1}{2} \frac{V - V_s}{V} \frac{V - V_s}{V_s} = 0.0052 \tag{10}$$

This value for a is to be compared with the value 0.00534 which is chosen to fit experimental data. The fraction $(n - 1)/Z$ results from the fact that a molecule expanding into the vacancy acquires $1/Z$ of its kinetic energy of melting and there are only $n - 1$ molecules to compete with the molecule in question. Our model thus fixes all the parameters in liquid theory except those which are properties of the solid.

"An essential point in any model of the liquid is that it explains the utilization of excess volume introduced by melting. A model which omits this explanation is either a superheated solid or chilled vapor theory and not really a liquid theory at all.

"Obviously, equation (9) is only approximate, but it does give a good estimate for the value of a. The error in the value of a is due to two causes. The quantity $E_s(V - V_s)/V$ gives a value for the heat of fusion which is about 10% too low. On the other hand the value $\frac{1}{2}$ obtained from the virial theorem for the needed kinetic energy is undoubtedly only approximate. A molecule in the liquid state is apt to lower its potential energy as it is pushed out of the excess volume. Therefore, the factor $\frac{1}{2}$ in equation (9) should be smaller. The errors in these two factors probably about compensate each other.

"The theory also leads to a radial distribution function. Knowing the molar volume of the solid and the type of packing in the solid phase, we can compute the size of the molecules. If we now arrange these molecules in the volume V in the most random way possible (in obtaining the fraction of solid- and gas-like molecules, we have assumed complete randomness), we can compute a radial distribution function. Due to the fact that the molecules are not rigid spheres, but rather are elastic molecules, and since there is a distribution of kinetic energies, the peaks of the distribution function will be smeared-out, as is observed experimentally.

"Using equations (5) and (6), equation (4) can be rewritten

$$f = \left\{ \frac{e^{E_s/RT}}{(1 - e^{-\theta/T})^3} \cdot \left(1 + n\frac{V - V_s}{V_s} e^{-aE_sV_s/RT(V-V_s)}\right)\right\}^{N(V_s/V)}$$

$$\cdot \left\{\frac{(2\pi mkT)^{3/2}}{h^3} \cdot \frac{eV}{N}\right\}^{N(V-V_s)/V} \quad (11)$$

This is the form in which the partition function for Significant Structure theory is most frequently written. Equation (11) is for liquids composed of monatomic molecules. Naturally for systems which possess internal vibrations and rotations, the appropriate expressions must be added to the solid- and gas-like portions of the partition function.

"Calculation of Thermodynamic Properties

"With the basic partition function given in equation (11) we are in an excellent position to calculate thermodynamic properties from the melting point to the critical point for a wide variety of substances ranging from such near-ideal liquids as argon to nonideal systems such as water. The relation between the Helmholtz free energy, A, and the partition function is

$$A = -kT \ln f \quad (12)$$

Since we now have A as a function of V and T, we can calculate all other thermodynamic properties from

$$S = -\left(\frac{\partial A}{\partial T}\right)$$

$$E = -T^2\left[\frac{\partial(A/T)}{\partial T}\right]_v$$

$$P = -\left(\frac{\partial A}{\partial V}\right)_T \tag{13}$$

$$C_v = T\cdot\left(\frac{\partial S}{\partial T}\right)_v = -T\left(\frac{\partial^2 A}{\partial T^2}\right)_v$$

$$\alpha = \frac{1}{V}\left(\frac{\partial V}{\partial T}\right)_P = -\left(\frac{\partial P}{\partial T}\right)_v\Big/\left[V\cdot\left(\frac{\partial P}{\partial V}\right)_T\right]$$

and similar expressions for the remaining thermodynamic properties.

"Inert Gases

"For the liquid inert gases we use the partition function given in equation (11). E_s, θ, and V_s are taken from the properties of the solid phase; n is determined from equation (8) and a is estimated from equation (10). Some of the results are summarized in Table 1. It will be noted that the calculated critical pressure is in all cases too high. Inspection of equation (11) produces

TABLE 1

*Calculated and Observed Thermodynamic Properties
of the Liquid Noble Gases*

	Ar	Kr	Xe	
T_m (°K)	(83.85)	(116.0)	(161.3)	calc
	83.85	116.0	161.3	obs
V_m (cm³ mole⁻¹)	28.90	33.11	42.30	calc
	28.03	34.13	42.68	obs
P_m (atm)	0.679	0.756	0.399	calc
	0.674	0.722	0.804	obs
ΔS_m (cal mole⁻¹ deg⁻¹)	3.263	3.456	3.415	calc
	3.34	3.35	3.40	obs
T_b (°K)	87.29	119.28	167.5	calc
	87.29	119.93	165.1	obs
V_b (cm³ mole⁻¹)	29.33	33.31	42.96	calc
	28.69	. . .	. . .	obs
ΔS_b (cal mole⁻¹ deg⁻¹)	19.04	19.27	19.43	calc
	17.85	17.99	18.29	obs
T_c (°K)	149.7	208.33	287.8	calc
	150.66	210.6	289.8	obs
V_c (cm³ mole⁻¹)	83.68	88.32	113.52	calc
	75.26	. . .	113.8	obs
P_c (atm)	52.93	69.68	74.89	calc
	48.00	54.24	58.2	obs

a possible explanation for this. As the critical point is approached, clustering becomes important. That is, concentrations of the dimer and trimer in the vapor phase become significant and thus should be included in the partition function. These clusters have the effect of decreasing the pressure. Equation (11) only includes monomers in the gas-like portion of the partition function. Presumably, inclusion of a dimer term would improve the results. . . .

"Liquid Hydrogen

"The theory has been applied with excellent results to liquid hydrogen, deuterium, and hydrogen deuteride. It provides an interesting test for this approach to liquids since changes in the concentrations of ortho and para hydrogen cause slight changes in the thermodynamic properties. Because these liquids exist at extremely low temperatures a Debye partition function is used for the solid-like degrees of freedom and equation (7) is used for n_h. The gas-like molecules are treated as a slightly degenerate gas which obeys Bose-Einstein statistics for the cases of hydrogen and deuterium and Fermi-Dirac statistics for the case of hydrogen deuteride. Henderson thus obtained the following partition function

$$f = \left\{ \frac{e^{E_s/RT}}{f_D} \left(1 + n_h e^{-aE_s V_s/RT(V-V_s)}\right) \cdot f_r \right\}^{N(V_s/V)}$$
$$\cdot \left\{ e^{(1-\ln y \pm y/2^{5/2})} \cdot f_r \right\}^{N(V-V_s)/V} \qquad (14)$$

where f_D is the Debye partition, f_r is the rotational partition function and depends upon the species, and y is related to the translational partition function. The reader is referred to the original paper for more details on the partition function, since it is inherently complex. Table 2 [see top of facing page] lists some calculated and observed properties at the melting, boiling, and critical point. . . ."[4]   ▲

Eyring's theory has been tested on diverse classes of substances such as rare gas liquids, diatomic liquids, organic liquids, molten metals, fused salts, and liquid hydrogen, deuterium, and hydrogen deuteride. In addition to hydrogen, the list of diatomic liquids includes nitrogen, chlorine, fluorine, bromine, and iodine. Quantum effects must be incorporated into the study of liquid helium and hydrogen. Studies of these two elements are further complicated since hydrogen exists in three isotopic modifications as well as in two forms, ortho and para, and liquid helium exists in two forms, I and II.

Eyring's theory covers an extensive list of properties, including transport phenomena, i.e. flow properties, as well as thermodynamic or equilibrium quantities. Melting, boiling, and critical values as related to temperature, pressure,

[4] H. EYRING and R. P. MARCHI, *J. Chem. Educ.*, **40**, 562 (1963).

TABLE 2

Calculated and Observed Thermodynamic Properties of Liquid Hydrogen

	p-H_2	n-H_2	H-D	o-D_2	n-D_2	
T_m (°K)	(13.84)	(13.94)	(16.60)	(18.63)	(18.73)	*calc*
	13.84	13.94	16.60	18.63	18.73	*obs*
P_m (atm)	0.07388	0.07589	0.1236	0.1706	0.1724	*calc*
	0.06942	0.07085	0.1221	0.1678	0.1692	*obs*
V_m (cm^3 mole^{-1}	26.213	26.093	24.491	23.262	23.155	*calc*
	26.176	26.108	24.487	. . .	23.162	*obs*
ΔS_m (cal mole^{-1} deg^{-1})	1.932	1.936	2.048	2.198	2.210	*calc*
	2.028	. . .	. . .	2.526	. . .	*obs*
T_b (°K)	20.58	20.70	22.29	23.65	23.75	*calc*
	20.261	20.365	22.14	23.59	23.67	*obs*
V_b (cm^3 mole^{-1})	28.829	28.692	26.525	24.955	24.830	*calc*
	28.482	28.393	. . .	. . .	. . .	*obs*
ΔS_b (cal mole^{-1} deg^{-1})	10.553	10.564	11.868	12.741	12.737	*calc*
	10.602	. . .	. . .	12.459	. . .	*obs*
T_c (°K)	35.9	36.2	37.6	39.4	39.7	*calc*
	32.994	33.24	35.908	38.262	38.24	*obs*
P_c (atm)	13.6	13.8	15.5	17.1	17.3	*calc*
	12.770	12.797	14.645	16.282	16.421	*obs*
V_c (cm^3 mole^{-1})	77.7	77.3	71.5	68.3	68.0	*calc*
	65.5	. . .	62.8	60.3	. . .	*obs*

and volume may be obtained, as well as surface tension and entropy changes.

In the practical application of the theory, the three quantities, E_s, θ, and V_s, must be determined from experiment. It would be possible to estimate these parameters if there were a suitable theory of the solid state. Two other parameters, a and n, are needed, and for a reasonably ideal liquid these might be obtained from a reduced equation of state. On this basis, all quantities could be approximated and no recourse to experiment would be required. No other theory is able to yield as reasonable results covering so many properties on such a variety of liquids. This work is the culmination of more than a quarter of a century of effort by Eyring to formulate a suitable theory of the liquid state. His work clearly exemplifies the dedication needed to solve some of the perplexing problems of nature.

The Cell Theory of Lennard-Jones and Devonshire

In the year following Eyring's original publication (1936), Lennard-Jones and Devonshire started a series of papers in which they developed a comprehensive theory covering dense gases, critical phenomena, and liquids.[5] They made use of the Lennard-Jones *12–6 potential* in which the attractive potential between molecules varies inversely with the sixth power of the distance r be-

[5] J. E. Lennard-Jones and A. F. Devonshire, *Proc. Roy. Soc., London*, **A163**, 53 (1937); **A165**, 1 (1938).

tween them, while at the same time the repulsive potential varies inversely as the twelfth power of r. The over-all potential may then be expressed as $U = b/r^{12} - a/r^6$, where a and b are constants. Figure 8 is a representation of the resultant potential for a typical pair of simple molecules (see also Figure 47, page 115). Since this is a potential energy curve, the minimum represents the point at which the molecules tend to be stabilized. If the molecules come closer together the repulsive action dominates, and if they move farther apart the attractive action will be stronger.

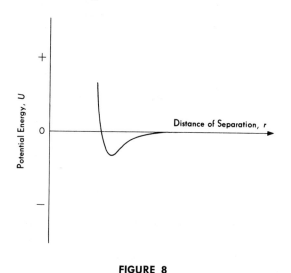

FIGURE 8

The over-all potential energy between two simple molecules as a function of the distance of separation.

In their first two papers, Lennard-Jones and Devonshire worked with the intermolecular forces in compressed gases whose molecules were depicted as being confined within a cell structure consisting of a shell of molecules. Each molecule was supposed to move about in its cell, and the potential energies were calculated for all positions within the cell. Simultaneously, all neighboring molecules were postulated as being at the centers of their cells, and the potential field was then averaged for spherical symmetry. Ordinary collisions were replaced by multiple encounters in the formulation of the theory which yielded an equation of state for such systems. The critical temperatures for the rare gases were then evaluated with reasonable success. This theory was extended to the liquid state which made it possible to calculate boiling points, vapor pressures, and heats of vaporization for liquids, and to interpret theoretically the rule of Trouton (see page 7). Developed to this stage, however, the theory does not make possible a distinction between a liquid and a solid. A third paper by these authors was devoted to this and other solid-liquid problems. LENNARD-JONES and DEVONSHIRE discuss their theory in the following excerpt from their classic article.

▼

"1. Introduction

"There have been many theories of the melting of solids but none has as yet given a satisfactory explanation of the change of phase from solid to liquid in terms of interatomic forces. They have usually been based on simple models and have attempted only to correlate the temperature of melting with other properties of the solid. . . .

"2. Order and Disorder in Liquid and Solid

"The first difficulty to be resolved in constructing a theory of melting of a normal substance is to find the essential difference between the solid and liquid states. The X-ray examination of liquids has shown that they have regions of order which are almost crystalline, at any rate just above the melting-point, while recent work on the structure of alloys has shown that certain types of disorder can occur in the solid state (Bragg and Williams 1934; Bethe 1935). The difference between a crystalline solid and a liquid can probably be attributed to the disappearance of long-distance order on melting, though some degree of short-distance order may still persist in the liquid and be lost gradually as the temperature rises or the volume increases.

"No theory of the gradual decrease of regularity has yet been given, though an interesting suggestion has been made by Eyring and his co-workers (Hirschfelder, Stevenson and Eyring 1937). They suggest that, whereas the atoms in a solid are localized most of the time, those in a liquid can continuously interchange places and can in consequence share the whole of the available volume. This latter property introduces an important change into the statistical treatment, for it changes a factor $(V/N)^N$, which occurs in the partition function of the solid, to $V^N/N!$ and this leads to a new term in the entropy of amount k (Boltzmann's constant), corresponding to the increased disorder of the liquid. There is nothing in the theory, as at present formulated, to indicate what are the conditions for this sudden change from perfect order to complete disorder, nor is there an explanation of the sudden change of volume which is known to occur at the melting-point. A satisfactory theory of melting should lead us to understand more clearly why for a given pressure melting occurs at a definite and precise temperature (and not gradually over a range of temperature) and why it is accompanied by an increase of volume. Eyring's suggestion does, however, focus attention on the essential difference between a solid and a liquid, namely, that a solid at most temperatures can be regarded as *ordered*, while a liquid for the most part is *disordered*.

"In this paper we attempt to construct a theory of melting by introducing a theory of disorder. We confine our attention to assemblies of atoms (or molecules), whose fields of force are spherically symmetrical, so that there are no specific points of attachment such as are believed to exist in abnormal liquids like water. Atoms with fields of this type probably form what are called normal liquids, though no strict definition exists as to what a normal liquid is. Usually a liquid is regarded as normal when it obeys certain empirical rules such as Trouton's rule. This latter rule was derived in terms of interatomic forces of the spherical type in a recent paper (Lennard-Jones and Devonshire, Paper II, 1937) and probably implies non-directed fields of force.

"We take over the theory and methods of the two preceding papers (Lennard-Jones and Devonshire 1937, under the title of 'Critical Phenomena in Gases I and II'), according to which each atom of a dense assembly, whether solid, liquid or gas, is regarded as moving in the field of force of its neighbours and confined by them to a small region of space equal to the average available volume per atom. This method proved surprisingly successful in providing direct calculations of critical temperatures and also of boiling-points in terms of interatomic forces. But the model as thus described does not differentiate a solid from a liquid. In the solid the cell in which an atom moves is localized whereas in a liquid it is not. There is a migration of the cell from one position to another. In a liquid therefore we must represent the motion of an atom as a vibration about a point which itself suffers displacement. This feature we introduce into the theory in this paper by considering the order and disorder of the sites (or centres of vibration) and discuss the relation between solid and liquid in terms of the disorder present.

"We picture a solid of one kind of atom (such as that of an inert gas) as an alloy of atoms and 'holes,' the atoms occupying at low temperatures all the available sites on a perfect lattice and the holes all the available sites on a similar lattice interpenetrating the first. A close analogy in two dimensions would be a draught or chess board, of which the white squares constitute the normal sites for the atoms and the black squares abnormal sites. We call the former α-sites and the latter β-sites. Each site is surrounded by z sites of the other type. When an atom is situated at an α-site and another at a contiguous β-site, we shall call them *close* neighbours, the term *immediate* neighbours being reserved, if need be, for the nearest sites of the same type.

"A measure of the disorder in such an assembly will be the number of atoms in abnormal sites. Figure 9, A shows a two-dimensional arrangement of α- and β-sites. Most of the atoms are ordered, but one or two are in β-sites. This arrangement corresponds to a state of long-distance order but local regions of disorder. A state of complete disorder is shown in Figure 9, B, where the atoms have been placed at random on α- and β-sites in such a way that there are equal numbers on each. In such an arrangement all evidence of a regular lattice structure has disappeared. We do not suggest

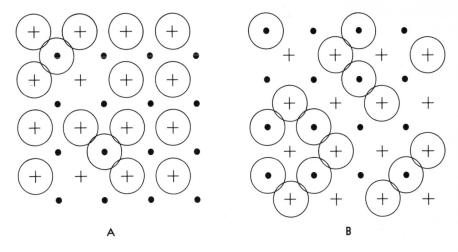

FIGURE 9

*A shows local displacements but long-distance order. (α-sites are repre-
sented by crosses, β-sites by dots, and atoms by circles.) B shows break up
of long-distance order, equal numbers on α- and β-sites. Adapted from J. E.
Lennard-Jones and A. F. Devonshire, Proc. Roy. Soc., A169, 318 (1939).*

that the actual configuration, shown in Figure 9, B, is a likely one. The
clusters will not remain congested while surrounded by empty sites, but will
expand until they occupy as much as possible of the available volume. This
aspect of the problem we shall consider later. What we want to do first is
to get a mathematical theory of disorder to give the *relative* positions of the
atoms surrounding any one, and then we shall be able to deal later with the
problem as to what will be their actual positions.

"The theory of disorder in alloys consisting of two kinds of atoms has been
considered by several authors and has been successful in accounting for
anomalous properties of these alloys at a certain temperature, called the
critical temperature (Bragg and Williams 1934–5; Bethe 1935; Williams
1935). This temperature is now interpreted as the one at which long-distance
order disappears. In this paper we shall consider a solid of one kind of atom
as an alloy of atoms and holes, and the migration of an atom to an abnormal
site as the interchange of an atom and a hole. We adopt with suitable modifications the method used by Bethe for alloys, but we take the energy necessary for an interchange of atom and hole to be a function of the volume of
the whole assembly. This makes the phenomenon a co-operative one in a
twofold sense and . . . the combination of these two concepts leads to a
theory of melting."[6]   ▲

[6] J. E. LENNARD-JONES and A. F. DEVONSHIRE, *Proc. Roy. Soc., London,* **A169,** 317 (1939).

Proceeding along the lines of the above introduction, Lennard-Jones and Devonshire developed their mathematical cell theory which provided a semi-quantitative picture of liquids. It is one of the most promising of the theoretical model concepts, and several physical quantities calculated on the basis of this theory come surprisingly close to the experimental values. Because of these early successes as well as the logical development of the theory, it was received with considerable enthusiasm and many attempts to improve upon it have since been made. In particular, recent developments by the following investigators may be cited: Rowlinson and Curtiss, Cernuschi and H. Eyring, Peek and Hill, and Ono. An appraisal of their results is given by HIRSCHFELDER, CURTISS, and BIRD, who state:

▼   "It is disappointing that these four hole theories show little improvement over the treatment of Lennard-Jones and Devonshire. It is particularly significant that the approximation of Rowlinson and Curtiss ... does not provide a better description of dense gases and liquids.... The fact that their approximation seems only slightly better than the others seems to indicate that little further progress can be made without removing some of the assumptions inherent in the fundamental theory."[7]   ▲

CELL CLUSTER THEORY

Two recently proposed theories which attempt to improve the cell ideas will be mentioned briefly. One is the cell cluster theory by de Boer and the other, the tunnel theory of Barker. Direct calculations are used by de Boer[8] to correct for the approximations in Lennard-Jones and Devonshire's original work. Even though a return to the cluster concept is involved, it is the cells themselves that are thought of as being clustered. There might be one, two, three, or more cells in a cluster, although calculations for more than two are difficult. The ability to make proper calculations of the communal entropy is an important advantage of de Boer's theory. Generalizations allowing for holes have been added by Dahler and Cohen.[9] One of the more satisfying cell theories has emerged from their work. Although no significant improvement over the previous, simpler hole theories has been obtained by these modifications, work is continuing in this direction.

[7] J. O. HIRSCHFELDER, C. F. CURTISS, and R. B. BIRD, *Molecular Theory of Gases and Liquids* (New York: John Wiley & Sons, Inc., 1954), p. 316.

[8] J. de Boer, *Physics*, **20**, 655 (1954).

[9] J. S. Dahler and E. G. D. Cohen, *Physics*, **26**, 81 (1960).

TUNNEL THEORY

The most recent hole theory to be developed involves the tunnel concept originated by Barker in 1960 and described in his excellent book on lattice theories.[10] His basic premise is that one-dimensional chains of molecules move through tunnels composed of neighboring molecules arranged in parallel lines or cylinders. Figure 10, A, is a ball-and-stick model of a straight section of a tunnel. The shadow picture in Figure 10, B, illustrates how a central core or chain of atoms might be placed within the tunnel. Figure 10, C, shows that the tunnels and cores need not be in straight lines. The tunnels move about with respect to one another, so there is essentially random motion or disorder in the molecules as they are observed from nearby tunnels. As part of Barker's postulates, the motions along the tunnels are considered to be distinguishable from those across the tunnels. The essentially one-dimensional character of this model permits calculation of the partition function. Since each subsystem

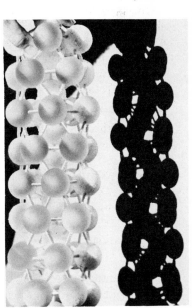

FIGURE 10

A, B, and C are ball-and-stick models of a postulated tunnel section of the molecules in a liquid.

[10] J. A. Barker, *The International Encyclopedia of Physical Chemistry and Chemical Physics*, Topic 10, Vol. 1, *Lattice Theories of the Liquid State* (New York: The Macmillan Company, 1963); *Proc. Roy. Soc., London,* **A259,** 442 (1961).

contains a large number of molecules, it is not necessary to take account of the fluctuations; hence the problem of calculating the communal entropy does not arise. Other physical properties such as compressibility coefficients and vapor pressures may be calculated with reasonable success, but estimated critical constant values are not satisfactory. This approach is new and more study is needed before an attempt to evaluate it can be made. An important discussion of the cell concepts is given by I. Prigogine in his book on solutions.[11]

The model theories have been developed, modified, and consolidated during the past several decades. Eyring has expended considerable sustaining effort to change and improve his original cell theory and gives a convincing outline in his recent publication (see pages 19–31). Many investigators have utilized the principles of Lennard-Jones and Devonshire in attempts to develop new theories, such as the tunnel theory of Barker. In discussing the lattice theories of liquids in 1963, Barker gives considerable emphasis to the Lennard-Jones and Devonshire theory.

One objection to many theories involving models is that it is impossible to make proper allowances for the errors arising from the necessary assumptions. Another is that further improvements of these theories is not easy. Nevertheless, the model concept is an intriguing one and investigation is continuing in this direction. Although the model method is not accepted universally, Row-LINSON feels that

▼ "... this lattice approximation is tractable and has been moderately successful in practice. It is still being refined, although much of its simplicity is being lost in the refining, and may yet prove to be the most satisfactory approach to a theory of liquids. However, it is neither the only approach nor even the most successful numerically in some cases, and its influence on the theory of mixtures, as apart from pure liquids, has often been unhelpful. Many of us must regret time spent in pursuing some of its less fruitful applications."[12]   ▲

Complete agreement is lacking as to the most desirable method of describing liquid structure. In reviewing the present state of the theory of liquids in 1962, I. Z. Fisher[13] maintains that a kinetic approach, such as that of Kirkwood or of Born and Green (page 49), offers the greatest potential for the development of a successful theory. Other proposals, such as the geometrical concept of Bernal, should not be neglected when searching for the answer to the structure of liquids.

[11] I. Prigogine, *The Molecular Theory of Solutions* (Amsterdam: North-Holland Publishing Company, 1957), Chap. 7.

[12] J. S. ROWLINSON, *Liquids and Liquid Mixtures* (London: Butterworth and Company, 1959), p. 5.

[13] I. Z. Fisher, *Usp. Fiz. Nauk.*, **76**, 499 (Mar., 1962); translated in *Soviet Phys. Uspekhi*, **5**, 239 (1962); *Statistical Theory of Liquids* (Chicago: University of Chicago Press, 1964).

CHAPTER 5

Distribution of

Molecules in Liquids

PACKING OF SPHERES AND LIQUID STRUCTURE

The model theories for liquids are based on a structure which involves some degree of order among the molecules. X-ray patterns such as those of Debye and Menke support the concept of short-range order in liquids. The question naturally arises as to the origin of this order. What are the relative effects of cohesion and kinetic activity in liquids? The role of temperature in the interplay of these two factors has already been expressed as an increase of kinetic action with an increase of temperature. It should be noted, however, that the fusion of a solid may take place with no change of temperature. All that is needed is to add heat energy and suitably stir a mixture of a solid and its liquid at the melting point to shift from the rigid ordered structure of the solid to the mobile, liquid state of little or no rigid order. In this transformation only the energy and volume have changed, not the temperature. Rigid spheres packed as closely as possible in a container will have an orderly structure similar to that of a simple crystal. If the container is enlarged and then shaken, the order will be destroyed. This is somewhat analogous to melting, with its attendant decrease in density. For the simplest solids, such as close-packed hexagonal or face-centered cubic structures, there are twelve molecules about any given molecule. As a solid changes to liquid there are fewer neighbors, eight to ten, about any given molecule; the space between them is greater than that in the crystal. The evidence for fewer than twelve nearest neighbors comes from X-ray studies such as those on liquid mercury by Debye and Menke.

Figure 11 is a ball-and-stick model of a unit cell of a cubic (or a hexagonal) crystalline solid structure with atoms arranged in a uniform fashion. Figure 12 shows a larger collection of balls, and their shadow photograph depicts the

FIGURE 11

A ball-and-stick model of a close-packed cubic (or hexagonal) unit cell of a crystalline solid.

FIGURE 12

A model similar to Figure 11 showing a larger number of balls and their shadow photograph.

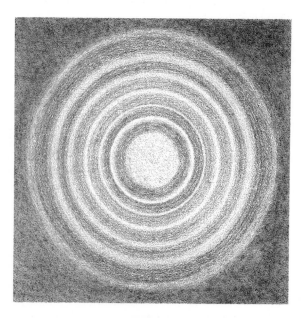

FIGURE 13

A sketch of a typical X-ray pattern of a crystalline solid.

orderly spacing of the particles. Macroscopic crystals of this nature yield clear-cut X-ray patterns as sketched in Figure 13. The model in Figure 14 consists of monatomic molecules in a more random arrangement such as might exist in a liquid.

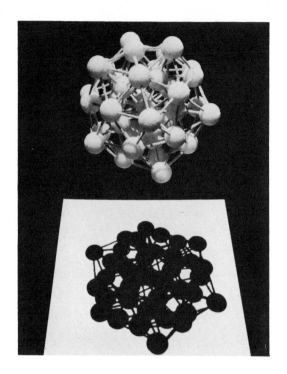

FIGURE 14

A ball-and-stick model with its shadow of monatomic molecules in a more random arrangement than is shown in Figure 12.

It is to be understood at the onset that X-ray diffractions are the result of interactions between X-ray photons and the electrons of the atoms. The X-rays do not interact in this fashion with the nucleus or with atoms as units. The shadows produced by light through the models are merely intended to portray on a plane the ordered arrangement of the particles in space.

A sketch of a typical X-ray diffraction halo of a liquid showing alternately heavier and lighter regions is illustrated in Figure 15. On the basis of such diffraction studies, Debye and Menke, and also Morrell and Hildebrand, set about to depict the structure of liquids in terms of a distribution function, W, which is more frequently designated as $g(r)$. Figure 16 portrays this function for liquid mercury. The degree of local and long-range order in solids is depicted by W. When a crystalline solid melts, the long-range order is lost, leaving

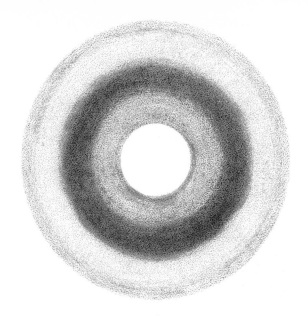

FIGURE 15

Sketch of a typical X-ray diffraction halo of a liquid.

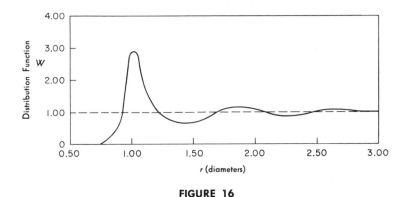

FIGURE 16

X-ray diffraction patterns as shown in Figure 15 may be interpreted in terms of the distribution density of molecules at various distances, r, from a central molecule.

only the possibility of short-range order for liquids. As can be seen in Figure 16, at distances (r) close to a given central molecule, W varies greatly from unity, but at greater and greater distances it approaches and finally remains one, at which point all order is considered to be lost. The maxima in the curve represent the coordination numbers for the molecules in shells around the central molecule.

Molecules do not overlap to any extent, and, because of the potential field, the simpler ones such as argon arrange themselves so that they are not in contact. In liquids, any central molecule is surrounded by a region devoid of molecules, then beyond that by a shell of molecules. The distance from the central molecule to this shell is roughly the same as the distance to the first maximum in the distribution curve. Considerably less ordering of molecules into shells appears to exist beyond this first shell, and the maxima are not so distinct after the first one. The nature and explanation of these distribution curves form a major problem of liquid structure elucidation.

In 1927, Prins and Zernike considered the possibility of relating the structure of liquids to the increase in volume upon melting at constant temperature. This same approach was investigated later by Menke, Frenkel, and Morrell and Hildebrand, among others. Frenkel related the loss of order to the change in space by considering loose packing for molecules in one dimension.[1] It is relatively simple to make calculations for this uncomplicated system. The molecules in a solid might be pictured as being evenly spaced in a line and provided with stops at each end as shown in Figure 17, A. Frenkel assumed that no attractive forces exist between the molecules or particles, and that they may adopt thermal motion similar to that of a gas, thus being capable of random distribution. The question arises as to what the distribution of particles would be if a stop were moved out, as indicated in Figure 17, B. In answering this question Frenkel was able to develop an exact mathematical relation which applies to molecules in one dimension. An extension of this treatment to the two- and three-dimensional cases should be possible. It is interesting to recall that in a different way Barker's tunnel theory makes use of a one-dimensional line or chain of molecules moving within the confines of a channel consisting of a tunnel of other molecules.

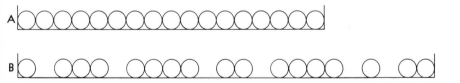

FIGURE 17

A shows a one-dimensional array of monatomic molecules confined as in a solid. B shows a distribution of the molecules under less confining conditions.

The more complex problem of two-dimensional packing was investigated by Prins in 1931 and Menke in 1932. These two investigators dropped seeds and steel balls, respectively, onto a plate or plane in order to determine the two-dimensional kinetic behavior of non-attractive particles.

[1] J. Frenkel, *Kinetic Theory of Liquids* (New York: Dover Publications, Inc., 1955), p. 126.

Morrell and Hildebrand studied the even more difficult three-dimensional problem by suspending hard gelatin spheres in a solution within a transparent box in an ingenious arrangement that eliminated the unwanted effect of gravity and allowed only kinetic activity to influence the distribution of the spheres. The procedure and results are described in their article "The Distribution of Molecules in a Model Liquid," which follows.

▼ "The number of molecules of a pure fluid in a spherical shell of radius r and thickness dr is $(N/V)4\pi r^2 dr$ (where N is Avogadro's number and V is the molal volume), provided r is large. When r becomes small, however, a function of r, which has been designated by W, must be introduced, because the positions of the molecules in the shell are influenced by the positions of their neighbors. The number of molecules in the shell is then $(N/V)4\pi Wr^2 dr$. We may define W as the average number of molecules per unit volume (v/N) at distance r from a central molecule.

"The determination of this distribution function, W, would permit important conclusions to be drawn regarding intermolecular forces and related problems such as solubilities. Experimental determination of the distribution function by the aid of X-ray diffraction has been carried out in the cases of mercury and liquid gallium by Menke, and at two different temperatures for water by Katzoff. Menke's distribution function for mercury is reproduced in Figure 18, A. Kirkwood's curve only roughly approximates this experimental curve.

"Another type of investigation which throws light upon the variation of W with r is the use of models and direct measurement. Thus Menke, by merely pouring steel spheres onto a flat surface and measuring each time the distance between two black ones, then tabulating these distances, obtained a curve for two dimensions which had the characteristics of his W curve for mercury. Very similarly, Prins poured seeds onto a glass plate and photographed them. He then drew concentric circles on the negatives around 'central' seeds, counted the numbers between circles, and obtained the two-dimensional 'W' for this case, or the number per unit area at various distances from the central seed. Here also, curves were obtained which at least roughly resemble the distribution function for mercury.

"The present work is an extension of this use of models, under conditions, however, which should more nearly duplicate those in an actual liquid. We have used three dimensions instead of two, practically neutralized the force of gravity on the individual particles, put the 'molecules' in motion, and have taken more measurements and at smaller intervals.

"The model 'molecules' were gelatin spheres. . . . A few black spheres were made by mixing lamp black into part of the hot gelatin. . . .

"An environment for the spheres was made by heating . . . clear gelatin solution over a water-bath for some 12–16 hours — until it no longer solidified when cooled. This solution retains practically the same density and

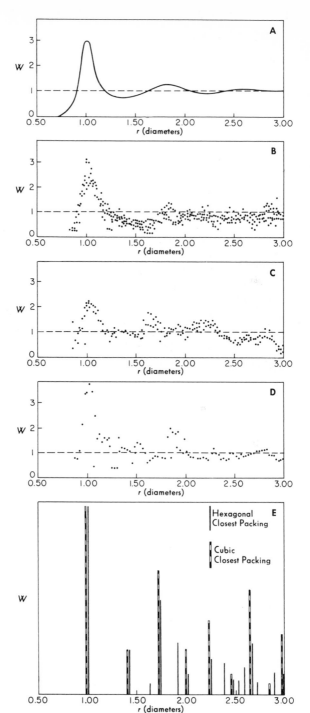

FIGURE 18

A, Menke's distribution function for mercury; B, two distribution functions, superimposed, obtained with gelatin spheres, "expansions" 1.84 and 19.2; C, "expansion" 2.84; D, "expansion" 1.45; E, discontinuous distribution functions for regular close-packed arrangements. Adapted from W. E. Morrell and J. H. Hildebrand, J. Chem. Phys., 4, 224 (1936); Science, 80, 124 (1934).

refractive index as the spheres, or can be adjusted to these conditions by the addition of a little water. The solid balls, then, when placed in this solution would neither sink nor rise to the surface and were practically invisible. On the other hand, the few black spheres put into the mixture were clearly and sharply defined.

"The solution and spheres were placed in a small plate-glass cell. Shadow pictures of the mixture were made by means of a mercury spark. . . .

"One of the resulting photographs is shown in Figure 19. . . .

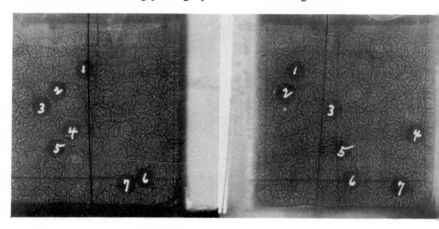

FIGURE 19

Adapted from W. E. Morrell and J. H. Hildebrand, J. Chem. Phys., 4, 224 (1936); Science, 80, 124 (1934).

"The distances between all possible pairs of black spheres [were] calculated from a series of photographs [and] the number of times that each distance occurred was tabulated. If this number be x, the total number of measurements obtained from the series can be designated $\sum\limits_{0}^{\infty} x$. Then $x/\sum\limits_{0}^{\infty} x$ is the relative frequency with which this particular distance occurred in the series, or it is the relative chance that a particular black sphere would at a certain time be found at a given distance r from a particular ball arbitrarily chosen as the central one. Since there are N spheres in the box, the chance that any of them, no matter which, would at that time be at distance r from the central one is $(N - 1)x/\sum\limits_{0}^{\infty} x$, or this is the probable number of balls which at any time would be found at distance r from the central one. The number which would probably be found within a spherical shell of inner radius r_1 and outer radius r_2 is $(N - 1)\sum\limits_{r_1}^{r_2} x/\sum\limits_{0}^{\infty} x$. The number per cc within this shell would be

$$(N - 1) \sum_{r_1}^{r_2} x \bigg/ \sum_{0}^{\infty} x \int_{r_1}^{r_2} 4\pi r^2 dr.$$

Hence the number of spheres per unit volume at distance r from the central sphere would be

$$V(N - 1) \sum_{r_1}^{r_2} x \bigg/ N \sum_{0}^{\infty} x \int_{r_1}^{r_2} 4\pi r^2 dr,$$

and this by definition is W. Integrating, the expression becomes:

$$W = 3V(N - 1) \sum_{r_1}^{r_2} x \bigg/ 4\pi N \sum_{0}^{\infty} x(r_2^3 - r_1^3). \tag{1}$$

"By means of this equation and the data obtained from the photographs, the value of W at each value of r was calculated. The results of four series of measurements are plotted in Figure 18, B, C, and D.

"In these figures the points represented by the solid dots were obtained by taking $r_2 - r_1 = 0.05$ cm, and the circles by using $r_2 - r_1 = 0.09$ cm. The points on D were determined only with $r_2 - r_1 = 0.05$ cm. The values of the various constant quantities occurring in Equation (1), together with other information concerning each series, are summarized in Table 3.

TABLE 3

Series	Total No. Measurements $\left(\sum_{0}^{\infty} x\right)$	Total No. Spheres (N)	No. Black Spheres	Diameter of Spheres	Volume of "System" (V)	"Expansion"
B	1121	614	7	0.422 cm	60 cc	1.84
B'	820	300	6	0.48 cm	45 cc	1.92
C	1120	371	7	0.432 cm	60 cc	2.84
D	1035	500	10	0.39 cm	30.5 cc	1.45

"The 'expansion' is the ratio of the total volume of the mixture to that which would be occupied by the balls, together with the space between them, if they were allowed to settle into a completely regular, closest-packed arrangement. In other words, it is the ratio of V to $0.707 D^3 N$, where D is the diameter of the spheres.

"The 'expansions' of two of the series, B and B', were practically equal, hence they were plotted together in B.

"It will be noted that the less expanded the mixture, the higher and sharper is the first maximum. This is exactly what should be expected, and agrees also with the results of Prins. The extreme case would be a regular, close-packed arrangement, either hexagonal close packing or cubic close packing. In these cases the distribution functions become discontinuous. These are given for comparison in Figure 18, E.

"These varying 'expansions' were introduced to simulate the effect of temperature. As a sample of the degree of expansion of an ordinary liquid we may cite carbon disulfide, whose volume at 25°C is 1.25 times its volume extrapolated to absolute zero. . . .

"In opposition to close-packed arrangements, very high expansions, or a gas-like structure, should give distribution functions with a very low first maximum or no peak at all, and practically no fluctuations from unity at distances greater than one diameter.

"Because of the smallness to the cell used in these experiments, the values of W tend to sag below the unity line at the larger distances, since these larger distances could not occur relatively as frequently as they would in a box of infinite size. This effect, within the region considered, could have been practically eliminated by the use of a larger container. This, however, would have greatly increased the number of observations necessary to supply the same number of measurements at the shorter distances, and it is at these smaller distances that the determination of the distribution function is of most value. Beyond a couple of diameters the function fluctuates little from unity, as Menke's curve shows. Within a couple of diameters this sagging effect plays very little part, so the added labor incident to the use of a larger cell was not considered worth while.

"Thus by the use of a model molecular assemblage we have been able to duplicate the principal characteristics of the molecular distribution function obtained for mercury. Presumably the atoms in liquid mercury are distributed much as are the spheres in these model liquids. This distribution, while practically random with respect to a central molecule at distances greater than a couple of diameters, is far from random at smaller distances. Within these shorter distances the distribution shows remnants of a regular, close-packed or crystalline structure. . . .

"It would be interesting and enlightening to extend the study of the distribution functions by means of model liquids to cases involving spheres of different sizes, and these at various 'mole fractions.' The method might also be extended to 'molecules' of other forms, such as sausage-shaped, where orientation as well as distance would have to be considered.

"A knowledge of these distribution functions for various types of liquids and solutions, and their variations with concentration and temperature, would permit a forward step in the study of the liquid state."[2]   ▲

2 W. E. MORRELL AND J. H. HILDEBRAND, *J. Chem. Phys.*, **4**, 224 (1936).

THE RADIAL DISTRIBUTION FUNCTION AND LIQUID STRUCTURE

The radial distribution curves obtained with the non-attracting spheres are surprisingly similar to those obtained by X-ray analysis of liquids. This similarity suggests an explanation for the radial distribution function based on volume or repulsive forces, rather than on attractive forces. Following the theoretical analysis of the one-dimensional case, the experimental studies of simulated two- and three-dimensional interactions have provided results in agreement with those of X-ray analysis. However, an exact formal equation for the three-dimensional problem has not been derived.

A need exists for a practical description of liquids based on known intermolecular forces, kinetic activity, and molecular geometry. Two obvious approaches are to set up a simple model with suitable parameters to fit the experimental results or to write out a perfectly general and proper mathematical theory. The first procedure has already been discussed rather extensively and is still under active study. Kirkwood, as well as Born and Green,[3] is among the leaders who have initiated and extended the second alternative with some success. In a series of papers starting in 1935, Kirkwood and his co-workers developed and extended general methods for the study of local order in terms of the molecular distribution function in liquids.[4] There are several ways to represent the distribution of molecules in a liquid. One is to use the radial distribution function, which may be determined experimentally from X-ray patterns by using the developments of Zernike and Prins, and Debye and Menke. A more recent experimental approach involves the use of neutron scattering which may prove to be superior to X-ray diffraction techniques for certain applications.[5] In introducing the article by Debye and Menke, pages 14–17, it was stated that the number of molecules in a spherical shell about a given molecule is given by $4\pi r^2 g(r)dr$, where the radial distribution function, $g(r)$ (or W), shows the average number of molecules at the radial distance, r, from the particular molecule. Kirkwood formulated an integral equation for the radial distribution function $g(r)$ in liquids and attempted its solution.[6] He made certain approximations and assumptions, such as postulating spherically shaped molecules and maintaining that attractive forces play only a minor role in the structure of liquids. The latter proposal is borne out by experiment which indicates that repulsive forces may be the important factor in determining the radial distribution function. The longer-range attractive forces are responsible, however, for matter remaining in the condensed state. Other important considerations in his theory are described below.

[3] M. Born and H. S. Green, *Proc. Roy. Soc.*, London, **A188,** 10 (1946); *A General Kinetic Theory of Liquids* (Cambridge: Cambridge University Press, 1949).

[4] J. G. Kirkwood and E. M. Boggs, *J. Chem. Phys.*, **10,** 394 (1942).

[5] O. Chamberlain, *Phys. Rev.*, **77,** 305 (1950).

[6] See the article by Kirkwood and Boggs in the Appendix.

All interactions among molecules depend on their relative positions. The force on a given molecule is the resultant of the attractive and repulsive forces of all the surrounding molecules, and a rigorous equation for $g(r)$ would require knowledge of all the interactions among all the molecules concerned. It is clear that such knowledge is practically impossible to obtain. Kirkwood, however, simplified the situation by assuming a "superposition approximation" in which the relationship between a molecule and its neighbors is defined so that the central molecule and only one of its neighbors need be considered at a time, that is, in pair fashion. Each pair is considered separately; then the effects are summed to obtain the resultant force on the central molecule.[7] This major simplifying approximation makes possible the evaluation of the distribution function, but the lack of close agreement with experiment introduces some doubt as to its validity. B. V. Derjaguin feels there is good reason to question the strict additive character of these forces, in view of the data obtained from his direct measurement of the attractive force between closely spaced objects.[8]

In addition to his key approximation, Kirkwood further maintained that the equation thus developed worked well not only for fluids of low densities, but for fluids of all densities. Subsequent investigations have shown that his concept must be modified. Considerable controversy over the usefulness and validity of the Kirkwood theory stems from approximations of indeterminable magnitude.

Of the two widely divergent approaches to a theory for the structure of liquids, Barker (1963), de Boer (1952), Rowlinson (1959), and others feel that the model concept is superior in terms of practical results. Rowlinson states that ". . . the direct calculation of the pair distribution function is stuck at the superposition approximation, and has produced surprisingly few numerical results . . . [and] it seems that little quantitative progress will be made in the approach to the theory of fluids of high density until the superposition approximation is abandoned."[9] The many attempts to circumvent the superposition approximation have met with little success.

Among the efforts to expand Kirkwood's theory is that of I. Z. Fisher, who introduced a "hypersuperposition" approximation.[10] This has permitted an extension of the range of validity of Kirkwood's equations. Fisher feels that "in spite of the approximate character of [the Kirkwood] theory, it is at present the best developed." Stuart A. Rice agrees and points out that "calculations have been carried furthest with Kirkwood's approach . . . even though the theory is only in semi-quantitative agreement with experiment. . . . The theory has no adjustable parameters, and all macroscopic properties are related di-

---

[7] H. S. Green, *The Molecular Theory of Fluids* (Amsterdam: North-Holland Publishing Company, 1952), p. 71. Chapter 1 contains a useful description of the mathematical technique used in the quantitative analysis of molecular behavior.

[8] B. V. Derjaguin, *Sci. Am.*, **203**, 47 (July, 1960).

[9] J. S. Rowlinson, *Liquids and Liquid Mixtures* (London: Butterworth and Company, 1959), p. 295.

[10] I. Z. Fisher, *Soviet Phys. Uspekhi*, **5**, 239 (1962).

rectly to the, presumably known, properties of the molecules. Moreover, the theory is internally consistent. . . . The distribution function method is the most satisfactory approach now available to a real theory of liquids."[11] H. S. Green maintains that "the kinetic theory of liquids can now be regarded as reasonably complete in its essentials: but of course formidable computational difficulties remain to be overcome."[12]

MONTE CARLO AND RELATED METHODS USING COMPUTERS

Even though complex and unwieldy, the possibility of writing an equation representing the state of an uncomplicated liquid has been indicated. In the molecular picture of liquids every particle is surrounded by others in its immediate neighborhood. The molecular effects, such as kinetic activity and collisions, attractive and repulsive forces, and space requirements must be accounted for in the equation. The complexity of these factors makes it difficult to describe with precision even a single pair of molecules, although reasonable success has been attained with such a system. Following this, an equation of state for liquids would be written by extending the methods used for the description of pairs to larger and larger numbers of molecules. The task seems hopeless at first because of the magnitude of the number of molecules in any weighable amount of material. One gram of argon contains 1.5×10^{22} particles. Macroscopic properties of matter involving such quantities are reproducible, however, because the average of a large number of molecules is measured, and under a given set of conditions the average values are essentially the same. Thus Morrell and Hildebrand were able to simulate molecular activity by using relatively few balls or spheres in their model. They attained reasonable success even though such factors as attractive forces were not included in the operations. On the basis of their experiments with a small number of spheres it is expected that studies in which somewhat similar methods are used might be feasible.

Monte Carlo Method

One proposal for depicting molecular activity applies the Monte Carlo technique to the problem of molecular distribution in a liquid in order to obtain a statistical estimate of the desired quantity by random sampling. An artificial population similar to the real system is set up. This approach should be suitable for liquids since the molecules are continually trying, in a random way, to occupy every conceivable position within their allotted space. With an adequate computer it should be possible to approximate the distribution of these molecules.

[11] Stuart A. Rice, *Intern. Sci. and Technol.*, No. 15, 64 (March, 1963).
[12] H. S. Green, *Proc. Phys. Soc.*, **A69**, 269 (1956).

In a program of this nature such factors as attractive and repulsive forces and the spatial requirements of molecules can be included.

A straightforward approach would be to choose a set of initial conditions for each molecule, such as the positions and velocities, or momenta; then the equation of motion could be used to determine the course of the molecular distribution with respect to time. This simple procedure is not feasible because of the great number of configurations needed. It would be possible, however, to decide upon a suitable number of configurations and use the Boltzmann factor as a means of weighting to average the properties over these configurations. This time-averaging procedure is the basis of the molecular dynamics method. The Monte Carlo method involves ensemble averaging and can be suitably modified for use with liquids. These two methods should give identical results for equilibrium properties. In the Monte Carlo procedure of N. Metropolis, A. W. Rosenbluth, M. N. Rosenbluth, A. H. Teller, and E. Teller,[13] the modification involves choosing configurations with a probability, $e^{-E/kT}$, and weighting them evenly, as contrasted with random choosing, then weighting in $e^{-E/kT}$.

An informative introduction to the Monte Carlo and molecular dynamics methods is given by Alder and Wainwright in their description of "Molecular Motions."[14] It might be profitable to read their discussion before considering the article of Metropolis and collaborators which follows.

▼ _____

"I. INTRODUCTION

"The purpose of this paper is to describe a general method, suitable for fast electronic computing machines, of calculating the properties of any substance which may be considered as composed of interacting individual molecules. Classical statistics is assumed, only two-body forces are considered, and the potential field of a molecule is assumed spherically symmetric. These are the usual assumptions made in theories of liquids. Subject to the above assumptions, the method is not restricted to any range of temperature or density. This paper will also present results of a preliminary two-dimensional calculation for the rigid-sphere system. . . .

"II. THE GENERAL METHOD FOR AN ARBITRARY POTENTIAL BETWEEN THE PARTICLES

"In order to reduce the problem to a feasible size for numerical work, we can, of course, consider only a finite number of particles. This number N may be as high as several hundred. Our system consists of a square containing N particles. In order to minimize the surface effects we suppose the

[13] N. Metropolis, A. W. Rosenbluth, M. N. Rosenbluth, A. H. Teller, and E. Teller, *J. Chem. Phys.*, **21**, 1087 (1953).
[14] B. J. Alder and T. E. Wainwright, *Sci. Am.*, **201**, 113 (October, 1959).

complete substance to be periodic, consisting of many such squares, each square containing N particles in the same configuration. Thus we define $\bar{d}_{AB}$, the minimum distance between particles A and B, as the shortest distance between A and any of the particles B, of which there is one in each of the squares which comprise the complete substance. If we have a potential which falls off rapidly with distance, there will be at most one of the distances AB which can make a substantial contribution; hence we need consider only the minimum distance $\bar{d}_{AB}$.

"Our method in this respect is similar to the cell method except that our cells contain several hundred particles instead of one. One would think that such a sample would be quite adequate for describing any one-phase system. We do find, however, that in two-phase systems the surface between the phases makes quite a perturbation. Also, statistical fluctuations may be sizable.

"If we know the positions of the N particles in the square, we can easily calculate, for example, the potential energy of the system,

$$E = \frac{1}{2} \sum_{\substack{i=1 \\ i \neq j}}^{N} \sum_{j=1}^{N} V(\bar{d}_{ij}). \tag{2}$$

(Here V is the potential between molecules, and $\bar{d}_{ij}$ is the minimum distance between particles i and j as defined above.)

"In order to calculate the properties of our system we use the canonical ensemble. So, to calculate the equilibrium value of any quantity of interest F,

$$\bar{F} = \left[\int F \exp(-E/kT) d^{2N}p\, d^{2N}q \right] \Big/ \left[\int \exp(-E/kT) d^{2N}p\, d^{2N}q \right], \tag{3}$$

where $(d^{2N}p\, d^{2N}q)$ is a volume element in the $4N$-dimensional phase space. Moreover, since forces between particles are velocity-independent, the momentum integrals may be separated off, and we need perform only the integration over the $2N$-dimensional configuration space. It is evidently impractical to carry out a several hundred-dimensional integral by the usual numerical methods, so we resort to the Monte Carlo method. The Monte Carlo method for many-dimensional integrals consists simply of integrating over a random sampling of points instead of over a regular array of points.

"Thus the most naive method of carrying out the integration would be to put each of the N particles at a random position in the square (this defines a random point in the $2N$-dimensional configuration space), then calculate the energy of the system according to Equation (2), and give this configuration a weight $\exp(-E/kT)$. This method, however, is not practical for close-packed configurations, since with high probability we choose a configuration where $\exp(-E/kT)$ is very small; hence a configuration of very low weight. So the method we employ is actually a modified Monte Carlo scheme, where, instead of choosing configurations randomly, then weighting them with $\exp(-E/kT)$, we choose configurations with a probability $\exp(-E/kT)$ and weight them evenly.

"This we do as follows: We place the N particles in any configuration, for example, in a regular lattice. Then we move each of the particles in succession according to the following prescription:

$$X \rightarrow X + \alpha\xi_1$$
$$Y \rightarrow Y + \alpha\xi_2, \tag{4}$$

where α is the maximum allowed displacement, which for the sake of this argument is arbitrary, and ξ_1 and ξ_2 are random numbers between (-1) and 1. Then, after we move a particle, it is equally likely to be anywhere within a square of side 2α centered about its original position. (In accord with the periodicity assumption, if the indicated move would put the particle outside the square, this only means that it re-enters the square from the opposite side.)

"We then calculate the change in energy of the system ΔE, which is caused by the move. If $\Delta E < 0$, i.e., if the move would bring the system to a state of lower energy, we allow the move and put the particle in its new position. If $\Delta E > 0$, we allow the move with probability $\exp(-\Delta E/kT)$; i.e., we take a random number ξ_3 between 0 and 1, and if $\xi_3 < \exp(-\Delta E/kT)$, we move the particle to its new position. If $\xi_3 > \exp(-\Delta E/kT)$, we return it to its old position. Then, whether the move has been allowed or not, i.e., whether we are in a different configuration or in the original configuration, we consider that we are in a new configuration for the purpose of taking our averages. So

$$\bar{F} = (1/M) \sum_{j=1}^{M} F_j, \tag{5}$$

where F_j is the value of the property F of the system after the jth move is carried out according to the complete prescription above. Having attempted to move a particle we proceed similarly with the next one.

"We now prove that the method outlined above does choose configurations with a probability $\exp(-E/kT)$. Since a particle is allowed to move to any point within a square of side 2α with a finite probability, it is clear that a large enough number of moves will enable it to reach any point in the complete square. Since this is true of all particles, we may reach any point in configuration space. Hence, the method is ergodic.

"Next consider a very large ensemble of systems. Suppose for simplicity that there are only a finite number of states of the system, and that ν_r is the number of systems of the ensemble in state r. What we must prove is that after many moves the ensemble tends to a distribution

$$\nu_r \propto \exp(-E_r/kT).$$

"Now let us make a move in all the systems of our ensemble. Let the *a priori* probability that the move will carry a system in state r to state s be P_{rs}. [By the *a priori* probability we mean the probability before discriminating on $\exp(-\Delta E/kT)$.] First, it is clear that $P_{rs} = P_{sr}$, since according to the way our game is played a particle is equally likely to be moved anywhere within a square of side 2α centered about its original position. Thus, if states r and s differ from each other only by the position of the particle moved and if these positions are within each other's squares, the transition probabilities are equal; otherwise they are zero. Assume $E_r > E_s$. Then the number of systems moving from state r to state s will be simply $v_r P_{rs}$, since all moves to a state of lower energy are allowed. The number moving from s to r will be $v_s P_{sr} \exp(-(E_r - E_s)/kT)$, since here we must weigh by the exponential factor. Thus the net number of systems moving from s to r is

$$P_{rs}\left(v_s \exp(-(E_r-E_s)/kT) - v_r.\right) \tag{6}$$

So we see that between any two states r and s, if

$$(v_r/v_s) > [\exp(-E_r/kT)/\exp(-E_s/kT)], \tag{7}$$

on the average more systems move from state r to state s. We have seen already that the method is ergodic; i.e., that any state can be reached from any other, albeit in several moves. These two facts mean that our ensemble must approach the canonical distribution. It is, incidentally, clear from the above derivation that after a forbidden move we must count again the initial configuration. Not to do this would correspond in the above case to removing from the ensemble those systems which tried to move from s to r and were forbidden. This would unjustifiably reduce the number in state s relative to r.

"The above argument does not, of course, specify how rapidly the canonical distribution is approached. It may be mentioned in this connection that the maximum displacement α must be chosen with some care; if too large, most moves will be forbidden, and if too small, the configuration will not change enough. In either case it will then take longer to come to equilibrium.

"For the rigid-sphere case, the game of chance on $\exp(-\Delta E/kT)$ is, of course, not necessary since ΔE is either zero or infinity. The particles are moved, one at a time, according to Equation (4). If a sphere, after such a move, happens to overlap another sphere, we return it to its original position.

"III. SPECIALIZATION TO RIGID SPHERES IN TWO DIMENSIONS

A. The Equation of State

"The virial theorem of Clausius can be used to give an equation of state in terms of $\bar{n}$, the average density of other particles at the surface of a particle. Let $X_i^{(tot)}$ and $X_i^{(int)}$ represent the total and the internal force, respectively, acting on particle i, at a position r_i. Then the virial theorem can be written

$$\left\langle \sum_i X_i^{(tot)} \cdot r_i \right\rangle_{Av} = 2PA + \left\langle \sum_i X_i^{(int)} \cdot r_i \right\rangle_{Av} = 2E_{kin}. \tag{8}$$

Here P is the pressure, A the area, and E_{kin} the total kinetic energy,

$$E_{kin} = N m \bar{v}^2 / 2$$

of the system of N particles.

"Consider the collisions of the spheres for convenience as represented by those of a particle of radius d_0, twice the radius of the actual spheres, surrounded by $\bar{n}$ point particles per unit area. Those surrounding particles in an area of $2\pi d_0 v \cos \phi \, \Delta t$, traveling with velocity v at an angle ϕ with the radius vector, collide with the central particle provided $|\phi| < \pi/2$. (See Figure 20.) Assuming elastic recoil, they each exert an average force during the time Δt on the central particle of $2mv \cos \phi / \Delta t$. One can see that all ϕ's

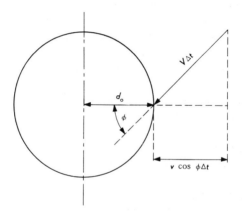

FIGURE 20

Collisions of rigid spheres.   Adapted from N. Metropolis et al., J. Chem. Phys., 21, 1087 (1953).

are equally probable, since for any velocity-independent potential between particles the velocity distribution will just be Maxwellian, hence isotropic. The total force acting on the central particle, averaged over ϕ, over time, and over velocity, is

$$\bar{F}_i = m\bar{v}^2 \pi d_0 \bar{n}: \tag{9}$$

"The sum

$$\left\langle \sum_i X_i^{(\text{int})} \cdot r_i \right\rangle_{Av}$$

is

$$-\frac{1}{2} \sum_i \left\{ \sum_{\substack{j \\ i \neq j}} r_{ij} F_{ij} \right\},$$

with F_{ij} the magnitude of the force between two particles and r_{ij} the distance between them. We see that $r_{ij} = d_0$ and $\sum_j F_{ij}$ is given by Equation (9), so we have

$$\left\langle \sum_i X_i^{(\text{int})} \cdot r_i \right\rangle_{Av} = -(Nm\bar{v}^2/2)\pi d_0^2 \bar{n}. \tag{10}$$

"Substitution of (10) into (8) and replacement of $(N/2)m\bar{v}^2$ by E_{kin} gives finally

$$PA = E_{kin}(1 + \pi d_0^2 \bar{n}/2) \equiv NkT(1 + \pi d_0^2 \bar{n}/2). \tag{11}$$

"This equation shows that a determination of the one quantity $\bar{n}$, according to Equation (5) as a function of A, the area, is sufficient to determine the equation of state for the rigid spheres.

B. The Actual Calculation of $\bar{n}$

"We set up the calculation on a system composed of $N = 224$ particles ($i = 0, 1 \ldots 223$) placed inside a square of unit side and unit area. The particles were arranged initially in a trigonal lattice of fourteen particles per row by sixteen particles per column, alternate rows being displaced relative to each other as shown in Figure 21. This arrangement gives each particle six nearest neighbors at approximately equal distances of $d = \frac{1}{14}$ from it.

"Instead of performing the calculation for various areas A and for a fixed distance d_0, we shall solve the equivalent problem of leaving $A = 1$ fixed and changing d_0. We denote by A_0 the area the particles occupy in close-packed arrangement (see Figure 22). For numerical convenience we defined an auxiliary parameter v, which we varied from zero to seven, and in terms of which the ratio, (A/A_0), and the forbidden distance, d_0, are defined as follows:

$$d_0 = d(1 - 2^{v-8}), \quad d = (1/14), \tag{12a}$$

$$(A/A_0) = 1/(3^{\frac{1}{2}}d_0^2 N/2) = 1/0.98974329(1 - 2^{v-8})^2. \tag{12b}$$

The unit cell is a parallelogram with interior angle 60°, side d_0, and altitude $3^{\frac{1}{2}}d_0/2$ in the close-packed system.

"Every configuration reached by proceeding according to the method of the preceding section was analyzed in terms of a radial distribution function

$N(r^2)$. We chose a $K > 1$ for each ν and divided the area between πd_0^2 and $K^2 \pi d_0^2$ into sixty-four zones of equal area ΔA^2,

$$\Delta A^2 = (K^2 - 1)\pi d_0^2 / 64.$$

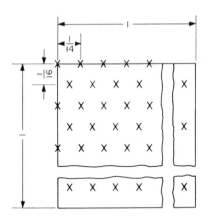

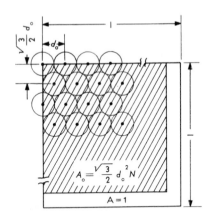

FIGURE 21

Initial trigonal lattice. Adapted from N. Metropolis et al., J. Chem. Phys., 21, 1087 (1953).

FIGURE 22

The close-packed arrangement for determining A_0. Adapted from N. Metropolis et al., J. Chem. Phys., 21, 1087 (1953).

We then had the machine calculate for each configuration the number of pairs of particles N_m ($m = 1, 2, \ldots 64$) separated by distances r which satisfy

$$(m - 1)\,\Delta A^2 + \pi d_0^2 < \pi r^2 \leq m\,\Delta A^2 + \pi d_0^2. \tag{13}$$

The N_m were averaged over successive configurations according to Equation (5), and after every sixteen cycles (a cycle consists of moving every particle once) were extrapolated back to $r^2 = d_0^2$ to obtain $N_{\frac{1}{2}}$. This $N_{\frac{1}{2}}$ differs from $\bar{n}$ in Equation (11) by a constant factor depending on N and K.

"The quantity K was chosen for each ν to give reasonable statistics for the N_m. It would, of course, have been possible by choosing fairly large K's, with perhaps a larger number of zones, to obtain $N(r^2)$ at large distances. The oscillatory behavior of $N(r^2)$ at large distances is of some interest. However, the time per cycle goes up fairly rapidly with K and with the number of zones in the distance analysis. For this reason only the behavior of $N(r^2)$ in the neighborhood of d_0^2 was investigated.

"The maximum displacement α of Equation (4) was set to $(d - d_0)$. About half the moves in a cycle were forbidden by this choice, and the initial approach to equilibrium from the regular lattice was fairly rapid.

"IV. NUMERICAL RESULTS FOR RIGID SPHERES
IN TWO DIMENSIONS

"We first ran for something less than sixteen cycles in order to get rid of the effects of the initial regular configuration on the averages. Then about forty-eight to sixty-four cycles were run at

$$\nu = 2, 4, 5, 5.5, 6, 6.25, 6.5, \text{ and } 7.$$

Also, a smaller amount of data was obtained at $\nu = 0, 1,$ and 3. The time per cycle on the Los Alamos MANIAC is approximately three minutes, and a given point on the pressure curve was obtained in four to five hours of running. Figure 23 shows $(PA/NkT) - 1$ *versus* $(A/A_0) - 1$ on a log-log scale from our results (curve A), compared to the free volume equation of Wood (curve B) and to the curve given by the first four virial coefficients (curve C). The last two virial coefficients were obtained by straightforward Monte Carlo integration on the MANIAC (see Sec. V). It is seen that the agreement between curves A and B at small areas and between curves A and C at large areas is good. Deviation from the free volume theory begins with a fairly sudden break at $\nu = 6(A/A_0 \simeq 1.8)$.

"A sample plot of the radial distribution function for $\nu = 5$ is given in Figure 24. The various types of points represent values after sixteen, thirty-two, and forty-eight cycles. For $\nu = 5$, least-square fits with a straight line to the first sixteen N_m values were made, giving extrapolated values of

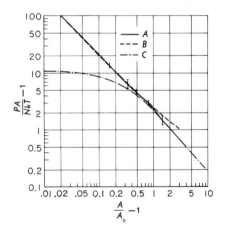

FIGURE 23

A plot of $(PA/NkT) - 1$ versus $(A/A_0) - 1$. Curve A (solid line) gives the results of this paper. Curves B and C (dashed and dot-dashed lines) give the results of the free volume theory and of the first four virial coefficients, respectively. Adapted from N. Metropolis et al., J. Chem. Phys., 21, 1087 (1953).

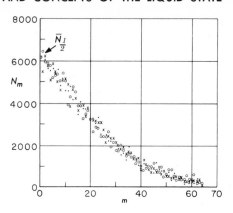

FIGURE 24

The radial distribution function N_m for $\nu = 5$, $(A/A_0) = 1.31966$, $K = 1.5$. The average of the extrapolated values of $N_{1/2}$ is $\bar{N}_{1/2} = 6301$. The resultant value of $(PA/NkT) - 1$ is $64\bar{N}_{1/2}/N^2(K^2 - 1)$ or 6.43. Values after 16 cycles, •; after 32, ✕; and after 48, o. Adapted from N. Metropolis et al., J. Chem. Phys., 21, 1087 (1953).

$N_{\frac{1}{2}}^{(1)} = 6367$, $N_{\frac{1}{2}}^{(2)} = 616^0$, and $N_{\frac{1}{2}}^{(3)} = 6377$. The average of these three was used in constructing PA/NkT. In general, least-square fits of the first sixteen to twenty N_m's by means of a parabola, or, where it seemed suitable, a straight line, were made. The errors indicated in Figure 23 are the root-mean-square deviations for the three of four $N_{\frac{1}{2}}$ values. Our average error seemed to be about 3 percent.

"Table 4 gives the results of our calculations in numerical form. The columns are ν, A/A_0, $(PA/NkT) - 1$, and, for comparison purposes, $(PA/NkT - 1)$ for the free volume theory and for the first four coefficients in the virial coefficient expansion, in that order, and finally PA_0/NkT from our results.

"V. THE VIRIAL COEFFICIENT EXPANSION

"One can show that

$$(PA/NkT) - 1 = C_1(A_0/A) + C_2(A_0/A)^2 \\ + C_3(A_0/A)^3 + C_4(A_0/A)^4 + 0(A_0/A)^5,$$

$$C_1 = \pi/3^{\frac{1}{2}}, \quad C_2 = 4\pi^2 A_{3,3}/9,$$

$$C_3 = \pi^3(6A_{4,5} - 3A_{4,4} - A_{4,6})/3^{\frac{3}{2}},$$

$$C_4 = (8\pi^3/135) \cdot [12A_{5,5} - 60A_{5,6}' - 10A_{5,6}'' \\ + 30A_{5,7}' + 60A_{5,7}'' + 10A_{5,7}''' - 30A_{5,8}' \\ - 15A_{5,8}'' + 10A_{5,9} - A_{5,10}]. \quad (14)$$

TABLE 4

Results of This Calculation for $(PA/NkT) - 1 = X_1$ Compared to the Free Volume Theory (X_2) and the Four-Term Virial Expansion (X_3). Also (PA_0/NkT) from our Calculations

ν	(A/A_0)	X_1	X_2	X_3	(PA_0/NkT)
2	1.04269	49.17	47.35	9.77	48.11
4	1.14957	13.95	13.85	7.55	13.01
5	1.31966	6.43	6.72	5.35	5.63
5.5	1.4909	4.41	4.53	4.02	3.63
6	1.7962	2.929	2.939	2.680	2.187
6.25	2.04616	2.186	2.323	2.065	1.557
6.5	2.41751	1.486	1.802	1.514	1.028
7	4.04145	0.6766	0.990	0.667	0.4149

The coefficients $A_{i,k}$ are cluster integrals over configuration space of i particles, with k bonds between them. In our problem a bond is established if the two particles overlap. The cluster integral is the volume of configuration space for which the appropriate bonds are established. If k bonds can be distributed over the i particles in two or more different ways without destroying the irreducibility of the integrals, the separate cases are distinguished by primes. For example, $A_{3,3}$ is given schematically by the diagram

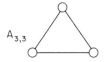

and mathematically as follows: if we define $f(r_{ij})$ by

$$f(r_{ij}) = 1 \quad \text{if} \quad r_{ij} < d,$$
$$f(r_{ij}) = 0 \quad \text{if} \quad r_{ij} > d,$$

then

$$A_{3,3} = \frac{1}{\pi^2 d^4} \int \dots \int dx_1 dx_2 dx_3 dy_1 dy_2 dy_3 (f_{12} f_{23} f_{31}).$$

The schematics for the remaining integrals are indicated in Figure 25.

"The coefficients $A_{3,3}$, $A_{4,4}$, and $A_{4,5}$ were calculated algebraically, the remainder numerically by Monte Carlo integration. That is, for $A_{5,5}$ for example, particle 1 was placed at the origin, and particles 2, 3, 4, and 5 were put down at random, subject to $f_{12} = f_{23} = f_{34} = f_{15} = 1$. The number of trials for which $f_{4,5} = 1$, divided by the total number of trials, is just $A_{5,5}$.

"The data on $A_{4,6}$ is quite reliable. We obtained

$$A_{4,6}/A_{4,4} = 0.752(\pm 0.002).$$

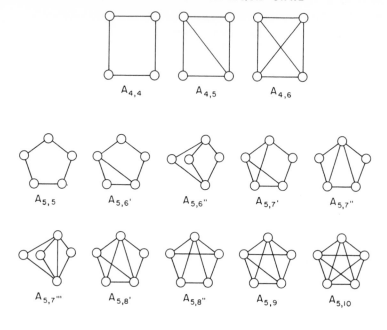

FIGURE 25

Schematic diagrams for the various area integrals.   Adapted from N. Metropolis et al., J. Chem. Phys., 21, 1087 (1953).

However, because of the relatively large positive and negative terms in C_4 of Equation (14), the coefficient C_4, being a small difference, is less accurate. We obtained

$$C_4 = 8\pi^3(0.585)/135(\pm \sim 5 \text{ percent}).$$

Our final formula is

$$(PA/NkT) - 1 = 1.813799(A_0/A) + 2.57269(A_0/A)^2 \\ + 3.179(A_0/A)^3 + 3.38(A_0/A)^4 + 0(A_0/A)^5. \quad (15)$$

This formula is plotted in curve C of Figure 23 and tabulated for some values of (A/A_0) in column 5 of Table 4. It is seen in Figure 23 that the curves agree very well with our calculated equation of state for $(A/A_0) > 2.5$. In this region both the possible error in our last virial coefficients and the contribution of succeeding terms in the expansion are quite small (less than our probable statistical error) so that the virial expansion should be accurate.

"VI. CONCLUSION

"The method of Monte Carlo integrations over configuration space seems to be a feasible approach to statistical mechanical problems which are as yet not analytically soluble. At least for a single-phase system a sample of several hundred particles seems sufficient. In the case of two-dimensional rigid spheres, runs made with 56 particles and with 224 particles agreed within statistical error. For a computing time of a few hours with presently available electronic computers, it seems possible to obtain the pressure for a given volume and temperature to an accuracy of a few percent.

"In the case of two-dimensional rigid spheres our results are in agreement with the free volume approximation for $A/A_0 < 1.8$ and with a five-term virial expansion for $A/A_0 > 2.5$. There is no indication of a phase transition."[15]   ▲

Molecular Dynamics Method

High speed computers make it possible to handle the mathematical difficulties of statistical mechanics, but they do not provide a simple description of liquids. Space limitations and attractive and repulsive forces, insofar as we understand them, can be introduced into the study. Allowance for temperature changes can be made, and the results can be used to calculate the pressure of the system. The distribution of molecules can then be simulated by the molecular dynamics method, as reported by Alder and Wainwright.[16]

Computers are capable of calculating the detailed trajectories of a fairly large number of particles. The various individual paths are followed until two particles come close enough for interacting forces to become effective. The computer describes their actions according to the programmed information. After the interaction the trajectories are followed again until a new collision occurs. Many particles are grouped together to produce a large cell and the entire space is then pictured as being filled by repetitions of these cells. The number of particles in a cell is kept at a constant value by utilizing a periodic boundary arrangement whereby a particle leaving a cell reenters through the opposite side with essentially no disruption. Except for the greater cell size, this system has much in common with the previously discussed cell models. A detailed description of the molecular dynamics method, along with some interesting results, including traces of the particles, is given by WAINWRIGHT and ALDER.

▼ "1. Introduction

"Statistical mechanical theories of many-particle systems encounter difficulties . . . [which are] compounded by the complicated and not well established law of interatomic force between the particles. This latter uncertainty makes any comparison of the theory with experimental data on real gases

---

[15] N. METROPOLIS ET AL., loc. cit.
[16] B. J. Alder and T. E. Wainwright, J. Chem. Phys., **27**, 1208 (1957); Sci. Am., **201**, 113 (October, 1959).

and liquids doubly unsure. With fast electronic computers it is possible to set up artificial many-particle systems with interactions which are both simple and exactly known. Experiments with such a system can yield not only the equilibrium and transport properties at any arbitrary density and temperature of the system, but also any much more detailed information desired. With these 'controlled' experiments in simple systems it is then possible to narrow down the problem as to what analytical scheme best approximates the many-body correlations. This is not to say that computations can not be performed on more realistic systems.

"The main disadvantage of such an artificial system is that only rather small numbers of particles can be treated in a reasonable calculating time. This means that the inherent fluctuations in the artificial system will be more limited than the fluctuations in a very large system. Also the boundaries might have an influence on the bulk properties; however, there is at present no evidence of this, except possibly in transition regions.

"2. Description of the method

"In calculations described here a system of particles, ranging in number from 32 to 500, is considered to be located in a rectangular box. The position and velocity of each particle is stored in the memory of the calculating machine, and the changes of all positions and velocities are arrived at by numerical solution of the classical many-body problem. The interaction potential is taken to be . . . that of smooth, rigid spheres. . . .

"The boundary conditions are such that a particle which passes out through one side of the box, reenters with the same velocity through the opposite side. Alternately, the system can be conceived of as an infinite array of identical boxes with penetrable walls. This is not unlike the cell model of liquids; however, the cells here contain many more particles than one is analytically capable of handling and the boundaries are not fixed. . . .

"At low densities, the number of particles in the box is unimportant; however, at high densities the number of particles in the box determines the kind of packing which is achieved. A few low-density calculations have been made with a cubic box and 100 particles. Both high and low-density calculations have been made with a cubic box and $4n^3$ particles (i.e. 32, 108, 256, and 500). In these cases the packing is necessarily face-centered cubic. A number of calculations have been made with 96 particles in a rectangular box whose edge lengths were such that the close-packed configuration is hexagonal.

"Since the interaction potentials are such that particles exert forces on each other only at certain specified separations, the entire dynamic calculation can be done by considering a succession of two-body collisions. A tally of the number of collisions as a function of time and also the sum of the absolute values of the momentum changes are occasionally printed by the machine as the calculation proceeds so that the collision rate and the pressure can be determined. The latter is calculated from the growth-rate of the momentum sum by means of the virial theorem. The velocity changes of each particle are recorded on magnetic tape so that the history of the system can later be reconstructed in order to calculate such things as radial distribution functions, diffusion coefficients, velocity distributions, *H*-functions, and velocity autocorrelation functions.

"3. Non-equilibrium properties

"Nearly all of the systems so far studied have been started with a particular non-equilibrium velocity distribution. The particles all have equal kinetic energies with velocities in random directions. . . . calculations have been made over a wide range of densities; in all cases the equilibrium value is reached monotonically in from 2 to 4 collisions per particle. The rapidity with which the velocity distribution equilibrates is made possible by the fact that large amounts of momentum can be exchanged in single collisions. . . .

"4. Equilibrium properties

"The equation of state of systems of rigid spheres has been investigated rather intensively, especially in the density range $1.5 < v/v_0 < 1.7$, where there is a strong indication of a first order transition [v is the specific volume and v_0 is the close-packed specific volume]. Figure 26 shows the number of collisions (circles) and the momentum sum, $\sum$ (triangles), for a system of 100 rigid spheres at $v/v_0 = 2$ as a function of time. $\sum$ is defined as

$$\sum_i (r_{a_i} - r_{b_i}) \cdot \Delta v_a , \tag{16}$$

where r_{a_i} and r_{b_i} are the positions of particles a_i and b_i which are involved in collision i. Δv_{a_i} is the change of velocity of particle a_i which is the same, except for sign, as the change in velocity of particle b_i. The pressure is determined by

$$\frac{pv}{kT} - 1 = \frac{1}{N\bar{v}^2} \frac{\Delta \sum}{\Delta t} , \tag{17}$$

where N is the number of particles in the system and $\bar{v}^2$ is the mean square velocity relative to the center of mass of the system. A straight line is drawn through the triangles and its slope measured to find $\Delta \sum / \Delta t$ and thus, $pv/kT - 1$. According to the theory of Enskog [see page 106] the collision rate is given by

$$\frac{\Delta C}{\Delta t} = \frac{N-1}{d} \sqrt{\frac{3\bar{v}^2}{\pi}} \left(\frac{pv}{kT} - 1 \right) , \tag{18}$$

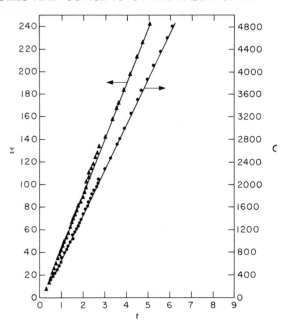

FIGURE 26

A plot of the virial (triangles), Σ, and the collision number (circle), C, as a function of time for a system of 100 hard sphere particles at $v/v_0 = 2.00$. The solid line for the collision rate is calculated from Enskog's theory. Adapted from T. Wainwright and B. J. Alder, Il Nuovo Cimento, 9, 116 (1958); J. Chem. Phys., 31, 459 (1959); 33, 1439 (1960).

where d is the diameter of a sphere. The straight line through the circles is drawn with this slope. It is found that this Enskog relationship between pressure and collision rate holds good even for quite high densities. . . . Figure 26 is typical of all systems regardless of density. . . .

"In a narrow intermediate range of densities the systems show a tendency to undergo spontaneous transitions between states of considerably different pressures. Thus, for all systems of $v/v_0 \geq 1.525$ and $v/v_0 <$ about 1.7 which are started out in a face-centered cubic configuration, the pressure remains steady at a low value for a more or less long period of time and then suddenly the collision rate increases (see Figure 27) and the Σ curve increases its slope indicating a transition to a higher pressure. The time required for the first such transition is as expected generally longer for the higher densities; however, there are large statistical variations. See Table 5. For $v/v_0 = 1.525$ the transition occurs after about 93,000 collisions, then at 203,000 collisions the system spontaneously goes back to the low pressure

TABLE 5

*Collision Number at Which the First Transition
to a Fluid Took Place*

v/v_0	32 particles	108 particles	256 particles
	C	C	C
1.5250	93,000	—	—
1.5300	76,000	—	—
1.53125	4,000	—	—
1.5325	9,000	—	—
1.5350	2,000	—	—
1.5400	400	—	—
1.5500	25,000	3000	—
1.6000	5,000	2100	1900
1.6500	—	800	—
1.7000	—	<100	—
1.7678	—	1200	4600

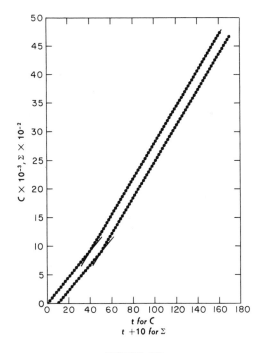

FIGURE 27

*The collision rate, C, and the virial, $\sum$, as a function of time for 32 hard
sphere particles at $v/v_0 = 1.5325$ showing a sudden jump at about 9,000
collisions. Adapted from T. Wainwright and B. J. Alder, Il Nuovo Cimento,
9, 116 (1958); J. Chem. Phys., 31, 459 (1959); 33, 1439 (1960).*

state and stays there for about 1,000 collisions before returning to the high pressure state. It is not known whether systems at even higher densities would finally go to the high pressure state if sufficient time were allowed. It is clear that configurational states can require extremely long times to equilibrate because the proper fluctuation among a set of particles may not occur frequently.

"A cathode-ray picture tube attached to the calculating machine was utilized to make traces in a plane projection of the positions of the centers of the particles in the 32 particle system $v/v_0 = 1.525$. Figure 28 shows the traces from collision 202,000 to 203,000 where the system is in the high pressure state. . . . Figure 29 and Figure 30 show the traces in the fluid and solid regions respectively for about 3,000 collisions. Evidently the system is not sufficiently large that the fluid and solid phases can exist in equilibrium, but rather a system in the appropriate density range exists part of the time in one phase and part of the time in the other.

"An extremely long calculation would be required to establish a time average over the two pressure states. Furthermore, the average pressure in the transition region thus obtained differs from the pressure of a large system which could contain crystals in equilibrium with fluid. We have, therefore, chosen to calculate pressures of the fluid and solid phases separately. Similar behavior has been found by Wood, Parker, and Jacobson in their Monte Carlo calculations on hard sphere systems. . . .

"The effect of the number of particles on the pressure is most noticeable in the transition region. For a larger and larger number of particles the system should approach more and more a horizontal line in the equation of state. Though no noticeable difference between 32 and 108 particles was obtained in the two branches, the true average between the two pressures may be different. From very preliminary results it may be possible that for 500 particles the system can partially contain the two coexisting phases simultaneously and thus yield a partially averaged pressure.

"Outside the two phase region no difference can be detected in the equation of state for various sized samples and this includes the 96-particle system with the hexagonal close packed structure in a rectangular box. In fact, it can be shown that the second, B, and third, C, virial coefficients have the following dependence on the number of particles, N, in a periodic system

$$B_N = B_\infty(1 - 1/N), \tag{19}$$

$$C_N = C_\infty(1 + \tfrac{1}{5}N - \tfrac{6}{5}N^2), \tag{20}$$

where the subscript ∞ is the ordinary virial coefficient for an infinite system. Hence, this is a small correction for even 32 particles.

"The pressure has also been calculated by means of the radial distribution function. The comparison with Equation (17) is within the accuracy of the

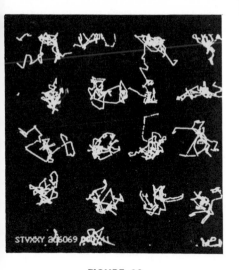

FIGURE 28

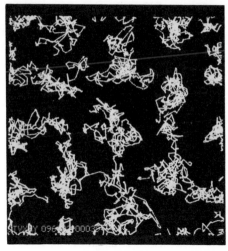

FIGURE 29

FIGURE 30

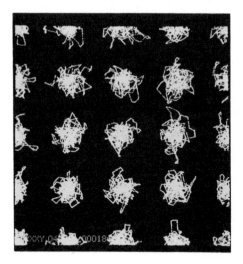

Figure 28 shows traces of the centers of 32 particles during 1,000 collisions in the dense liquid region of hard spheres. Figure 29 shows projected molecular trajectories for rigid spheres with $V/V_0 = 1.525$; 32 particles in a cubic box performing 3,000 collisions in the fluid region. Figure 30 shows projected molecular trajectories for rigid spheres with $V/V_0 = 1.525$; 32 particles in a cubic box performing 3,000 collisions in the solid region. Adapted from T. Wainwright and B. J. Alder, Il Nuovo Cimento, 9, 116 (1958); J. Chem. Phys., 31, 459 (1959); 33, 1439 (1960).

calculation. The radial distribution functions disagree somewhat, however, with the ones calculated from the superposition theory at intermediate densities although that theory predicted a transition for hard spheres at $v/v_0 = 1.48$."[17]

▲

Equilibrium data may be provided by both the Monte Carlo and molecular dynamics methods. In addition, the latter method is capable of yielding information about dynamic processes. The opportunity to view or follow the motions of molecules is intriguing, to say the least. At this point it might be in order to add a precautionary note such as that expressed by WIGNER:

▼ "If I had a great calculating machine, I would perhaps apply it to the Schroedinger equation of each metal and obtain its cohesive energy, its lattice constant, etc. It is not clear, however, that I would gain a great deal by this. Presumably, all the results would agree with the experimental values and not much would be learned from the calculations."[18]

▲

It is possible to carry out laborious mathematical computations involving the best estimates of 12–6 type potentials, molecular diameters, and other factors, all of which make this technique a significant aid in liquid investigation. There is need for improvement in the equipment itself as well as in the methods of application. Calculating speed is a limiting factor in the application of computers, although a fairly large number of particles, of the order of 10,000, may be handled. This quantity is still extremely small in terms of the immense number of molecules actually involved in macroscopic systems. The consensus is, however, that only a comparatively small number of particles is needed to duplicate closely the behavior of a fluid. Other drawbacks such as the inability to determine the partition function and the entropy still need to be overcome.

[17] T. WAINWRIGHT AND B. J. ALDER, *Il Nuovo Cim.*, **9,** 116 (1958); see also *J. Chem. Phys.*, **31,** 459 (1959); **33,** 1439 (1960).

[18] E. P. WIGNER, *Handbuch der Physik*, **PH XIII** (Berlin-Göttingen-Heidelberg: Springer-Verlag, 1962), p. 217.

CHAPTER 6

Spatial Model

GEOMETRICAL APPROACH TO THE STRUCTURE OF LIQUIDS

Another application of the computing machine to the problem of structure in liquids was provided by J. D. Bernal, who adapted it to geometrical models.[1] He devised a method to compute the coordinates of centers of random assemblies of hard spheres so as to get a minimum energy for each relative position of the points, and from this to evaluate the radial distribution functions.

One unexpected result of the geometrical study is the possibility of a natural arrangement of matter in the fluid state into five-sided units. It is accepted that five-fold symmetry is impossible in any crystal lattice structure for solids. However, if a soft substance such as lead, putty, or other plastic material is formed into spheres, then put under pressure until flow takes place, many of the spheres will be distorted into units having some five-sided faces. Figure 31 is an enlarged sketch of ordinary lead shot balls after having been placed in a steel cylinder fitted with a solid piston and put under pressure in an arbor press. Similar distorted particles may be seen on breaking expanded, rigid Styrofoam plastic material.

Bernal contends that, while a five-fold structure is prohibited for solid crystals, such is not the case for all of nature. Pentagonal arrangements may well be the rule for irregular, non-crystalline material. In this way he is freed from the limitations imposed by the restrictions of crystallography and can approach the structure of liquids from the standpoint of a new geometrical concept. BERNAL'S interesting development is reproduced in the following two articles.

[1] J. D. Bernal, *Nature*, **183**, 141 (1959); **185**, 68 (1960); *Sci. Am.*, **203**, 124 (August, 1960).

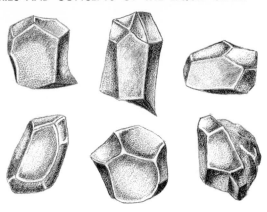

FIGURE 31

Enlarged sketches of lead shot balls after being subjected to pressure. About 100 balls were used to provide ample space for flow. Some five-sided faces are clearly visible.

▼ "Most of the vast literature on the liquid state is based on attempted explanations of experimental observations of the thermal, mechanical, and other properties of actual liquids. Compared with the progress of the molecular theories of gases and the lattice theory of crystalline solids, there has been little success in accounting for the phenomena of the liquid state in terms of the position and the known laws of the interaction of their constituent molecules. This is evidently because of the extreme difficulty of arriving at a model of the structure of a liquid which corresponds to the arrangements of its molecules and which at the same time is susceptible to mathematical computation. Most recent theories are frankly attempts to adapt the known structures of gaseous and crystalline matter to the intermediate state of the liquid. They are consequently physically very implausible, whether they are the kinetic multiple molecular contact theories of Kirkwood, [or] Born and Green, the cell theories of Lennard-Jones and Devonshire, the hole theories of Frenkel, Eyring and Furth, or the cybotactic hypothesis of Stewart. The last three indeed assume that a large part of a liquid consists of crystalline material, which is in contradiction to the essential negative property of liquids — their lack of long-range order.

"Meanwhile, evidence on the actual molecular structure of liquids has been accumulating, starting with the classical work of Prins and Stewart based on X-ray, and now on neutron, diffraction of liquids, which shows them to possess only a short-range order, practically limited to molecules in the first and second spheres around a given molecule. Very little use has been made of this evidence in constructing theories of the liquid state, essentially because of its complexity — of a kind unfamiliar to theoretical physicists or chemists.

"It has occurred to me recently that, in view of this and a renewed interest in the properties of liquids, it might be worthwhile to take up the sketch of a theory I first put forward twenty years ago, and to see whether it is capable of leading to a physically acceptable theory of liquids. I cannot yet claim that it is at the same time adapted to mathematical treatment, but I have hopes that at least it can be adapted to computing machines in the way that has already been used by Alder and Wainwright for kinetic studies of gases.

"The essential feature of this theory is that it treats liquids as *homogeneous*, *coherent* and *essentially irregular* assemblages of molecules containing no crystalline regions or holes large enough to admit another molecule. In most of what follows I shall be dealing with ideally simple liquids such as those of the rare gases (except helium), but the arguments used can apply with minor modifications to all liquids. What characterizes any particular liquid arrangement is its radial distribution function $g(r)$ which expresses the probability of finding a molecule at a distance r from any other. The determination of the distribution function from diffraction data is subject to error in detail, but its main features are beyond doubt. All show a strong peak indicating 8–12 neighbours at a distance r_0, very little different from the closest approach in the corresponding crystalline solid. The interpretation of the structures corresponding to any radial distribution function is an exercise of an almost unknown subject 'statistical geometry,' which I recommend to mathematicians. There must be theorems limiting the possible forms of distribution functions of any array of points whatever. For example, in a dense irregular assembly, each point is linked in general by fourteen vectors to its neighbours, while only six are needed to fix its position precisely, each vector being counted twice. It would be most desirable to find the true minimum number of parameters or parametral functions defining the statistical structure of any homogeneous irregular assemblage in the way that the lattice vectors define a regular one. I suggested — but could not prove in my original paper — that three parameters suffice to determine the whole of a distribution function: N_1, the number of neighbours, r_1 the mean distance, and λ_1 the variance of r between the neighbours. Whether this be so or not geometrically, it is evident that physically most of the properties must be determined by the arrangement of neighbouring molecules, on account of the rapid fall-off of attractive intermolecular potentials as $1/r^6$ for apolar molecules.

"What I am attempting to do now is to examine more closely the neighbour relations in irregular assemblies of molecules. In any definite assembly of points whatever, the neighbours of any one point can be precisely indicated. If planes are drawn bisecting the distances between each point and any other, then we can call those points corresponding to the sides of the smallest convex polyhedron surrounding the point the *geometrical neighbours* of the point. There seem to be, in irregular as in regular arrangements, some fourteen of these, and in any approximately dense assembly of molecules, they will lie between r_0 and $\sqrt{2}r_0$, where r_0 is the distance of closest approach. In the ball-and-spoke model (see Figure 33 below), this number was found to be 13·6 and in the 'Plasticene' model 13·3.

"Many of the properties of liquids can be most readily appreciated in terms of the packing of irregular polyhedra — as in a foam (Figure 32). For example, the total volume, V, of a liquid of n molecules is $\sum v_q$, where v_q is the volume of the qth molecular polyhedron. To obtain an expression for v_q, or rather for $\bar{v}$, the mean polyhedron volume, in terms of molecular dimensions and arrangement, it is not convenient to use the number of geometrical neighbours, which is insensitive to these factors. It is easier to use the number N of *physical neighbours* which can be defined, arbitrarily, as those of the geometrical neighbours which lie at distances between r_0 and $\frac{5}{4}r_0$ (for beyond the latter distance the Van der Waals attraction falls to less than a quarter of its maximum value). The mean volume can then be expressed as $r_0{}^3 f(N)$, where $f(N)$ is a function not yet determinable for the case of irregular packing, but which cannot differ widely from its value in regular packing as shown in Table 6. The equivalences of N with reduced temperature T† are derived from de Boer's results.

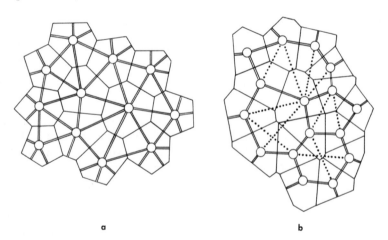

a   b

FIGURE 32

Diagram of neighbourhood polyhedra, geometrical and physical, for two-dimensional arrays of points. a, high co-ordinated; ═, physical neighbours. b, low co-ordinated; . . . . , geometrical neighbours. Adapted from J. D. Bernal, Nature, 183, 141 (1959).

TABLE 6

N	12	10	8	6	4	3
f(N)	5.66	5·9*	6·4*	8	12·3	18
f(N)/f	1·0	1·04	1·16	1·41	2·17	3·18
T†	0	0·8	0·9	1·0	1·2	1·27
			Tm			Tc

* Interpolated values

"The irregularity of the neighbourhood polyhedra is the essential condition for liquid as against crystalline structures. It can be seen to underly their thermal and mechanical properties. It implies first of all the absence of long-range order and of symmetry other than statistical. The conditions that a set of quasi-equal irregular polyhedra must satisfy to fill space completely must be stringent, but I have not been able to define them mathematically. Instead I have tried to approach them by physical and mathematical model-building in a somewhat different way from that employed by Morrell and Hildebrand. In the first place, I have constructed models of balls and spokes as irregular as possible using spokes of lengths from 2·75 to 4·0 in. in the proportions roughly the same as observed in liquid distribution functions (Figure 33). From such models it is possible to draw conclusions

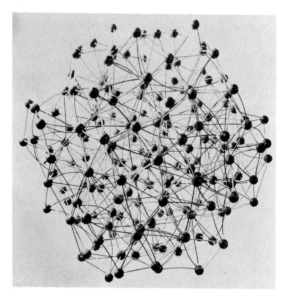

FIGURE 33

Photograph of ball-and-spoke model of irregular structure. Adapted from J. D. Bernal, Nature, 183, 141 (1959).

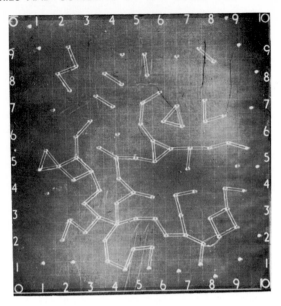

FIGURE 34

Two-dimensional random crystal model at intermediate stage.   No two points are at a distance smaller than the 8-cm. long links joining most of the points.   Adapted from J. D. Bernal, Nature, 183, 141 (1959).

on volume and energy of the corresponding arrangements of actual molecules. I have also built models from which the human element is eliminated as far as possible by 'Monte Carlo' constructions. The first of these which I attempted ten years ago was purely mathematical. . . .

"The second 'Monte Carlo' approach I have tried with physical models is analogous to the formation of irregular close-packed liquids by compression from a gas. A set of points is chosen at random in the large cell of a two- or three-dimensional lattice (Figures 34 and 35). If these are thought of as being rigid spheres of unit radius, the compression of such a cell is exactly equivalent to expanding a sphere surrounding each point. No new points are added. Starting with the nearest pair, the points are moved apart by small successive stages so that at each stage no two points are nearer than a pre-specified distance. There is a limit to the process, however. At a length corresponding to about 0·9 of the closed-packed distance in two dimensions and 0·95 in three dimensions, no further movement is possible without introducing long-range order. In other words, at densities beyond a certain limit, only crystalline arrangements of incompressible spheres are possible. Two-dimensional aggregates crystallize more easily than do three-dimensional aggregates. This is a point of the greatest importance, because the possibility

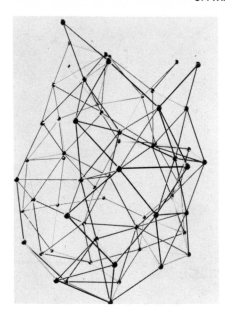

FIGURE 35

Three-dimensional hanging-ball model at intermediate stage. Adapted from
J. D. Bernal, Nature, 183, 141 (1959).

of irregular coordinations are multiplied in three dimensions. The whole
process of compressions can be carried out by rules adapted to the iterative
action of an electronic computer; but this has yet to be done, and it may
turn out to be blocked by the occurrence of impossible moves or 'moving
corner' ambiguities. However, enough has been done to bring out clearly
that indefinite irregular assemblies can be constructed having about the same
volume, internal energy and distribution function, as tested by the Lipson
diffractometer, as simple liquids. The possibility of forming such statically
stable, dense irregular molecular aggregates in three dimensions follows indeed from the great variety of polyhedra of 10–14 sides that can be escribed
about the same sphere. Such arrangements, though they must have slightly
greater energy than the corresponding regular assembly, are so much more
numerous as to provide for greater entropy.

"I have also attempted to describe the irregular character of such distributions both mathematically and by models. I am reasonably sure that the
enumeration of topologically distinct convex polyhedra having in general
three edges meeting at a point must have been carried out by some mathematicians, though I cannot trace it. The subject appears not to be of interest
to modern mathematicians, and I have found little on it later than Cayley

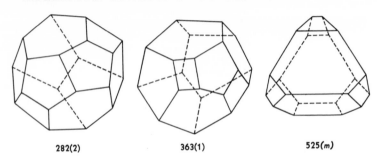

282(2)   363(1)   525(*m*)

FIGURE 36

Three typical polyhedra with twelve faces.   Adapted from J. D. Bernal, Nature, 183, 141 (1959).

and Kirkman, who were only interested in symmetrical solutions, except in the very valuable studies of Toth.   The derivation of the irregular polyhedra is straightforward but tedious.   There are certainly 46 distinct polyhedra with up to 12 faces composed of polygons of 4, 5 and 6 edges (Figure 36). There are probably, though I have not exhausted the list, some 150 of up to 14 faces.   To work out the angles and closest approach of spheres to all these would be a formidable task.   Before attempting it I thought it would be well to discover which of them were likely to occur in nearly close-packed assemblies of spheres.   For this I used a rough empirical method adapted from that developed by the botanist, Marvin, to determine the shapes of cells in plants.   Balls of 'Plasticene' rolled in chalk were packed together irregularly and pressed into one solid lump.   The resulting polyhedra (Figure 37) were analysed for arrangement of their polygon faces, with the results shown in Table 7.   Two results are noticeable: first, the wide variety of polyhedra — the 65 studied showed 32 different combinations of polygonal faces and only two were found with the same permutations of these faces; secondly, the absolute predominance of pentagonal faces.   In all but six cases, no polygon appeared more often than a pentagon.   These observations, taken together, are the key to the geometrical nature of irregular aggregates of equal spheres and also, in my view, of the molecular arrangements in liquids.   Regular three-dimensional arrangements have symmetries limited to multiplicities of 2, 3, 4 and 6.   Pentagonal arrangements can only occur in very complex structures such as some of the alloy structures classified by Frank.   My central geometrical thesis is that *irregular dense packing and pentagonal arrangements are necessarily connected.*   Though I have no proof of this theorem for lack of an adequate statistical geometry, I think it is related to two simple geometrical facts: first, that twelve spheres touching an equal sphere are most regularly distributed in a way in which one just

FIGURE 37

*A portion of a "plasticene" hemisphere showing polyhedra. Adapted from
J. D. Bernal, Nature, 183, 141 (1959).*

TABLE 7

*Number of Each Polygon Combination Type Arranged in the Order of the
Number of Pentagonal Faces*

			Number of pentagonal faces						
12	10	9	8	7	6	5	4	3	1
0 12 0 (2) 0 12 2	1 10 2 (4) 1 10 4 (2)	1 0 9 3 2 9 5 1	2 8 1 (2) 2 8 2 (3) 2 8 3 (3) 2 8 4 (4) 2 8 6	3 7 2 1 (3) 3 7 3 1	3 6 2 3 6 3 (5) 3 6 4 (5) 3 6 5 (3) 3 6 6 (5) 4 6 4 2	1 2 5 3 4 5 3 1 4 5 4 1 (2)	1 3 4 3 1 1 3 4 4 1 (2) 1 3 4 5 1 (3) 1 3 4 6 1 4 4 2 4 4 4 4 4 5 4 4 6	5 3 3 1	1 4 1 5
3	6	2	13	4	20	4	11	1	1

Total number of polyhedra, 65. Number of polyhedron categories, 32.

Explanation: The numbers for each polyhedron are put in the order of the polygonal
faces. For example, 1 3 4 5 1 stands for a polyhedron with 1 triangular, 3 quadrangular, 4
pentagonal, 5 hexagonal, 1 heptagonal face. The last row gives the number in each category.

fails to touch five others in its shell — it has a surface co-ordination of 5, to
follow Frank's terminology. This results in a pentagonal icosahedron, a
shape which cannot be used to fill space. Secondly, in those forms which
can fill space, the twelve co-ordinations corresponding to hexagonal or cubic

close packing, each sphere is in actual contact with only four others in its shell, a very stable but improbable arrangement. This is on the basis of a rough examination of the number of possible arrangements of 10–15 circles on the surface of a sphere. This may be susceptible to exact statistical treatment, or could be adequately worked out on a computer.

"The irregular dense arrangement occupies a volume per sphere of some 10 per cent more than close packing. This is the figure first found by Osborne Reynolds in his studies of the dilatancy of closed-packed sand.

"I have always found it impossible to construct irregular arrangements of any intermediate density. I believe this is a necessary consequence of the irregularity, and that there is *an absolute impossibility of forming a homogeneous assembly of points of volume intermediate between those of long-range order and closest packed disorder.* Regular and irregular close packing are evidently arrangements of quite different local co-ordination, and a transition between them is necessarily as abrupt as that between two regular phases of different structure such as occurs in the α- (body-centred) and γ- (face-centred) phases of iron.

"Translated into physical terms, this geometrical difference expresses the absolute discontinuity between the liquid and the crystalline phases and accordingly the need for a first-order transformation between them. This is in accord with Simon's general findings that the melting entropy of solids increases indefinitely with the temperature, showing therefore no tendency towards a critical point. The fact that the polyhedra of irregular and regular packing differ only slightly in volume for the same values of N would seem to justify, at least as a working hypothesis, the idea that a liquid structure near the melting point is only an irregular but absolutely distinct variant of a crystalline one. In this irregular structure, molecules are vibrating about positions of equilibrium for times so long compared to their period of vibration that for all thermal properties the time variations of molecular positions — so important for all transfer phenomena — can be neglected in the first instance. The lower specific heat of simple liquids compared with the corresponding solid at the same pressure is accounted for by the irregular and wider shape of the equilibrium minima: at constant volume there is little difference between the specific heats of solids and liquids. On this basis, finding the equilibrium structure of a liquid is the same as finding that of a crystal. For liquids having molecules with attraction rapidly diminishing with distance — such as rare gases and organic liquids, but not for liquid metals or water — the solution equates minimum energy with minimum volume. If the internal energy U varies as $1/r^6$, it must vary as $1/v^2$, as Van der Waals had intuitively supposed. The types of irregular arrangement arrived at by all the methods described above, except that leading to maximum coherent volume, are of minimum volume and should be near to true models for a liquid near the melting point. Indeed, by using a potential function of the form

$$U = \frac{A}{r^{12}} - \frac{B}{r^6}$$

they are found to give the right orders of magnitude for the heat of fusion.

"The chief advantage that a theory based on the intrinsic irregularity of liquid structures has over most cell or hole theories is that it gives a natural qualitative explanation for the high entropies of liquids compared with solids which these theories have failed to do as de Boer has pointed out. Unfortunately, it is not yet possible to put this on a quantitative basis. The fundamental difficulty is to know what to count as a configuration in order to build a partition function. It is evident that in an irregular structure there is a wide variation in the potential energy associated with each molecule. . . .

". . . we can make a qualitative picture of the energy states in a liquid as a function of temperature. In the first place, from near the melting point downwards through the range of super-cooling, the approximate close-packed disorder is maintained, for it cannot change without crystallization, which, for the reasons already given, is always a discontinuous phenomenon. However, at all temperatures the thermal state of a liquid is fundamentally different from that of a solid, for the rise in temperature leads not only to higher vibrational levels, as it does in a solid, but also to changes in the equilibrium configuration, increased disorder, and, at constant pressure, also to greater volume, lower co-ordination numbers, and consequently lower mean-lattice energy. A liquid, over this range of temperature, corresponds more to a series of polymorphic phases with heats of transformation between them than to a single phase, as explained in my original paper. Instead of heats of transformation, the process is smeared out to give an accelerated rise in the specific heat at constant pressure which I called the 'configurational specific heat.'

"This has been recently studied in detail by Jones and Walker for liquid argon. Their observations of the specific heat seem to me of fundamental, but hitherto unrecognized, importance. They find that, well above the critical pressure, the specific heat at constant pressure, starting at 10·8 cal./mol./deg. C., increases rapidly with temperatures to values of nearly 50, reaches a sharp maximum and then falls to the normal value 3 for a gas. This is the condition for a higher-order transition (λ-point) between the liquid and the gaseous state. The line of transition in the pressure-temperature diagram continues that of the boiling-point line indefinitely beyond the critical point. I would suggest calling this line the *hyper-critical line*. Its existence shows that liquid and gas do not form, as previously thought, a single 'fluid' phase. They are distinct states of matter, though one may pass into the other without visible discontinuity. (The discontinuity is, however, 'audible,' as shown by heavy absorption of sound in this region and is also

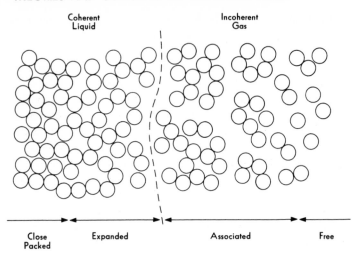

Coherent
Liquid

Incoherent
Gas

Close
Packed

Expanded

Associated

Free

FIGURE 38

*Diagram of transition of molecular arrangements passing from close-packed
liquid to gas through the hyper-critical line. Adapted from J. D. Bernal,
Nature, 183, 141 (1959).*

shown by a minimum in the velocity of sound and in the viscosity.) This is
probably a very general phenomenon applying not only to all liquids and
gases but also to all critical mixtures above their critical points.

"It finds a ready explanation along the lines of the theory I have just been
putting forward. In this picture, a liquid will continue to expand with temperature until it is slightly more than three times its original close-packed
volume. The *physical* co-ordination number falls to between 4 and 3, which
is the limit for 'coherent' structure — one in which the molecules are linked
together without a break throughout the whole volume (Table 6 and Figure
38). Above the hyper-critical temperature it becomes 'incoherent,' consisting
of associated groups of molecules in free space. As this temperature is approached, therefore, at constant pressures at or above the critical pressure,
more and more co-ordination links are broken, leading to a rise in specific
heat. This falls again beyond the hyper-critical point as fewer and fewer
links remain to be broken. Just below and above this temperature, the number of intermolecular links undergoes no abrupt change; hence there is no
heat of transformation, but continuous regions become discontinuous and
vice versa. This is analogous on a micro-scale to the sharp transition between
oil-in-water and water-in-oil emulsions. At temperatures and pressures
approaching the critical point, the coherent-incoherent structures become
also inhomogeneous with macroscopic cavities and drops leading to the
critical opalescence, the study of which has been recently taken up again
by Debye.

"The fundamental structural characteristic of liquids — the irregular arrangement of their molecules — can be seen also to be the basis of their characteristic physical property — their fluidity. In a way impossible for a crystalline solid, the neighbourhood relations of molecules in a liquid are necessarily in continual flux. This is easiest to understand by considering the relationships of the polyhedra which define the closest interacting neighbours. The elementary process by which a molecule loses a neighbour is represented by the closing in of the face common to both; how it gains another is by the opening up of a new, in general, triangular face (Figure 39).

"Such processes must occur constantly by thermal motion on account of the sustained inequality of energies between molecules. By repetition they

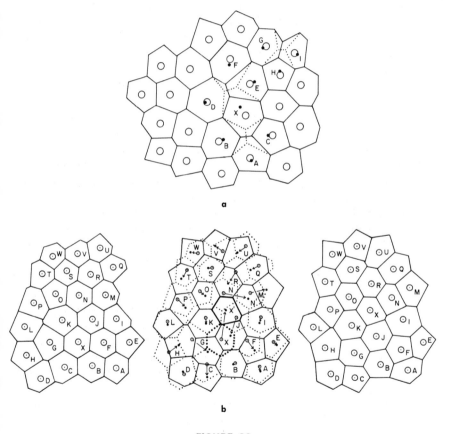

FIGURE 39

Diagram to illustrate molecular movements in liquids through neighbour exchange. a illustrates individual moves; b illustrates the extent to which one molecule can be displaced after five moves. (The two-dimensional representation greatly exaggerates the distortion required for a single move.) Adapted from J. D. Bernal, Nature, 183, 141 (1959).

give rise to self-diffusion and show themselves on the macroscopic scale in fluidity. In this view, the *fluidity of a liquid is a consequence of its molecular irregularity and not vice versa.* The construction of a theory of viscosity based on such a mechanism would be formally almost identical with that of Eyring, based on the hole theory and the analogy to rates of chemical reaction. Another consequence of the intrinsic irregularity of liquid structures is their powers of accommodating molecules of different sizes, and consequently accounting for the solvent powers of liquids and their mutual miscibility.

"This picture of the liquid state, based on the properties of the simplest spherical molecules such as those of the rare gases, is readily extended to other types of liquid. It can take into account the effects of shape, as in most organic liquids (for example, it would explain the quasi-crystallinity of two-dimensionally packed long-chain hydrocarbon molecules); the presence of hydrogen bonds, as in water, alcohols and acids, leading to the formation of non-equilibrium liquids or glasses; the presence of oppositely charged ions, simple or complex, as in fused salts where low co-ordination also leads to glasses; and that of free electrons, as in metallic liquids where, as I have already proposed, the metal ions occupy a smaller part of the volume, leading to greater fluidity and smaller change of volume on melting.

"This theory, or rather sketch of a theory, of liquid is put forward not because it accounts better for their properties than the numerous formal mathematical theories that have been in use in the past twenty years. The success of many of these, often radically different from each other, only goes to show how insensitive to theory are such expressions as the equation of state or the laws of viscosity. I am putting it forward rather because, as a crystallographer, I find it more satisfactory to try to build theories of liquids on the basis of a model of an instantaneous molecular structure that is at least plausible. I feel that we now have ample evidence that the essential nature of the liquid state is the existence of statistical molecular configurations with varieties of co-ordination patterns geometrically necessarily different in kind from any that can occur in a regular solid. Any theories that do not take this into account — and few have hitherto — are likely to lead to predictions which are the wider from the facts the more the properties concerned, such as vapour pressure or critical constants, depend directly on the molecular arrangements.

"What I have done, and I hope even more the programme of research that should follow it, should show that an approach to a theory of liquids based on irregularity is not so formidable mathematically as to discourage quantitative studies. If this should prove to be the case, it seems probable that the new theory should not only explain known facts but also point the way to unsuspected new phenomena."[2]

[2] J. D. BERNAL, *Nature*, **183,** 141 (1959).

"Since the work referred to in my communication to *Nature* early in 1959, it has been possible to approach the problem in a more quantitative way by the use of computers and geometrical models. Following up the concept of a liquid as an essentially irregular assembly, I have been able to realize a mathematical model of such an assembly, thanks to the help of Dr. A. D. and Mrs. Booth at Birkbeck College, and of the University of London Computer Unit through the work of my son, Dr. M. J. M. Bernal. A method was devised for computing the co-ordinates of centres of random assemblies of hard spheres with the one condition that no two centres should approach at less than a minimum distance. It proved possible to arrange these in systems with varying densities, the chief interest being, however, in the arrangements of highest density. Later it was possible to build up such arrangements with as many as seventy-five spheres in various ways, to compute from these their mutual energies on the simple Lennard-Jones $-A/r^6 + B/r^{12}$ potential rule and also to determine their effective volumes.

"The general picture which emerged was that each particular random arrangement could be altered in absolute scale so as to get a minimum energy for each mutual relative metric position of the points. It could further be modified without preserving these metrical relations but yet maintaining the same topological neighbourhood relations so as to get even lower energy values.

"From these minimum energy arrangements it is possible to calculate mean radial distribution functions (Figure 40). These resembled roughly those obtained experimentally by X-ray and neutron diffraction from monatomic liquids. Dr. Furukawa has shown that nearly all metals show the same distribution function if these are calculated from their observed diffraction curves in the same way. The distribution functions derived from the random arrangement described are similar to this with the significant difference that the first or principal maximum is considerably broader in the model. Now this is exactly what should be expected from the way the model was derived by emphasizing minimum rather than most probable distances of neighbours, for it proved impracticable at this stage to devise a programme which ensured arrangements with a maximum of molecular contact.

"To overcome this difficulty, I used a semi-empirical device by building an actual physical model corresponding to the machine-calculated distances. Then, after joining neighbouring points by links of variable length, devised by my technical assistant, Mr. J. Mason, I was able, by a process of manipulation, to reduce most, by but no means all, of the distances between neighbouring points to approximately identical minimum values. This gave a new kind of distribution function (Figure 40) with much sharper peaks, sharper actually than those given by metallic or molecular liquids (Figure 40) but more closely approximating to them than in the first model. It also gave a density of packing of 0·61, approaching the value of 0·63 determined by

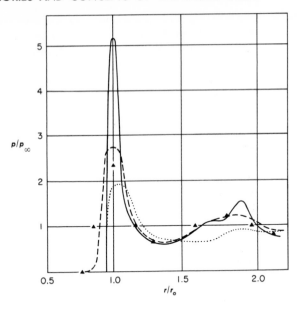

FIGURE 40

Density distribution function: ρ/ρ_∞ variation of mean particle density as a function of r/r_0. ......, derived from calculated random model; ———, derived from squeezed random model; - - - -, calculated for lead by K. Furukawa (Nature, 181, 1209 (1959)); ▲, *calculated for liquid argon by neutron diffraction.*

G. D. Scott (a private communication) for irregularly close-packed spheres.

"It is evident that this model, by an intermediate degree of equalization of the shorter bonds, could be made to provide radial distribution functions approximating, within experimental limits, to those calculated from diffraction curves. This agreement provides strong support for the principles of construction of the geometrical model proposed for liquid structure. Although, on account of the inherent phase ambiguity of diffraction studies, it is impossible to *prove* the correctness of the model by these means, it equally cannot be disproved, and it must correspond more closely to the real distribution than any model hitherto proposed. Its closest affinity is, in principle, to that of Furukawa, who was the first to explain the location of the second peak of the distribution function.

"A contemplation of the bond-equalized model led me to the radically new conception of the *ideal structure of a liquid*, ideal in the sense that in such a structure all the distances between closest neighbours are equal. This ideal corresponds to the ideal structures in crystallography by which, for example, Pauling worked out the structures of the silicates. Actual structures, however, differ, and it is certain that no actual liquid structure can be an ideal one, though it may be close to it.

"Examination of the model showed that it could be considered most profitably as broken down into a set of *polyhedral* holes between molecules. These polyhedra are necessarily small because, by definition, in any coherent *close-packed* liquid there are no holes large enough for another molecule to be inserted. All have in common faces composed of equilateral triangles, or, in other words, *all their edges are equal.* They can, in fact, be derived from five ideal basic shapes: two platonic, two regular archimedean polyhedra, and one of lower symmetry. These are the tetrahedron, the octahedron, the trigonal prism, the archimedean antiprism, and another eight-cornered form, the tetragonal dodecahedron (Figure 41). These forms can be combined in

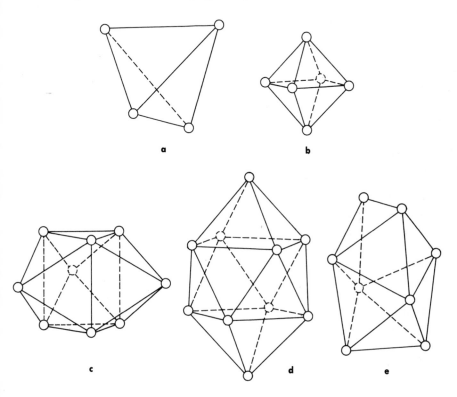

FIGURE 41

Forms of holes in ideal equidistant molecule model of a liquid. a, tetra-hedron; b, octahedron; c, trigonal prism capped with three half octahedra; d, archimedean antiprism capped with two half octahedra; e, tetragonal dodecahedron. (Note prevalence of five-fold surface co-ordination in c, d, and e.) Adapted from J. D. Bernal, Nature, 185, 68 (1960).

an unlimited number of ways through the sharing of triangular or square faces (here the half octahedron can appear as a pyramid on a square base). There are no other forms with equal edges, though a relaxation of this rule allows a few other kinds of holes to occur. However, *in general*, such packing cannot fill space without breaking, though to a degree limited to some 15 per cent, the condition of the equality of nearest neighbour distances. The introduction of archimedean polyhedra prevents any long-range order and also prevents a realization of the ideal structure precisely; for the sums of the dihedral angles of the polyhedra can never (except in the case mentioned below) be made exactly to amount to four right angles. In one particular case, that where only tetrahedra and octahedra occur, the packing can be regular, giving rise to varieties of cubic or hexagonal close-packed crystals.

"It is possible, therefore, to formulate the geometrical hypothesis of the structure of liquids as follows:

"In an *ideal* liquid structure, the molecular centres lie at the apices of a set of empty polyhedra (holes) with equal edges (r_0), or a combination of them. These polyhedra are: platonic regular (1) tetrahedra; (2) octahedra; archimedean (3) trigonal prisms; (4) archimedean antiprisms; and (5) tetragonal dodecahedra. The presence of the three latter forms prevents any long-range order and thus permits fluidity appropriate to temperature, while their proportion determines the configurational volume of the structure at different temperatures. For any temperature the structure is characterized only by the mean value $\bar{N}$ of molecular neighbours, varying from 11 to 3 as the temperature rises, and by the variance (λ) of the intermolecular distance (r_0), which increases with temperature.

"This concept of the ideal structure also opens the way to a real statistic of liquid structure, the relative numbers of the platonic and archimedean polyhedra, depending on the temperature, giving the possibility of determining a mixing entropy to account for the large entropy of the liquid state. This would seem to provide a geometrical basis for Eyring's partition function in his new thermodynamic theory of liquid structure. It can be seen that this geometric view contains the essential features of many earlier theories of liquids, including that of Born and Green based on gas laws, the hole theory of Kirkwood and Frenkel and the crystallite theory of Eyring and others, and points to their eventual reconciliation.

"With regard to the last of these, it is apparent from the model that even the most irregular structure contains regions composed of a number of tetrahedra sharing faces. Even though their density may be greater than close packing, as Boerdijk has shown, they are not in general crystalline, but are asymmetric or have forbidden symmetries, such as pentagonal (Figure 42). They cannot lead to three-dimensional repeat structures and consequently cannot function during the time of their stability as nuclei of crystallization. This may indeed provide the explanation of the phenomena of

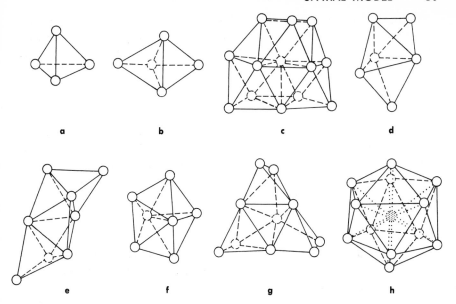

FIGURE 42

Crystal nuclei and pseudo-nuclei: built from equidistant or quasi-equidistant molecules. Crystal nuclei: a, single; b, double tetrahedra; c, close-packed layers, four tetrahedra and three octahedra. Pseudo nuclei: d, three; e, four tetrahedral elements of super close-packed spiral chain; f, five tetrahedra in pentagonal bipyramid; g, seven tetrahedra with elements of three spiral chains; h, twenty tetrahedra as fitted in an icosahedron. (In f, and h, all the intermolecular distances cannot be precisely equal.) Adapted from J. D. Bernal, Nature, 185, 68 (1960).

nucleation and crystal growth in super-cooled liquids. The character of these pseudonuclei near their melting point may well be dependent on whether they are formed from the melting of a crystal or from the cooling of a liquid heated to a high temperature. This may also explain some observed hysteresis phenomena in liquids near the melting point. It also implies that with poly-atomic molecules there may be several degrees of melting or break-up of such non-crystallographic aggregates which may help to account for viscosity anomalies with temperature which will appear not as discontinuities but changes of higher order. Further, the existence of such condensations indi-cates the necessity of fluctuations in density in normal liquids of the dimen-sions of several interatomic distances as postulated by Furth.

"A fuller account of this work will be published elsewhere."[3]   ▲

---

[3] *Ibid.*, **185,** 68 (1960).

The Bernal concept differs from other cell models, since it is based on an irregular ideal structure which in itself provides for the lack of an ordered lattice. Disorder is the key feature of the model. His is a refreshing approach, for it depicts liquids from the liquid state rather than from the gas-like or solid-like state. The conclusions about liquid structure and crystallization reached by Turnbull[4] in connection with his investigations of the undercooling of liquids agree with the postulates of Bernal.

Many points of clarification and extension are needed before an appraisal may be given of this proposed geometrical structure for liquids. Apparently there are a number of difficulties which may require extensive development. The attractive forces between molecules must be great enough to distort the molecular groups into five-fold symmetry, at least temporarily. At a recent symposium, HILDEBRAND proposed as defects of Bernal's concept:

▼   ". . . that it is based upon the number of contacts of hard spheres. . . . [and] that it does not allow for any expansion except that between 'random close-packing' and crystalline close-packing. The result is that integral numbers are built into the model, which is not the case with liquids in ordinary degrees of expansion. Carbon tetrachloride, for example, is expanded over a close-packed structure not by 15 percent, as in Bernal's model, but by about 30 percent."[5]   ▲

[4] D. Turnbull, *J. Phys. Chem.*, **66,** 609 (1962); *Sci. Am.*, **212,** 38 (January, 1965).
[5] J. H. HILDEBRAND (private communication).

CHAPTER 7

Critique of Model Theories

The theories and concepts of the liquid state described in the preceding chapters show that the principal efforts have been directed toward a cell model interpretation of liquid structure. Apparently a majority of investigators feel that the simplest road to a practical solution to the problem lies in this direction. Cell models ordinarily connote some semblance of regularity and the idea of at least a small degree of orderliness is a rather persistent one. It does not appear easy to discard the model approach to a theory of liquid structure. The tunnel theory of Barker is the most recent proposal; although basically a model concept, it does have a degree of disorder built into it which could afford a greater measure of success than has been found with other model theories.

One of the leading opponents of the cell, hole, or cage theory is Joel H. Hildebrand who has consistently argued against any model which introduces the aspects of a lattice structure.

Several items substantiating Hildebrand's views about lattice structures are described in his book with R. L. Scott on solutions.[1] HILDEBRAND's objections are succinctly summarized in the article reproduced below.

▼   "For dealing with the theory of the liquid state, some authors have assumed quasi-crystalline models, as implied in such terms as: 'lattice,' 'cells,' 'holes,' 'vacancies,' and 'dislocations.' Eyring, in a series of papers in these *Proceedings*, postulates that a liquid consists of a mixture of 'solid-like' and 'gas-like' molecules.

[1] J. H. Hildebrand and R. L. Scott, *Regular Solutions* (Englewood Cliffs: Prentice-Hall, Inc., 1962), Chap. 5.

"The senior author has adduced a number of experimental facts that seem inconsistent with any sort of 'solid-like' structure in liquids. The following are the most significant:

"1. The X-ray scattering by solid gallium gives the line-spectrum characteristic of crystals, while the liquid at nearly the same temperature gives no trace of lines.

"2. The X-ray scattering by mercury, determined years ago by Debye and Menke, indicated a structure closely agreeing with that of an artificial model designed by Morrell and Hildebrand in which the simulated molecules were in a state of maximum disorder.

"3. The partial molal volume of iodine, whose molal volume as liquid is 59 cc, is identical, 66.6 ± 0.1 cc, in solvents of such different molal volumes as CCl_4, 97.1 cc, and $c\text{-}(CH_3)_8Si_4O_4$, 312 cc. The iodine molecules do not find any larger 'holes' ready to receive them in the latter than in the former; they make their own equal-sized 'holes.'

"4. Phosphorus, whose molecules, P_4, are regular tetrahedra, melts at 44.2°C, but drops of the liquid in a vacuum have been cooled as far as $-70°$ before all of them crystallized.

"5. Dahler and Hirschfelder have concluded that 'a major factor contributing to this failure of the cell theory is the artificially high degree of order built into the model. Although it has often been supposed that this order could be disrupted by introducing holes or empty cells into the theory, we find that the slight increase of entropy which accompanies the introduction of such a hole is more than offset by the enormous amount of energy required for its production.'

"6. Alder has stated results of his studies of the liquid state in part as follows:

'Our Molecular Dynamics studies give no support to the lattice concept of the liquid state. . . . The solid is regularly ordered, with excursions from lattice points taking place, but they are never large enough for the molecule to escape. The transition occurs when such an excursion is simultaneously accompanied by movement of surrounding molecules out of the way. Once this has happened, the whole region becomes disorganized, and subsequently no discernible order is present, and no holes can be observed.'

"The purpose of this paper is to present one more piece of simple, direct evidence.

"Meta- and para-xylenes, in the liquid state, differ but slightly in their thermodynamic properties. They boil within 0.8°C, and their heat capacities, determined by Pitzer and Scott, are identical within the limit of error. Their molal volumes, calculated from densities by Massart, plotted against temperature in Figure 43, are parallel within 0.5 cc between 100° and the freezing point of p-xylene 13.2°. Meta-xylene continues as liquid down to $-47.9°$.

"In order to make it clear that 'solid-like' aggregates, if present, would diminish molal volume, we determined the molal volume of solid p-xylene.

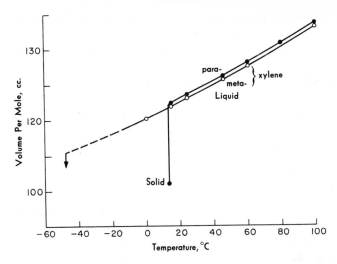

FIGURE 43

The molal volumes of meta- and para-xylenes plotted against temperature. Adapted from J. H. Hildebrand and G. Archer, Proc. Nat. Acad. of Sci., 47, 1881 (1961).

A sample melting within 0.5° of the 'best' value was placed in a dilatometer consisting of a cylindrical tube 1 cm in diameter provided with a capillary stem of 2 mm internal diameter.

"The dilatometer was filled with liquid, approximately 7 cc. This was degassed by alternate freezing and melting under moderate vacuum. It was then frozen very slowly from the bottom up by gradually lowering it into a bath at a temperature of ~10°. By this procedure, the liquid above the solid flowed down and filled the space produced by the contraction accompanying freezing. The position of the surface of the solid was read on an attached scale; the solid was melted, and the position of the liquid meniscus read. Repeated determinations agreed in giving the shrinkage on freezing as 16.8 ± 0.1 per cent. Taking the molal volume of the liquid at its melting point according to Massart's figures as 122.5 cc, the molal volume of the solid just below the melting point is 101.9 cc, as shown in Figure 43.

"The near identity of the molal volumes and of the heat capacities of these two isomers above 13.2°, contrasting with the enormous difference in their freezing temperatures, is surely inconsistent with any content in either isomer of 'solid-like' aggregates. The p-xylene is not 'aware,' even at 15°, of what it is about to undergo at 13.2°; the freezing is a completely discontinuous process."[2]   ▲

---

[2] J. H. HILDEBRAND AND G. ARCHER, *Proc. Nat. Acad. Sci.*, **47**, 1881 (1961).

In a more recent publication by Smith and Hildebrand, the viscosities of meta- and para-xylenes are reported: "It is evident that as in the comparison between molal volumes, the properties of liquid *p*-xylene are quite unaffected by nearness to its melting point. We therefore assert again, with even more assurance, that 'the freezing is a completely discontinuous process.' "[3]

The emphasis on attempts to improve and develop new cell and hole theories indicates that they are not acceptable in their present state.[4] The agreement of these theories with experimental evidence from X-ray and neutron scattering and physical property measurements is not entirely satisfactory. Actually any concept involving aspects of a lattice arrangement is likely to portray solid rather than liquid structure. Many physical properties of liquids are not greatly different from those of the corresponding solids. This fact may be partly responsible for the success achieved by some of the cell theories, since the degree of precision attained by calculations made on the basis of these concepts is not great enough to make the necessary distinction between the properties in the two states.

An examination of the theories presented shows that the situation at the melting point has not been resolved. There is evidence that all aspects of the characteristic crystalline order are lost as the solid is transformed to the liquid during melting. One point of controversy centers around the possibility of short- and long-range order for molecules in the liquid state. In their recent article, Eyring and Marchi restate the longheld view that X-ray data on liquids indicates that the molecules immediately surrounding a given molecule are arranged in an orderly manner, but there is a total lack of long-range order.[5] Instead of maintaining that long-range order is possible in solids, it might be asserted that a crystal lattice requires long-range order and that this, in turn, allows short-range order to exist in crystalline solids.

For central-force molecules the particles could be arranged about a central molecule in a hexagonal or a face-centered cubic structure, or as an icosahedral shell of twelve molecules. There is a tendency for molecules to stabilize at the point of balance between the forces of attraction and repulsion, both with respect to the central molecule and to one another in the shell. Spatial limitations are encountered, however, as well as the dislocations brought on by the relatively intense kinetic activity which exists in liquids. These effects preclude the formation of any but the first shell of molecules and actually the full complement of twelve molecules is seldom realized; experiment indicates an average of eight to ten. The difficulties encountered by molecules in attempting to arrange themselves in an orderly fashion may be anticipated on the basis of such evidence as Hildebrand's experiment with rigid spheres, 'Monte Carlo' and molecular dynamics analyses, certain physical property information, and X-ray

[3] E. B. Smith and J. H. Hildebrand, *J. Chem. Phys.*, **40**, 909 (1964).

[4] D. Henderson, *Ann. Rev. of Phys. Chem.*, **15**, 31 (1964).

[5] H. Eyring and R. P. Marchi, *J. Chem. Educ.*, **40**, 562 (1963).

diffraction halos.   For simple central-force molecules, repulsive rather than attractive forces appear to be the major factor in determining the radial distribution functions.

X-ray patterns provide the basis for assuming some degree of short-range order in liquids. Certain experimental data which have not been discussed extensively indicate that X-ray scattering for highly compressed gases both immediately above and below the critical temperature is quite similar to that of the corresponding liquid.[6] No such pattern is found for simple, less dense gases at ordinary conditions. Perhaps the interpretation of X-ray data should be reexamined in the light of this evidence and of information from the newer technique of neutron scattering by liquids.   It is possible to use neutrons with velocities of the order of that of the molecules in liquids, and this technique has certain advantages over X-ray studies.   Unfortunately, the necessary mathematics has not been worked out for this technique.   Furukawa has recently published a detailed discussion and review of the radial distribution curves of liquids by diffraction methods in which these techniques are described.[7]

[6] A. Eisenstein and N. S. Gingrich, *Phys. Rev.*, **62,** 261 (1942).
[7] K. Furukawa, *Rep. on Progr. in Phys.*, **25,** 395 (1962).

▪ PART TWO

Physical Properties
and Intermolecular Forces

Discussions of structure have centered around liquids of the simplest monatomic molecules such as the rare-gas elements xenon, krypton, and argon. The
theories proposed to date for such nearly ideal liquids have been only modestly
successful in explaining the nature of this state of matter; and the final theory
does not appear to be immediately forthcoming. Under such limitations it
might appear impractical to consider more complicated liquids. The great
majority of liquids are more complex than those indicated above, and an approach is needed that will be satisfactory for these substances also. It is hoped
that any theory which is satisfactory for the uncomplicated liquids might be
suitably altered to characterize those which are more complex.

The molecules in liquids are so close together that the various interactions
such as van der Waals' forces, electronic fields, and ionic attractions assume
considerable significance. Because these factors are not easy to evaluate, it is
expedient to rely heavily on experimental information in characterizing liquids.
The data may be classified according to the equilibrium and non-equilibrium
conditions of the fluid. The considerable collection of thermodynamic properties makes up the first category, while the second involves transport phenomena.

A liquid can be described as a collection of particles in constant, rather
violent motion of translation, rotation and vibration. Such motion is sufficiently
intense to cause the units to fly off in every direction were it not for the restrain-
ing forces of cohesion. The molecules in the liquid move about spatially, and
it is postulated that these particles vibrate in one position for some time before
jumping randomly to another place within the body of the liquid. The physical
properties of liquids may be considered with this picture in mind.

CHAPTER 8

Physical Properties

LIQUIDS IN EQUILIBRIUM WITH SURROUNDING FORCES

A liquid under a given set of conditions of temperature and pressure, but otherwise free from external forces, occupies a specific volume depending upon its mass, has a certain density, maintains a fixed shape (spherical), and possesses a certain amount of energy which it received in attaining the given state.

Volume and Density

Cohesive forces hold the molecules of a liquid together, and, unlike gases, the volume occupied by a gram molecular weight of a liquid is characteristic of each substance and depends on the volumes of the constituent atoms. The space allotted to an atom in a molecule is essentially constant, regardless of the compound of which it is a part. The sum of the atomic volumes yields a molar volume value which agrees reasonably well with that obtained from density measurements. It has been found that agreement between experimental and calculated results is best when determinations are carried out at the boiling point of the liquid. The rule is especially applicable to organic compounds. Thus in any homologous series, the molar volume increases regularly by about 22 ml. for each CH_2 group added. The assigned atomic volume for carbon is 11 ml., leaving 5.5 ml. for each hydrogen atom. On this basis, the estimated molar volume of pentane, $CH_3 \cdot CH_2 \cdot CH_2 \cdot CH_2 \cdot CH_3$, should be 120 ml. A value of 117 is obtained from density measurements on *sec*-pentane. The molar volume of water is 18 ml., and, from this, an atomic volume of 7 ml. may be deduced for oxygen. Other values may be obtained in this way. H. Kopp (1842) first noted the approximate correlation between the molar volume and chemical composition in one of the earliest attempts to relate physical properties to chemical constitution.

The molar volume may also be determined as the product of the molecular weight, M, and the experimental specific volume, v, the volume of 1 gram of the material. Density, D, is the reciprocal of v, and therefore the molar volume is M/D.

Density is among the first physical quantities to be determined for any new liquid compound. Many equations depicting the behavior of matter require a density value. A property in point is surface tension, or capillarity, as it is sometimes referred to because of the way liquids rise or fall in small-bore tubes. As will be shown in the next section, the maximum rise depends on several factors, one of which is density.

Surface Tension

A liquid left to itself will not only attain a definite fixed volume but will also attempt to reduce any exposed surface to a minimum, as evidenced by the tendency of drops to assume a spherical shape when no external forces are acting on the material. Work must be expended to increase the surface, and the ratio of work to the change in area, $w/\Delta A$, is designated as γ. This quantity, called surface tension, may also be determined as the ratio of force (F) per length (l), i.e., $\gamma = F/2l$. From thermodynamics the energy change in any process is $\Delta E = q + w$, where q is the heat absorbed by the system and w is the work done on the system. If the area of a liquid surface is increased by tension, there will be a tendency for the temperature to drop, and heat must be added if it is desired to maintain a constant temperature. The mechanism of increasing the surface area involves moving molecules from the body of the liquid into the outermost layer. The work to do this, $dw = \gamma dA$, is the change in free energy dG for constant temperature and pressure, i.e., $dG = \gamma dA$.

One of the frequently used methods of measuring surface tension is to note the amount of rise of a liquid in a capillary tube. For a rise, dh, of the liquid, there will be a change of surface area of $dA = 2\pi r dh$. The change of free energy of the surface will be proportional to dA and equal to $2\pi \gamma r dh$, where r is the internal radius of the capillary tube. The free energy will balance the gravitational free energy, $\pi r^2 D g h dh$, of the liquid column at the equilibrium height, giving $2\pi \gamma r dh = \pi r^2 D g h dh$. From this equality, the proportionality constant, $\gamma = \frac{1}{2} r D g h$, may be obtained, where g is the gravitational constant and D is the density of the liquid; the latter must be determined experimentally for each substance.

Intermolecular forces of attraction are responsible for the surface effects of liquids, and much effort has been put forth in an attempt to understand the nature of the forces. The brief description of intermolecular forces in Chapter 9 supplies ample evidence for the complexity of these factors.

Energy

The internal energy, E, of a liquid manifests itself chiefly as atomic and molecular motions of translation, rotation, and vibration. Where radiation is available from the surroundings, this internal energy is sustained by an interplay of photons between the matter and its environment. In the state of equilibrium between absorption and emission of photons, the internal energy remains constant and the molecules maintain essentially the same average arrangement postulated earlier. The proximity and continual motion of the liquid particles result in many collisions and near-hits so that it is frequently possible for pairs of molecules to be situated near the position of lowest energy assumed for this state of matter.

The position of lowest energy is not quite the same as the point of minimum potential predicted by the Lennard-Jones 12-6 law. The molecules are not averse to changing from one location to another, and they will do so according to the following factors: the geometry, the kinetic activity, and the potential energy of the system. The 12-6 law requires a certain distance of separation between the molecules. When several molecules are grouped about a central molecule, restrictions of geometry make it impossible for all of them to be positioned at the proper distances predicted by the 12-6 relation. In solids, a compromise position is accepted and maintained, but in liquids the vigorous kinetic bombardments by neighboring molecules make it impossible for such an accommodation to be maintained. Liquids are unique, since only in this state are all three factors simultaneously significant.

LIQUIDS UNDER IMPRESSED FORCES

A liquid may respond to its environment by expanding, contracting, freezing, vaporizing, boiling, vibrating, or deforming. These responses to impressed forces may be investigated in terms of the thermodynamic properties of the substance. The above properties, and several to be mentioned below, make up the thermodynamic quantities. A discussion of transport phenomena such as viscosity, diffusion, and thermal conductivity will follow that of the thermodynamic properties.

Heat Capacity

Whenever the environment changes enough to supply heat photons to a body at a greater rate than they are being lost from the body, either the temperature of the substance rises or a phase change takes place. The amount of heat required to increase the temperature of 1 mole of any material 1 degree Celsius (1°C.) is the heat capacity, C. Under constant volume conditions $C_v = \dfrac{(\partial E)}{(\partial T)_v}$, and for constant pressure $C_p = \dfrac{(\partial H)}{(\partial T)_p}$, where H is enthalpy. The variation of heat capacity with temperature has been satisfactorily characterized in a general way for simple crystalline solids and ideal gases by equations of the form $C_v = a + bT + cT^2 + \dots$ indicating a reasonably uniform change with temperature. Similar empirical equations depict the heat capacity behavior for liquids at ordinary conditions of temperature and pressure. At higher temperatures, however, C_v values for liquids increase rapidly with temperature and attain a maximum at the critical point, then drop down again at still higher temperatures. This unexpected behavior appears to be related to density fluctuations, but confirmation is difficult since it is not easy to carry out experiments in the critical region.[1] Because the theory of the heat capacity of liquids has not been fully developed, it is necessary to rely on experimental data when working with this property. Here, then, is another example which shows that there is no paucity of problems in the study of liquids.

A basic part of the kinetic theory postulates that the molecules of a liquid are in continual motion and maintain their average kinetic energy at constant temperature. Whenever the kinetic activity of the particles is increased, energy must be absorbed, and the kinetic theory suitably explains the direct proportionality between temperature rise and the corresponding increase in kinetic energy. In the usual development of the kinetic theory, however, there is no description of the actual mechanism of the interaction between the relatively low energy heat photons and the molecules whereby the translational motion of the molecule is increased. Thus, it is valid to inquire about the manner in which heat energy is absorbed by matter, with the subsequent increase in kinetic energy. The answer involves the interplay between the photons of the environment and the electrons associated with the molecules, but such a discussion is beyond the scope of this work.

Vapor Pressure

It is possible to add heat to a liquid and at the same time maintain a constant temperature if the more energetic molecules are allowed to escape from the surface. The vapor pressure of the material is a measure of this escaping tendency at any given temperature. If the system is enclosed, equilibrium between the vapor and the liquid will be established, and such an equilibrium arrangement can be used in measuring vapor pressure. Several techniques for the experimental determination of this pressure appear to be quite simple to carry out, but personal experience shows that accurate values are difficult to obtain — a view shared by other investigators in the field.[2]

---

[1] J. S. Rowlinson, *Liquids and Liquid Mixtures* (London: Butterworth and Company, 1959), p. 109.

[2] R. R. Dreisbach (ed.), *Pressure-Volume-Temperature Relationships of Organic Compounds*, 3rd ed., (Sandusky, Ohio: Handbook Publishers, Inc., 1952), Preface; F. Hovorka and D. Dreisbach, *J. Am. Chem. Soc.*, **56**, 1664 (1934).

If the temperature is allowed to rise as heat is added, the vapor pressure will increase. The change of pressure with temperature is a function of the volume change as indicated by the proportion:

$$\frac{dP}{dT} \propto \frac{1}{\Delta V}$$

where $\Delta V = V_{\text{vapor}} - V_{\text{liquid}}$. This proportionality transforms into the important equation

$$\frac{dP}{dT} = \frac{\Delta S}{\Delta V} \tag{1}$$

where ΔS is the entropy change on vaporization.

Figure 44, A shows the relations between temperature and pressure for a typical pure substance. Equation (1) may be applied to any of the three curves TA, TD, or TC. The vapor pressure curve, TC, for the liquid ranges from the critical point, C, at the upper limit to the triple point, T. Between these two unique points is the normal boiling point, B, at one atmosphere of pressure.

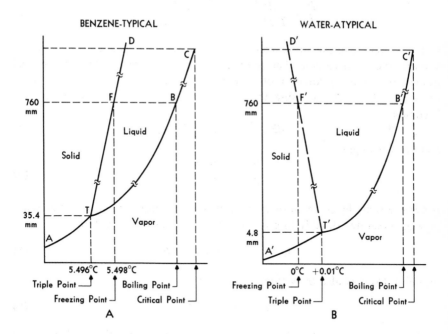

FIGURE 44

Equilibrium diagrams of single-component systems. The freezing point curve for almost all substances slopes away from the ordinate as shown by curve TD in figure A. The abnormal behavior of water is depicted by T′ D′ in figure B. The slopes of TD and T′ D′ are exaggerated.

Boiling Point

There is substantial change in volume during vaporization, and therefore the boiling point is quite sensitive to pressure changes, as may be deduced from Equation (1). This sensitivity exists even though a relatively large entropy change, of the order of 21 calories per mole, occurs in most liquids. The large value of the entropy of vaporization shows a significant increase in disorder as the liquid changes to the vapor state.

The considerable increase in volume on vaporization makes possible an important modification of Equation (1). Clapeyron, in 1834, originally derived Equation (1) in a slightly different form, basing his analysis on the untenable caloric theory. In 1850, Clausius, the originator of the concept of entropy, derived Equation (1) on the accepted ideas of mechanical and thermal energies proposed and substantiated by Mayer and Joule in the early 1840's. Clausius then integrated his equation to extend its applicability over a wider temperature range. The entropy of vaporization may be written in terms of the enthalpy change, $\Delta S = \Delta H/T$, so that Equation (1) becomes

$$\frac{dP}{dT} = \frac{\Delta H}{T \, \Delta V} = \frac{\Delta H}{T(V_{vapor} - V_{liquid})} \tag{2}$$

Here the volume of the liquid may be neglected since it is negligible in comparison with the vapor volume. The volume of the vapor is obtainable from the ideal gas law or any other equation of state, such as the virial equation, $PV = a + bP + cP^2 + \ldots$. By using the ideal law, $V_{vapor} = RT/P$, Equation (2) becomes

$$dP/dT = P \, \Delta H/RT^2 \tag{3}$$

and on rearranging,

$$\frac{dP}{P} = \frac{\Delta H}{R} \frac{dT}{T^2} \tag{4}$$

If ΔH is essentially constant over the desired temperature range, the expression may be integrated directly to give the Clausius-Clapeyron equation

$$\ln P = -\Delta H/RT + B \tag{5}$$

Equation (5) may also be written in the form

$$P = Ae^{-\Delta H/RT} \tag{6}$$

In these equations, ΔH is the enthalpy or heat of vaporization and A and B are constants. Equation (6) is representative of a type which is applied extensively in diverse fields of science. Such a relation is indicative of a process in which an energy barrier must be overcome. In the derivation, ΔH is assumed to have a negligible change, but it actually diminishes slowly with an increase in temperature and becomes zero at the critical point, the upper limit for the vapor-liquid equilibrium. The integrated equation is restricted to the vapor-condensed phase transitions, vapor-liquid and vapor-solid, since the volume of the condensed state is neglected in the derivation. The less common solid-vapor transition along TA in Figure 44, A, represents the sublimation curve, which may be analyzed by means of the Clausius-Clapeyron equation. Equations (5) and (6) are subject to the following limitations imposed in their derivations: deviation from the ideal gas law, variation of ΔH with temperature and any significant condensed state volume relative to the vapor volume. No such restrictions apply to the differential form (1), which may be applied to all phase transitions including that from one allotropic crystalline form to another. It may not be applied over an extended temperature or pressure range, however.

One of the frequently used applications of Equation (1) is that of correcting the boiling point of a liquid from the laboratory pressure to the standard pressure of 760 mm. of mercury. According to the rule of Trouton, ΔS of vaporization is about 21 calories per mole of liquid. By inverting Equation (1),

$$\frac{dT}{dP} = \frac{\Delta V}{\Delta S} = \frac{\Delta V}{21}$$

If $V_{\text{liquid}} \ll V_{\text{vapor}}$,

$$\Delta V \sim V_{\text{vapor}} \quad \text{and} \quad \frac{dT}{dP} = \frac{V_{\text{vapor}}}{21}$$

Using the ideal gas law, $V_{\text{vapor}} = RT_b/P$ and

$$\frac{dT}{dP} = \frac{RT_b/P}{21} = \frac{2T_b}{21 \times 760} = 0.00012T_b$$

where T_b is the boiling point on the absolute scale, and the gas constant, R, is approximately 2 calories per mole. For small pressure changes and ΔP in mm. of mercury, the temperature correction is given by the relation

$$\Delta T_b = 0.00012T_b \, \Delta P$$

Freezing Point

In order to apply Equation (1) to the other curves in Figure 44, A, the proper ΔS and ΔV quantities must be chosen. The entropy of fusion and the volume difference between liquid and solid would be used along the line TD. Point F is at one atmosphere, the condition for the normal melting point of a substance. The melting point is another, much used characteristic physical property and is determined whenever feasible. Although there is considerable variation, the entropy of fusion is of the order of 2 calories per gram formula weight for some substances, such as monatomic solids, connoting some aspect of universality in the freezing process. The entropy of a substance decreases on freezing, which shows that this process involves an increase in the ordered arrangement of the particles as the substance shifts from the liquid to the solid state.

The melting point almost always increases with pressure as denoted by the positive slope of curve TD. For benzene, $dT/dP = 0.029°$ per atmosphere. This reflects the fact that ordinarily the volume of the liquid is greater than that of the solid. Equation (1) indicates that dT/dP is proportional to the volume change ΔV. Water is unusual on two counts, having a curve with a negative slope and a liquid volume smaller than ice (Figure 44, B). Since the difference between the volumes for the two condensed states is relatively small, a considerable pressure change is needed to affect the freezing point significantly.

Recent investigations of the mechanism of freezing indicate great resistance to the initiation of crystallization.[3] When a liquid has no foreign particles — is mote-free — it is necessary for an unexpectedly large number of atoms to be associated in a unit before crystals can form. For example, it is estimated that to form a crystal nucleus of mercury 10 degrees below the normal freezing point, approximately 100,000 atoms would need to come together. It is highly improbable that so many atoms could properly orient themselves to form a crystal, and therefore "clean" mercury would be expected to remain a supercooled liquid indefinitely at this temperature. Fewer than 100,000 would be needed at still lower temperatures; thus freezing is aided by further cooling.

A very small amount of impurity may initiate crystallization; as little as one part of foreign material in 10^{15} may form the nucleus for a crystal in bulk liquids. It is practically impossible to eliminate such small quantities of impurities or motes and for this reason essentially all ordinary freezing is initiated by the mote effect. According to common experience, bulk liquids contain sufficient impurities to permit solidification to take place.

In very carefully controlled crystallization experiments it has been possible to produce a solid in which a great majority of the nuclei are homogeneous, that is, mote-free. Turnbull has related the results of such experiments to the concepts proposed by Bernal (Chapter 6) in one of the more fruitful explanations of the baffling crystallization process.

Triple Point

The triple point is a unique, characteristic quantity for each substance at which the temperature and pressure are fixed and all three states — solid, liquid, and vapor — are in equilibrium. This point is so specific and reproducible that it is now used in thermometry to establish the freezing point of water. The triple point for water is 273.16° on the absolute (Kelvin) scale and the freezing point is 0.01° lower or 273.15°K. This latter temperature is 0° on the Celsius scale. Purified water may be placed in an insulated flask which is then evacuated to remove all air. The flask is closed, and a portion of the water is frozen by means

[3] D. Turnbull, *J. Phys. Chem.*, **66,** 609 (1962); *Sci. Am.*, **212,** 38 (1965).

of a cooling coil. As long as liquid, solid, and vapor are present, a constant temperature of 273.16°K. and a pressure of 4.85 mm. of mercury will be maintained automatically.

One of several unusual physical properties of water is that its freezing temperature, indicated by F′ in Figure 44, B, is lower than the triple point. This anomalous behavior is related to the slope of T′D′, which points toward the pressure axis rather than away from it as is the usual behavior. The freezing points of almost all other substances are higher than their respective triple points. Benzene, with a freezing point about 0.02° higher than the triple point of 5.496°C., at 35.4 mm., is a typical example of a compound in which the curve TD has the usual slope shown in Figure 44, A. The slopes of these two curves are exaggerated in the figures.

Triple point temperatures for various substances range from nearly absolute zero to very high values, with no apparent upper limit. Triple point pressures are usually low, being less than one atmosphere for most substances. The triple point represents a natural lower limit for the existence of a liquid. Since it is unlikely that any two materials would have the same set of values, the triple point for a substance establishes its identity with certainty. It is unfortunate that the published data are so meager for this important and useful physical quantity.

TRANSPORT PHENOMENA

When matter is subjected to a thermal or mechanical stress, migration of one form or another tends to take place. The Greek philosopher Heraclitus (*c.* 500 B.C.) believed that "everything flows." This property is characteristic of matter in the fluid state. Transport phenomena embrace three important types of flow: (1) thermal conductivity, the transport of energy; (2) diffusion, the transport of mass; (3) viscosity, the transport of momentum.

When applied to dense gases and liquids, the transport properties represent a departure from equilibrium thermodynamic systems by involving irreversible non-equilibrium processes which are accompanied by an increase in entropy. Non-equilibrium radial distribution functions are used much like the previously discussed equilibrium radial distribution functions applied to equations of state. In comparison with equilibrium processes, the situation is more complicated under non-equilibrium conditions. Here again, it is necessary to use a simplifying method, such as the superposition approximation, to make it feasible to carry out the desired calculations. Owing to the complexity of these processes and the difficulties in interpreting them, the calculations yield results of only limited validity.

Four approaches to a theory of transport phenomena in dense gases and liquids are described by Hirschfelder, Curtiss, and Bird.[4] The first involves

[4] J. O. Hirschfelder, C. F. Curtiss, and R. B. Bird, *Molecular Theory of Gases and Liquids* (New York: John Wiley & Sons, Inc., 1954).

correlations in which known properties of one substance may be used to predict the properties of other materials. This procedure follows the principle of corresponding states. For the majority of practical problems, it is the only suitable method of attack; unfortunately, the lack of experimental data prevents this approach from attaining its potential stature. The ideas adopted in this method have been summarized by Condon.[5]

The second approach involves a rigorous, statistical mechanical development such as that of Kirkwood or Born and Green which will undoubtedly lead to a satisfactory, perhaps ultimate, theory; but results at present leave much to be desired. Several seemingly insurmountable obstacles must be overcome to achieve success in this direction.

The third method, a molecular theory by Enskog,[6] has had extensive development and is one of the most fruitful theoretical approaches to studying transport processes (see page 65). An essential feature of his procedure is the incorporation of the actual volume of the molecule into the relations. The volumes of the molecules may be neglected in dilute gases but not in dense gases and liquids since, under these conditions, the intermolecular distances are not significantly greater than the molecular diameter. Except for this difference, the analysis follows that for gases under ordinary conditions. The resulting relations have been applied successfully to systems consisting of the simpler, monatomic rare-gas liquids and dense gases.

Finally, in a model approach, Eyring (see pages 19–21) uses reaction rate concepts as the basis for one of the earliest successful theories for liquids. Many changes and improvements have been made, making this one of the most useful theories of transport phenomena. His procedure yields relationships on the macroscopic level rather than on the microscopic, or individual molecule, level. The fundamental transport process equation for the rate constant is

$$K' = \left(\frac{kT}{h}\right) e^{-\Delta G^{\ddagger}/kT}$$

where k and h are Boltzmann's and Planck's constants, respectively, and $\Delta G^{\ddagger}$ is the activation free energy for the process. In traveling from one position to another, a molecule is impeded in its motion, since it must move through regions densely populated with other molecules. If the molecule has sufficient kinetic energy, it can overcome the restrictive cohesive potential and move to the new location. The foregoing is related to the concept of activation energy employed in absolute reaction rate theory for chemical reactions.

Thermal Conductivity

Thermal conductivity is concerned with the rate at which heat is transported

---

[5] E. U. Condon and H. Odishaw (eds.), *Handbook of Physics* (New York: McGraw-Hill Book Company, Inc., 1958), pp. 5–61.

[6] Hirschfelder, *et al.*, *op. cit.*, pp. 634 ff.

from a region at a higher temperature to a region at a lower temperature. In a gas the faster (hotter) molecules will distribute their extra energies among the slower (cooler) molecules until a uniform distribution is established. In dilute gases a molecule travels a significant distance before contacting another; therefore, the principal mode of transport of thermal energy is for a molecule with higher energy to move freely in the space between molecules until collision takes place. Part of the extra energy will then be transferred to the contacted molecule, thus increasing its energy. By this mechanism the factors affecting the molecular motion have a major effect on thermal conductivity. Thermal transport is due to a heat gradient. The rate of flow, or flux, in the x-direction is proportional to the temperature gradient, dT/dx, in that direction. The flux then equals $-\lambda \dfrac{dT}{dx}$, where the proportionality constant, λ, is called the thermal conductivity.

In a liquid, however, cohesive restrictions prevent molecules from traveling quickly and freely from one position to another, and a different mechanism for the conduction of heat becomes necessary. The extra energy in a warmer region is transported by a potential energy interchange from one molecule to a close neighbor, thus transferring the thermal energy to the cooler region. The energy is transferred rapidly through the molecules themselves, and the time consumed by the molecules traveling through free space is greatly reduced since the molecules are so close together.

Thermal conductivity in liquids may be related to the speed of sound, since in both cases there appears to be essentially instantaneous transmission of these quantities from the center of one molecule to the center of a colliding molecule. In a liquid, sound travels about five times faster than small molecules moving under kinetic action at ordinary temperatures. The relation

$$\lambda = \sqrt{\frac{8}{\pi\gamma}}\, kn^{\frac{2}{3}}c$$

equates λ to the speed of sound, c, where $\gamma = \dfrac{C_p}{C_v}$ (the ratio of the heat capacity at constant pressure to that at constant volume), n is the number of molecules, and k is the Boltzmann constant. This equation may be used for simple liquids, but adjustments are necessary before it may be applied to more complex substances.

Diffusion

Just as thermal energy is transported through a liquid without requiring a mass flow of the fluid, diffusion of molecules may take place even though there is no bulk flow. The effects of attractive forces, as well as of geometry, will be at a minimum if the diffusing molecules have essentially the same parameters as the bulk material. In an experimental study, two isotopes of the heavier elements could be used, since in this instance the two species would be quite similar.

The molecules of a liquid move continually from region to region in all directions, and, where there is a concentration gradient, there will be an excess rate of flow or flux. This is caused by the imbalance in the concentration, c, and will be proportional to dc/dx for the flow considered in the x-direction. If the flux, J, is the amount diffusing per second across a square centimeter of surface,

$$J = -D \frac{dc}{dx},$$ D being the diffusion coefficient. There are several ways to

evaluate D. In a gas, for example, $D = klv$, where k is a constant close to unity, l is the mean free path, and v the average velocity of the molecules.

Diffusion is a much slower process than thermal conduction in liquids. For a solute in a liquid solution, $D = \sigma^2/2t$, where σ is the standard deviation of the Gaussian curve (normal, "bell-shaped" distribution curve) of dc/dx versus distance, x, perpendicular to a boundary between the solution and pure solvent. Time, t, is measured after the initially sharp boundary is established. The concentration gradient, dc/dx, through this diffuse boundary layer affects the light transmission of the medium.[7] The refractive index gradient, dn/dx, is proportional to the concentration gradient. Since dn/dx is more readily measured, it is frequently used to determine the value of σ. Some typical approximate values for D in cm^2 per second in very dilute solutions are: potassium chloride, 200×10^{-7}; sugar, 50×10^{-7}; and a protein, ovalbumin, 10×10^{-7}. In general, calculated diffusion coefficients are of limited reliability. The best results appear to be those obtained from Eyring's equation in which

$$D = \frac{kT}{\zeta\eta \left(\dfrac{V_s}{N}\right)^{\frac{1}{3}}}$$

The effective number of neighbors, ζ, about a given molecule in one plane is approximately six; V_s is the molar volume of the corresponding solid, N is Avogadro's number, k is Boltzmann's constant, and η is the coefficient of viscosity.[8]

It is not possible to detect self-diffusion when the molecules in a liquid are all alike. The diffusion coefficient will be nearly that of self-diffusion if the molecules are essentially similar. Unfortunately, it becomes more difficult to measure this quantity as the two chosen constituents become more nearly alike. As indicated previously, isotopes may be used to determine self-diffusion values. Heavier isotopes are more suitable, for there is less difference between such particles. Substances in which ortho and para modifications exist provide an-

[7] F. Daniels and R. A. Alberty, *Physical Chemistry* (New York: John Wiley & Sons, Inc., 1961), p. 354.

[8] H. Eyring, *J. Chem. Educ.*, **40**, 570 (1963).

other possible means for studying the property of self-diffusion. Eyring's equation expresses the interdependence of D and η, and, although few diffusion coefficient data exist, extensive tables of viscosities are available from which the corresponding values for D can be calculated.

Viscosity

When a substance is subjected to a stress, the normal distribution of the molecules will be distorted, and they will rearrange to a configuration of higher potential energy. At this point, one of several phenomena may occur. If the magnitude and time of application of the stress are small enough, upon release of the stress, the molecules will return to their original average positions and the previous potential energy level will be restored. This is an elastic process which takes place in solids and very viscous fluids where the return to the original conditions is a first order action and is reported in terms of a relaxation time. For a less viscous fluid to exhibit elastic properties, the perturbation must be smaller and the restoration time shorter. For many liquids, vibrations in the ultrasonic range will set up periodic strains of the order of magnitude of the natural restoring frequencies. The use of ultrasonics is one of the newer techniques being applied in the study of fluids. For greater stresses and longer times of application, restoration may not be possible, and viscous flow may take place. In this case the over-all operation will be irreversible, the radial distribution of molecules about a central molecule will be disrupted, and the translating and rotating motions of the molecules will assume new values. In the irreversible process the work expended will not be recovered but will be dissipated as heat.

A new factor, bulk flow of matter, is introduced by the transport process of viscous flow. Momentum is the quantity being transferred, and this transfer will have significance only if one segment of the fluid moves relative to an adjoining portion of the material. Momentum will be exchanged randomly by individual pairs of molecules, but the net movement will be in a forward direction for the bulk of the fluid. The chance for a reversal on the bulk, or macroscopic scale, is essentially zero. As stated by H. S. Green, "the irreversibility of natural processes is the outcome of enormous statistical preponderances rather than any inviolable law."[9]

In viscous flow the portion of fluid near the center of a pipe or channel moves with a greater velocity than that close to the walls, with a resultant velocity gradient from the center outward. The force causing the flow in the x-direction of one segment of fluid past another one parallel to it produces the gradient, dv/dy, and $f = -\eta \dfrac{dv}{dy}$. The proportionality constant η is the coefficient of viscosity. The gradient is in the y-direction, perpendicular to the x-direction.

[9] H. S. Green, *The Molecular Theory of Fluids* (Amsterdam: North-Holland Publishing Company, 1952), p. 13; (New York: Interscience Publishers, Inc.).

Two factors, temperature and velocity, affect fluid flow in special and perhaps unexpected ways. The viscosity of gases *increases* with increased temperature as may be seen from the relation[10]

$$\eta_{\text{gas}} = \frac{2}{3\pi d^2} \left(\frac{mkT}{\pi} \right)^{\frac{1}{2}}$$

while the viscosity of liquids *decreases* with increased temperature as shown by the equation

$$\eta_{\text{liquid}} = nhe^{a\Delta U_{\text{vap}}/RT}$$

In these equations, constant a is experimentally determined, ΔU_{vap} is the energy of vaporization, n is the number of molecules per unit volume, h is Planck's constant, d and m are the diameter and mass of the molecule, respectively, and k and R are the gas constants for a single molecule and a mole of molecules, respectively, and T is the absolute temperature.

To explain the above anomalous viscosity variation with temperature, it is necessary to consider the mechanism of momentum transfer in these two states. Molecules must collide for a momentum interchange; in dilute gases, collisions are infrequent due to the distance a molecule must travel before contacting another one. An increase in molecular speed will increase the collision rate and, hence, will increase the viscosity. The kinetic theory provides for an increase in molecular speed with a rise in temperature; therefore, the accompanying increase in viscosity is to be expected for gases.

When molecules are close together, as in liquids, the effect of molecular speeds is insignificant compared to its role in gases. It is postulated that there is essentially instantaneous transfer of momentum from the center of a molecule to the center of its collision partner and, thus, collisional transfer becomes the important factor in the transport of momentum where the molecules are so closely associated. Just above the melting point, there is an average of 10 to 11 molecules about any given molecule as indicated by a frequently cited coordination number, 10.6. This number decreases to about 4 as the temperature approaches the critical point. Since an increase in the temperature reduces the number of molecules about a given central molecule, momentum transfer will become more difficult and the viscosity of a liquid will decrease with a rise in temperature. Thus it is apparent that the mechanism of viscous flow for liquids is different from that for gases.

If a straight transparent tube, B, and a reservoir, A, of liquid are arranged as in Figure 45, A so that the fluid will travel through the tube at a modest velocity, the flow will be straight-line or viscous. This laminar character can be demonstrated by arranging an opaque dye solution so that a tiny jet, C, will be in the tube, as shown in Figure 45, B. As the jet is moved across the diameter of the tube, a fine stream, or thread, of dye parallel to the center axis of the tube

[10] E. U. Condon and H. Odishaw (eds.), *Handbook of Physics* (New York: McGraw-Hill Book Company, Inc., 1958), pp. 5–13, 5–59.

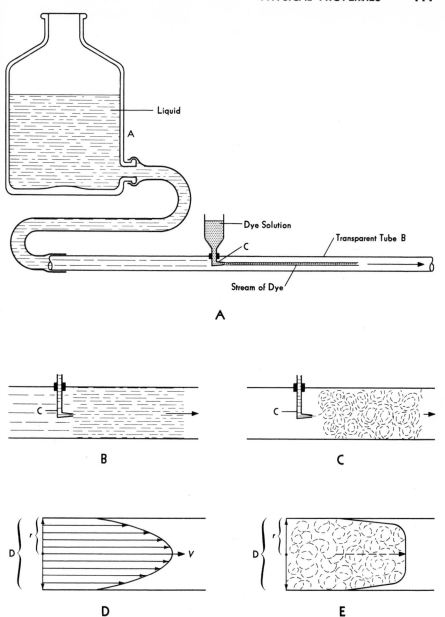

FIGURE 45

*Demonstration of viscous and turbulent fluid flow. Viscous flow is repre-
sented by A and B while turbulent flow is shown by C. The relative velocities
at various distances from the center of a tube are indicated for viscous flow
in D and turbulent flow in E.*

may be seen at any position of the jet orifice. Bottle A may be raised to increase the rate of flow through the tube. If the rate is increased slowly, a point will be observed where there is a sudden break from laminar flow to a new non-regular flow pattern in the dye stream, as in Figure 45, C. This non-laminar flow is called turbulent flow.

Reynolds (1883), in a study of fluid flow, discovered experimentally that the sudden shift from laminar to turbulent flow could be expected at a specific velocity if other conditions were kept constant. A quantity called the Reynolds number, Re, is customarily used to predict the point of change. $Re = D\bar{v}\rho/\eta$ is used for flow through a circular pipe of diameter, D. The average linear velocity of the fluid is $\bar{v}$, its density is ρ, and its viscosity is η. The quantity Re is a dimensionless number for which any consistent set of units may be used. The significant range of values for Re is from 2,100 to 4,000; all flow below 2,100 is viscous while all above 4,000 is turbulent. The condition of the tube, the material from which it is constructed, as well as other factors, dictate the exact number at which the change takes place. The shift is sudden, occurring at a specific number rather than taking place over a range of Reynolds number values. Turbulent flow is considerably more complicated than viscous flow, but, fortunately, it does not occur in most ordinary fluid transport operations.

Viscosity is usually measured by timing the flow of fluid through a capillary tube, but other methods are also used, such as the falling ball experiment in which measurement is made of the time it takes for a heavy sphere, such as a steel ball bearing, to fall through a given column of liquid. The calculation involves Stokes's law,

$$v = \frac{2}{9} \cdot \frac{g}{\eta}\, r^2(\rho - \rho_0)$$

where v is the steady velocity of the falling ball, g is the acceleration due to gravity, η is viscosity, r is the radius of the sphere which has a density, ρ, and ρ_0 is the density of the liquid. These methods demonstrate that for viscous flow, either the fluid may flow through a fixed channel or an object may move through the fluid. It has also been found that, regardless of which is moving, turbulence is always encountered at sufficiently high relative velocities in accordance with Reynolds' findings. When the size of the pipe is limited, as in a fixed installation, there is an advantage to turbulent flow since more material can be transferred per unit time; this is due primarily to the fact that a much higher proportion of the material is moving at the maximum velocity, as seen in Figure 45, D and E. There is a compensation, however, because greater energy is required to move a fluid in turbulent flow.

The greater complexity and energy requirements for turbulent flow introduce special problems for the operations of high speed airplanes, rockets, and missiles. Empirical methods are employed to a considerable extent for the calculations of these flow problems since there is no simple relation between fluid shear stress and the average linear velocity in turbulent flow.

CHAPTER 9

Intermolecular Forces

The existence of gravitational, magnetic, and electrical forces of attraction between portions of matter are well known. Since gravity is too weak to account for such processes as the condensation of vapors to liquids or to solids, it is necessary to look to the remaining forces for the explanation of this and other molecular interaction phenomena.

The magnitude of the forces necessary to bring about simple condensation may be estimated from the internal pressure, or tension, of a liquid. The thermodynamic equation of state

$$\left(\frac{\partial E}{\partial V}\right)_T = \left(\frac{\partial P}{\partial T}\right)_V - P$$

may be used to calculate this quantity. The term on the left is the internal pressure, or cohesion; the first term on the right represents kinetic action, or thermal pressure; and P is the external pressure. The terms on the right may be determined experimentally, and their difference is the internal pressure. At ordinary conditions this tension has a magnitude of a few thousand atmospheres for most substances. Typical values are: ethyl ether, 2,400; carbon tetrachloride, 3,300; and benzene, 3,600. All values are given in atmospheres and are only approximate.

In ·comparison with ordinary external pressures of the order of one atmosphere, calculated internal pressures are significantly larger, indicating that the attractive forces of cohesion are quite large. Figure 46 is a typical curve showing the effect of increased external pressure on the tension within a liquid as the molecules are forced from their normal positions into closer association. Very high external pressures are needed before any significant change occurs in the internal pressure. When the external pressure exceeds several thousand atmospheres, and continues to increase, the internal pressures reduce rapidly, reach zero, and continue downward quite steeply with no indicated lower limit. In Figure 46, the portion of the curve below zero represents the region of repulsion. Under normal conditions the cohesive forces are so great that ordinary external pressure variations cause very little change in the average positions of the molecules in the liquid. With greater and greater external pressure, however, the molecules are crowded closer together until the repulsive forces become significant. Tension decreases as repulsion sets in, and, on closer approach, opposition to the applied external pressure builds up quite rapidly.

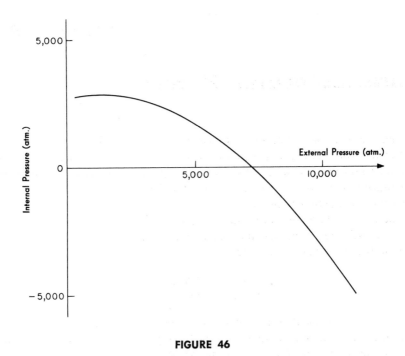

FIGURE 46

Figure 46 is an approximation of the effect of high external pressure on the internal pressure of a liquid.

MOLECULAR ATTRACTION-REPULSION

Two non-reacting atoms may be forced together until they are positioned at the point of closest contact. Due to repulsion, the potential energy between the atoms in this position will be very high. Some overlap of the electron clouds may be effected, but it is unlikely that this can proceed indefinitely or that any overlap of the nuclei may occur. At such close contact, the interactions between the electrons, as well as the positive charges on the nuclei, cause the atoms to attempt to separate with considerable vigor. The situation has been studied by a number of investigators, including Lennard-Jones, Buckingham, and Stockmayer, who estimate that the initial high repulsive potential drops off at a very rapid rate as the molecules separate. This potential, U, is inversely proportional to some power, n, of the distance of separation, r; n is usually given a value in the range 9 to 12, with 12 being used most frequently. The decrease of potential is illustrated by the upper curve in Figure 47, where $U_{\text{repulsive}} \propto \dfrac{1}{r^{12}}$.

The repulsive action of the like charges may be expected on the basis of experience with electrical charges. At the same time, the atoms are under another potential influence which is attractive in nature. Although this attractive action is well known, its explanation is not easy, and not until 1930 was it satisfactorily explained by F. London on the basis of quantum mechanics. The attractive potential varies inversely as the sixth power of the distance r: $U_{\text{attractive}} \propto \dfrac{1}{r^6}$. The smaller exponent results in a more gradual decrease in the attractive potential, as shown in the lower curve of Figure 47. The attractive action becomes dominant at greater distances of separation, while the repulsive potential is the controlling factor when the particles are quite close together.

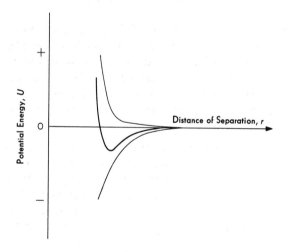

FIGURE 47

Figure 47 is a typical representation of the variation of potential energy with distance of separation for a pair of simple atoms. The upper curve portrays repulsive potentials, the lower curve shows attractive potentials, and the intermediate curve is the resultant of the other curves.

As the two atoms separate, a point will be reached where the two opposing potentials balance and the particles will tend to oscillate about this equilibrium position. The distance of separation at equilibrium is of the order of a molecular diameter for simple molecules. The resultant of the two potentials is represented by the middle curve in Figure 47, where the minimum indicates the point of stability near which the atoms oscillate. The resultant potential values are obtained from the relation $U_{\text{resultant}} = \dfrac{b}{r^{12}} - \dfrac{a}{r^6}$, described on page 32. The quantities a and b are constants.

The *force* between molecules is the gradient of the potential, i.e., $f(r) = -\dfrac{\partial U}{\partial r}$. Thus the attractive force is inversely proportional to the seventh power of the separating distance, $f \propto \dfrac{1}{r^7}$, and the force of repulsion is inversely proportional to the thirteenth power, $f \propto \dfrac{1}{r^{13}}$. In general discussions it is customary to describe the intermolecular actions in terms of forces, but, in the derivations and applications of the equations involving the interactions between molecules, it is more convenient to use potentials, like the Lennard-Jones (12–6) potential.

FORCES BETWEEN MOLECULES

Most attempts to develop a theory of liquid structure have been directed toward simple substances consisting of molecules behaving like hard spheres and having attractive forces which are directed toward the center of the sphere, i.e., non-directive forces. The vast majority of liquids, however, are more complex and consist of polyatomic non-spherical molecules in which additional types of molecular forces operate. As expressed by J. S. ROWLINSON:

▼   "The best possible description of the energy of a pair of polar polyatomic molecules of low symmetry and of anisotropic polarizability would be a formidable expression, bristling with undetermined parameters. The calculation of the bulk properties of an assembly of such molecules would be impossible, or at the best very tedious, and the comparison of such calculations with experiment would not determine uniquely all the parameters of the potential."[1]   ▲

Little more than a simple listing of the possible types of forces or potential energies between particles of matter is needed to demonstrate the magnitude of the problem involving the interactions of the molecules in diverse types of liquids.

---

[1] J. S. ROWLINSON, *Liquids and Liquid Mixtures* (London: Butterworth and Company, 1959), p. 250.

Ionic Bond

Following the electrochemical experiments and writings of Davy and others shortly after 1800, Berzelius elaborated on the postulate that chemical combination is due to electrical attractions between oppositely charged particles. Berzelius exerted considerable influence in the field of chemistry and his writings were not effectively challenged until additional detailed information about the electron and proton made possible a more satisfactory explanation for the formation of molecules. W. Kossel (1916) developed the first successful theory of chemical reactions on the basis of an *ionic bond* in which an electron leaves one of a pair of reacting atoms and goes to its partner. The resulting atoms, or ions, are oppositely charged and are held together by electrostatic attraction.

When chlorine vapor is brought into contact with molten sodium or potassium, a vigorous reaction takes place.[2] The energy needed to remove an electron from an atom such as potassium is designated as the ionization energy of the atom. The halogens, on the other hand, have a tendency to accept an electron and to assume a lower energy state. The energy liberated when a halogen atom accepts an electron and becomes a halide ion is termed the *electron affinity* of the halogen. As a chlorine atom in the gaseous state approaches a vaporized potassium atom, their electron clouds become distorted and, on colliding, the electrons may shift to form the K^+ and Cl^- ions. Energy is required to bring about the redistribution of electrons since the ionization energy of potassium which must be supplied is 4.3 electron volts, whereas the electron affinity given off by chlorine is 3.8 electron volts. The difference is one-half of an electron volt, so that the total energy in the ions is greater than that of the atoms, indicating a lower stability for the ions. There is an added electrostatic attraction between the oppositely charged particles, however, which holds them together in a stable ionic bond. The potential for these two ions varies inversely as the distance between them, i.e., $U \propto \dfrac{1}{r}$, which allows the attractive bond to remain effective over a considerable distance of separation. Ions are essentially spherical and possess central-force attractions for ions of opposite charge. When more ions are formed, they will symmetrically surround ions of the opposite charge to form the characteristic crystal, in this instance, cubic. The attractive force between the ions is coulombic and is of considerable magnitude; it is not easy to separate the particles of the crystal lattice, as the high melting point (790°C. for KCl) indicates. The ions persist in the molten salt, and the continued strong attraction accounts for the high boiling point (1500°C.) of liquid potassium chloride.

The K^+ and Cl^- ions have the argon electronic structure in which there are eight outer electrons in a stable arrangement. If the ions were to be moved too close together, the electron clouds would overlap, and, since the outer orbitals are filled, one or more of the electrons would need to move to a higher quantum

[2] R. N. Hammer, *J. Chem. Educ.*, **34**, A265 (1957).

level to accommodate the inter-penetrating electrons. This requires considerable energy and accounts for the steep ascent of the repulsion curve (see Figure 47).

Although this concept was used by Kossel to explain chemical combination, it is also useful in understanding the strong interionic attractions, as well as the high electrical conductivity, of anhydrous molten salts. The ionic bond is one of the most easily understood intermolecular forces; it will be considered further in Chapter 13. Other less obvious and usually weaker forces, such as dipole-dipole, also exist.

Dipole-Dipole Forces

In ionic bonding there is a displacement of an electron from one atom to another. On close approach, some tendency to a distortion of the electron cloud occurs in most molecules consisting of dissimilar atoms. The electrons will spend more time nearer the atom with the greater electron affinity, causing the other atom to be correspondingly positive in nature. These electrical effects are weaker and not so definite and specific as in ionic substances, but they are strong enough to constitute a dipole, which is a positive and negative charge separated by a small distance. There is a positive region and a negative region to a molecule having a dipole. These dipoles, referred to in this case as permanent dipoles, exist as long as the molecules are stable. Such molecules will be affected by external electrical and magnetic fields as well as by nearby charged particles. The distance between the centers of these charges multiplied by the magnitude of the charges is the dipole moment. This is a directed quantity, causing two molecules which are approaching one another to have varying electrostatic effects on each other, depending on their orientation.

Since attractions and repulsions are not symmetrical, there is an over-all force of attraction between all molecules possessing a dipole. Such molecules are called polar molecules and the potential energy between polar molecules varies inversely as the sixth power of the distance of separation, r, i.e., $U \propto \dfrac{1}{r^6}$.

This attractive effect is quite widespread and is found to some degree in almost all molecules except those that are symmetrical, such as H_2, N_2, carbon tetrachloride and benzene.

Dipole-Induced Dipole Forces

The electron clouds about the nuclei of molecules are not stationary and fixed, but are mobile and therefore capable of being shifted. Any applied electrical field will tend to disturb the average electronic arrangement by pulling the electron cloud toward a positive charge and by repelling it from a negative one. If a molecule with a dipole, such as alcohol, is brought near a molecule without a dipole (non-polar), carbon tetrachloride for instance, a dipole may be induced in the latter. The net result will then be a force of attraction between the two unlike molecules. The mutual solubility of alcohol and carbon tetrachloride attests to the existence of such attractive forces. These induced effects are found in many systems where two different species are involved. The action is similar to the permanent dipole-dipole and the potential varies in the same way: $U \propto \dfrac{1}{r^6}$. Dipoles may also be induced by ions.

London Dispersion Forces

On reviewing the forces listed above, no obvious explanation is forthcoming for the mechanism by which a symmetrical atom such as argon might attract other argon atoms to produce a liquid or solid. Cohesive forces must exist since all substances condense and freeze at sufficiently low temperatures.

The first successful explanation for the attraction between simple substances was reported by F. London (see page 115). In order to understand his concept it is necessary to recall that all tiny particles are in continual motion, regardless of whether they are a part of animate or inanimate matter. This contention is amply developed in *The Restless Universe* by Max Born.[3] In an atom, the negatively charged electrons are bound to the positive nucleus, and these electrons are in continual motion relative to the nucleus. At a given instant, as two atoms approach each other, the majority of the electrons of one atom may be on the side next to the other atom. The electrons in the second atom will then be repelled and will shift away from the first atom. The next moment the opposite arrangement may occur; in this way the electron clouds may oscillate in phase with each other, inducing dipoles of a temporary nature to be set up in the pair of atoms. London was able to show how this could lead to an over-all attraction. He found the potential between the two atoms to be of the order $U \propto \dfrac{1}{r^6}$, which is similar to that for the other dipole potentials. A comparison of the different dipole forces is illustrated in Figure 48.

Although other forces are sometimes included, it is customary to refer to the three dipole effects as the van der Waals' forces of attraction. For completely symmetrical molecules it is clear that the London force is the sole reason for attraction. With other substances, some or all of the forces may be superimposed on the London forces. Other forces, such as metallic bonding and hydrogen bonding, may also play significant attractive roles for certain classes of materials.

Metallic Bonding

Non-metallic elements have too few electrons to complete the rare gas configuration except by sharing electrons to form directed covalent bonds. Metallic

[3] M. Born, *The Restless Universe* (New York: Dover Publications, Inc., 1951).

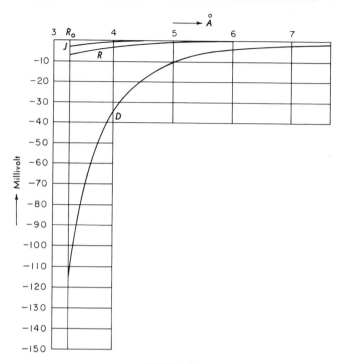

FIGURE 48

The components of molecular attraction for hydrogen bromide. J denotes the induction effect; R denotes interaction of permanent dipoles; D denotes the "dispersion effect" or dynamic interaction of the two electron systems. Adapted from J. H. Hildebrand, Solubility of Non-Electrolytes (New York: Reinhold Publishing Corporation, 1936).

elements have a slight excess of electrons above those needed for the rare gas structure and, therefore, will not form bonds in a manner similar to that of the non-metals. While electropositive metallic atoms share electrons, they do not have enough extra electrons to fill all the orbitals. Orbitals are available for more electrons than are present, and the covalent bonds that are formed resonate among the atoms of the metal lattice. The resulting crystalline structure is stable and the crystal is not easily fused. Since orbitals are available, there is no specific or directed orientation for some of the electrons. The nuclei are thus afforded the opportunity to choose a low energy arrangement such as the close-packed, face-centered cubic or hexagonal structure. The nuclei are arranged in an orderly pattern and are surrounded by electrons. At any given time, some electrons may not be associated with any particular nucleus. Such electrons are highly mobile and may be responsible for the high electrical conductivity of metals.

The electron field in a metal allows a nucleus to shift from one position to another and adjust readily to the new electrons which surround it. The ductility and malleability of metals are characteristics to be expected from this proposed structure. The high catalytic activity of metals results from the unsaturated character of the electron field at the surface, which permits other atoms to be readily attached to them prior to reaction. Other properties may be related to the structure of metals; for example, the special, attractive nature of crystalline metals permits them to melt readily with destruction of the crystal lattice, yet the atoms retain a strong attraction for each other as is indicated by the relatively high boiling points of liquid metals.

Hydrogen Bonding

An exposed hydrogen atom covalently bonded to a molecule may have a positive character, particularly if it is part of an OH or NH group. An electrostatic attraction may occur between the positive hydrogen and an electronegative atom such as fluorine, oxygen, or nitrogen. One of the strongest bonds of this nature occurs in the acid fluoride ions, HF_2^-, which form a chain as indicated in the following structure:

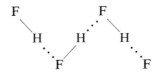

The regular molecular bonds (solid lines) and the hydrogen bonds (dotted lines) are equal. Water and alcohols (ROH) are typical of the extensive group in which oxygen is the electronegative atom giving rise to the structure

$$\overset{\displaystyle R}{\underset{}{|}}\quad\overset{\displaystyle R}{\underset{}{|}}$$
$$O{-}H\cdots O{-}H\cdots O{-}H$$
$$\underset{R}{|}$$

where R represents a group such as CH_3, C_2H_5, C_3H_7, etc. Hydrogen bonds are usually weaker than the regular bonds, as indicated by the longer dotted lines. The one notable exception is the HF_2^- structure, in which the bonds are equal. The relatively weak attractive forces of this type cause an association of molecules which results in liquids with abnormally high boiling points, water being the classic example. Hydrogen bonds are sensitive to temperature and tend to break as the kinetic activity of the molecules increases at higher temperatures.

Hydrogen bonding may also take place between different species of molecules, as illustrated by acetone and chloroform at the top of the following page:

$$CH_3 \diagdown \atop CH_3 \diagup C{=}O \cdots H{-}\underset{\underset{Cl}{|}}{\overset{\overset{Cl}{|}}{C}}{-}Cl$$

Although only pairs of molecules are involved, there is an increase in the solubility of such liquid-pair systems. Also, the boiling point of the constant boiling mixture is 65°C., which is higher than that of either of the pure substances; acetone boils at 56° and chloroform at 61°C. An increase of this nature in the boiling point of mixtures is indicative of molecular association.

Much of the discussion of intermolecular forces centers around pairs of molecules in the relatively simple gaseous state. These forces are effective in the liquid state, and the situation is complicated even more when the molecules are crowded together so that several are attempting to interact at one time. Nevertheless, the principles developed above will help in attempting to understand and explain the nature of liquids and solutions. There is little doubt that a complete description, on the basis of intermolecular forces, of such complex systems as solutions is not anticipated in the near future. One obvious obstacle is that the actual nature of these forces is not thoroughly understood. Much information about solutions has been published and many correlations have been worked out on the basis of intermolecular forces. Some of the relations resulting from such work will be described in Part Three.

■ PART THREE

Solutions

The chemical classification of matter includes elements, compounds, and mixtures. The elements make up the simplest category, and the least complicated of the elements are the rare gases whose molecules are composed of single atoms. These atoms are separate and independent of one another in the gaseous state, with very little interaction between them. When condensed to the liquid or solid state, the atoms are in more or less intimate contact with nearby atoms and are under the influence of interatomic forces, as described in the discussion on liquids.

Except for faults or defects, the atoms in a crystal are arranged and remain in an orderly neighbor-to-neighbor fashion. In a solid consisting of only one elemental species there is a minimum of stress in the symmetrical field of force about each particle. The question naturally arises as to the situation in a mixture of two or more substances when the neighboring atom is one of a different species. Spatial and force-field distortions may exist which would make it more difficult for the normal crystal to continue to grow about a nucleus. When the different species of the mixture are similar, a *solution* may result if the particles fulfil the necessary requirement of being distributed in a homogeneous molecular manner.

According to the above definition of a solution, it becomes obvious that the chemical nature of the different substances is of considerable significance in permitting dispersion of the particles in order to form a solution. The individual characteristics of the polyatomic elements, as well as of compounds, become increasingly important as the substances become more complex. The way in which materials mix has been investigated extensively. Many correlations and rules have been developed, and perhaps the most useful statement relating chemical constitution and solubility is the simple rule: *like dissolves like*. This rule applies to all states of matter but finds its widest use with liquid solutions.

In addition to the chemical nature of the constituents, the physical state is a further complicating factor in studying solutions. The order of mixing must be considered; for example, gases may dissolve in liquids or solids, but not the reverse, if vapors are neglected. Of the nine possible combinations, the seven listed are feasible:

Solute   *Solvent*

$$
\text{Gas in} \quad \begin{cases} \text{gas} \\ \text{liquid} \\ \text{solid} \end{cases}
$$

$$
\text{Liquid in} \quad \begin{cases} \text{liquid} \\ \text{solid} \end{cases}
$$

$$
\text{Solid in} \quad \begin{cases} \text{liquid} \\ \text{solid} \end{cases}
$$

Gas-in-solid and liquid-in-solid solutions are found infrequently. Of the five remaining systems, the gas-in-gas is the least significant, while the solid-in-solid class warrants a separate discussion. Finally, the three liquid solutions which make up the most important group of mixtures may be described together.

Because the constituents of gaseous mixtures are completely miscible, solutions of gases probably represent the simplest class of solutions and their behavior has been characterized by many laws and theories. Dalton's law of partial pressure illustrates the behavior of two or more gases which have been placed in the same container. Since the total pressure, P, in a volume of a mixture of gases is equal to the sum of the individual or partial pressures, P_1, P_2, P_3 ..., regardless of the nature of the gases, Dalton expressed this relation in the following form:

$$P = P_1 + P_2 + P_3 \dots$$

Other laws, such as those of Boyle, Gay-Lussac, Charles, and Graham, can be applied to gaseous solutions with essentially the same precision obtainable with the pure constituents under the same conditions. A natural consequence of the structure of gases is that their mixtures form solutions more nearly ideal than condensed systems. There are no deviations in solutions consisting of ideal gases, since no cohesive forces exist between molecules in such systems. Deviations exist for real substances and no adequate theory for the prediction of the degree of non-ideality of gaseous solutions is available, although considerable effort is being expended on this problem.

CHAPTER 10

The Phase Rule

The majority of known solutions in which one solid dissolves in another exist in the field of metallurgy, where they play important roles in the formation of alloys. There are not many examples of completely miscible solid solutions. A few notable ones are the binary mixtures of copper and gold, copper and silver, and manganese and gold. The other extreme, in which the solids are practically insoluble, is encountered more often, even though their liquid forms are usually miscible. A useful method of depicting solid-liquid systems is the thermal diagram in which the freezing temperature is plotted in relation to the composition of the mixture. Figure 49, A–D, represents equilibrium curves obtained for simpler systems consisting of two components.

The theory underlying the interpretation of thermal analysis diagrams was first developed by J. W. Gibbs in 1875, in his heterogeneous equilibrium studies.[1] These investigations led to his formulation of the Phase Rule, which may be used in explaining the conditions existing in the different regions of the phase diagrams and at the equilibrium lines bounding these regions. Gibbs's relation specifies the conditions for equilibrium as related to the number of components and phases. The possible variables, or degrees of freedom, F, may be calculated from the equation

$$F = C - P + 2$$

taken from Gibbs's theory. Such quantities as pressure, temperature, concentration, etc., may vary. In the system being analyzed, C is the number of components or distinct chemical substances, and P is the number of phases or

---

[1] J. W. Gibbs, *Trans. Conn. Acad.*, **3,** 108 (1875); *Collected Works*, Vol. I (New York: Longmans, Green & Company, Inc., 1931).

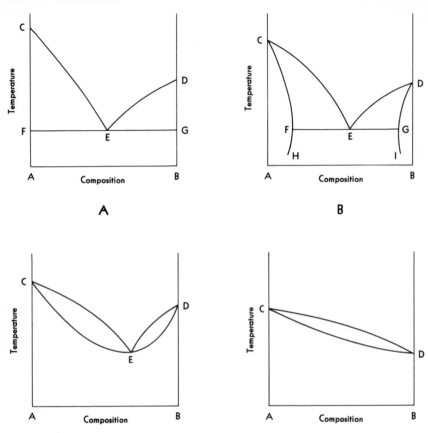

FIGURE 49

Equilibrium diagrams for two-component systems. The simple eutectic is shown by A; B portrays partial solid solubility; C and D represent different types of behavior in completely miscible solid systems.

separate physical states. When only one component is under investigation, $C = 1$ and

$$F = 1 - P + 2 = 3 - P$$

One of the simplest applications of his rule concerns one-component or single-substance systems. A material may exist in one, two, or three physical states or phases simultaneously, part or all of which may be in equilibrium if the conditions are right. When all three states — gas, liquid, and solid — are in equilibrium, the system is at the triple point and $F = 3 - 3 = 0$. The system is thus invariant at this unique point. Figure 44, A (page 101) illustrates the triple point and other phenomena associated with phase changes. To illustrate, two phases are in equilibrium along the lines, TA, TC and TD, and $F = 3 - 2 = 1$, that is, one degree of freedom. Along any line, such as TC, it is possible to choose any temperature at will, but the corresponding pressure must then be accepted; conversely, a chosen pressure must be accompanied by its required temperature. Finally, in any of the regions bounded by lines, such as that between TC and TD, both temperature and pressure may be adjusted as desired. There is only one phase and two degrees of freedom. In this and similar regions the heterogeneous quality is absent and the system is homogeneous.

SOLID-LIQUID DIAGRAMS

An analysis similar to the one-component discussion may be applied to mixtures, such as alloys, where two or more components are involved. The vapor pressure near the melting point of most molten substances is quite low and may be neglected, making it possible to change the Gibbs equation to the following form for solid-liquid equilibrium studies:

$$F = C - P + 1$$

Figure 49, A represents a system with solids A and B as components, where A might be cadmium and B, bismuth. The liquids dissolve in all proportions, but the solids do not mix to form solid solutions. Since the two liquids are miscible, there is only one liquid phase, indicated by the area above CED. With the two components in this region,

$$F = C - P + 1 = 2 - 1 + 1 = 2$$

The two allowable variables are temperature and composition; both may be chosen at will within the homogeneous CED region. Along the line CE the liquid is in equilibrium with solid crystals of pure A. There are two phases and only one degree of freedom. A given composition has a definite saturation temperature which may be found at the proper point on the line CE. This is the freezing point of the liquid solution, where crystals of pure solvent, A, first appear on cooling. The behavior along DE is similar to that along CE. Region CEF consists of a "slush" of crystals of pure A in the liquid solution. It is not possible to move into this area and still maintain equilibrium; this area may be reached only by quenching the melt. Point E is unique in that it is the only place where the liquid is in equilibrium with the two solid crystalline components, A and B. Here, there are two solid phases, one liquid phase, and no degrees of freedom; both temperature and composition are fixed. Point E is called the *eutectic*, or lowest freezing point, and it has a characteristic value with a definite composition and temperature for each system of this nature.

The remaining parts of Figure 49, B–D, represent varying degrees of solid solubility with complete liquid miscibility in each case. Figure 49, B portrays partial solid solubility in the region to the left of CFH where solid B is dissolved in solid A, and to the right of DGI where solid A is in solid B. On cooling the melt, crystals separating out along CE will consist of a solid solution of B in A, rather than pure A as in the simple eutectic system. Except for the solid solutions, this system is much like that of the simple eutectic.

The solid constituents are completely miscible in Figure 49, C and D. The simplicity of these curves indicates considerable similarity between the substances in these two systems. There is a minimum of stress when atoms of B are interspersed in a crystal of otherwise pure A and vice versa.

The information required to construct thermal diagrams is obtained experimentally by simply taking the desired quantities of the two substances, melting the mixture, and allowing the liquid to cool until crystals appear. The variation of temperature with time is recorded during cooling and a characteristic break, or hold, appears in the cooling rate at the freezing point. This approach is a powerful tool for solution studies, for it is a simple matter to record the readings automatically. An extensive array of thermal diagrams is available in the literature.[2]

[2] International Critical Tables, Vol. II (New York: McGraw-Hill Book Company, Inc., 1927).

CHAPTER 11

Liquid Solutions

When a gas dissolves in a liquid, the resulting mixture is usually a liquid. Two different physical states are involved, and two dissimilar chemical materials are mixed in producing these solutions. Such rather complicated systems were studied by WILLIAM HENRY (1803), who found a significant relation covering this class of solutions. He stated:

▼ "... That under the same circumstance of temperature water takes up the same volume of gas, whether it be condensed, or under ordinary pressure; but, as the spaces occupied by gases are inversely as the weights compressing them, it follows, that water takes up of gas condensed, by one, two, or three additional atmospheres, a quantity which is equal to twice, thrice, or four times the quantity taken up under the ordinary pressure.[1] ▲

His findings may be expressed by the equation

$$P = kX \tag{1}$$

where P is the partial pressure of the gas, X is its concentration in solution, and k is a constant, characteristic for each system. Although over a century and a half have elapsed since the discovery of this relatively simple relation, it is still being studied and clarified.[2]

[1] W. HENRY, *Phyl. Mag.*, **16,** 90 (1803).
[2] R. R. Davison (private communication).

Many dilute mixtures of liquids in liquids also obey Henry's law reasonably well. A similar relation,

$$P_1 = P_1^0 x_1 \tag{2}$$

discovered by F. M. Raoult in 1887, is usually used for investigations of liquid-in-liquid solutions. The quantities P_1 and x_1 are the partial vapor pressure and mole fraction of the solvent, respectively, and P_1^0 is the vapor pressure of the pure solvent. It is customary in solution studies to use subscript 1 to represent the solvent, the substance in which the solute, represented by subscript 2, dissolves. The mole fraction x_1 is the number of moles of the solvent divided by the total number of moles in the solution. The two laws stated above are found to apply to solutions so dilute that each solute molecule has a uniform environment in which it is completely surrounded by solvent molecules./ These laws are also obeyed when the constituents mix to form ideal solutions, i.e., where cohesive forces are uniform throughout./ An important criterion for ideal liquid-in-liquid solutions is that no heat shall be absorbed or evolved when they are formed. There are many degrees of variation from ideality even among those mixtures that are completely miscible. Solutions of liquids that are only partially miscible and, in particular, of those that are essentially immiscible deviate most widely from ideal behavior.

Solids have a limited solubility in liquids, and usually systems of solids in liquids do not follow the laws of ideal solutions very closely. Heat is ordinarily absorbed when a solid dissolves in a liquid; and, when the two substances are similar in chemical makeup, this heat is the enthalpy of fusion of the solid solute. Similarly, in the dissolution of gases in liquids, there is a heat effect, which is the heat of condensation of the gas. These are clearly the heats due to the changes in physical states and are not the result of interactions involved in the formation of the solution.

The study of solutions has been aided by suitably classifying them on the basis of deviations from ideal behavior. The deviations are exceptional in one group consisting of an acid, base, or salt solute dissolved in a specified solvent. Water is the solvent for ordinary acids, bases, and salts, such as hydrochloric acid, sodium hydroxide, and sodium chloride, respectively. Only a limited number of substances have the proper characteristics to act as solvents in a manner similar to that of water. Anhydrous liquid ammonia, phosgene, thionyl chloride, liquid sulfur dioxide, and fused salts are examples of such solvents. Analogous to water, any acceptable pure solvent must ionize slightly and be polar in nature, as exemplified by phosgene:

$$COCl_2 = CO^{++} + Cl_2^{=}$$

$CO \cdot Al_2Cl_8$ is an acid and $CaCl_2$ is a base on the phosgene system. A neutralization reaction produces solvent molecules and a salt ($CaAl_2Cl_8$):

$$COAl_2Cl_8 + CaCl_2 = COCl_2 + CaAl_2Cl_8$$

As with water and phosgene, there are specific interactions in all similar solvent systems between the solute and solvent in which the solute molecule or crystal separates into two or more electrically charged particles or ions. Solutions of ions exhibit such extensive and characteristic deviations from the ideal that it is desirable to set such systems aside as a separate group, called *solutions of electrolytes*. All solutions other than electrolytes are designated as solutions of non-electrolytes. The latter are discussed in the following chapter.

CHAPTER 12

Solutions of Non-Electrolytes

Systems in the non-electrolyte category exhibit a wide variety of behavior and range from nearly ideal solutions to those with great deviations from the ideal. Mixtures of substances which are not completely miscible exhibit the greatest deviations. One of the objectives of solution investigation is to find a unified approach that will provide information for systems which vary so greatly.

IDEAL SOLUTIONS

Pure liquids which are quite similar exhibit little in the way of measurable effects upon being mixed; the resulting solution is similar to the original substances. Such solutions have physical properties which are the average of the values for the individual constituents. As an example, the partial vapor pressure of the solvent is directly proportional to its mole fraction in solution, regardless of the nature of the solute. Raoult discovered this relation and first reported it in connection with his work on ethereal solutions.[1] His data were depicted by the equation

$$100 \, \frac{P}{P_1{}^0} = 100 - KN \tag{1}$$

where P is the total vapor pressure of the solution, $P_1{}^0$ is the vapor pressure of the pure solvent, K is a constant somewhat independent of the nature of the solute, and N is the number of solute molecules in 100 molecules of solution. The following table lists the values of K for various solutes in ether solutions.

[1] F. M. Raoult, *Comptes Rendus*, **104**, 1430 (1887); *Z. Physik. Chem.*, **2**, 353 (1888).

Solute	K
Turpentine	0.90
Aniline	0.90
Ethyl benzoate	0.90
Methyl salicylate	0.87
Nitrobenzene	0.70

The familiar Raoult equation, $P_1/P_1{}^0 = x_1$, results when the above studies are interpreted in terms of mole fractions. The linear relation between the partial pressure, P_1, of the solvent and its mole fraction, x_1, in an ideal solution is shown in Figure 50. The partial pressure, P_2, for the solute also varies linearly from its vapor pressure, $P_2{}^0$, in the pure state to zero when there is only pure solvent. The total pressure, P_{total}, for any desired composition is obtained by adding the two partial pressures. The series of points representing such sums yields a straight line ranging from pure solvent, with pressure, $P_1{}^0$, to pure solute, $P_2{}^0$, showing another linear vapor pressure relation for an ideal solution.

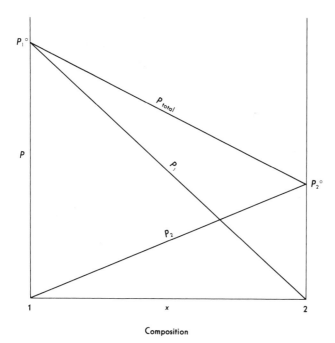

FIGURE 50

The vapor pressure-composition diagram of an ideal two-component system obeying Raoult's law. The upper curve P_{total} represents the directly measurable pressures. The partial pressure of the solvent is indicated by P_1 and that of the solute by P_2.

The relationships in the above analysis have been proposed as a basis for defining an *ideal solution*. Because of the linear relations, a minimum of experimental information will completely describe such a system. To calculate the complete total and partial vapor pressure curves for the entire system, only the vapor pressures, P_1^0 and P_2^0, of the pure constituents at the desired temperature are needed. The significance of vapor pressure studies as related to solutions will become more evident in the following discussion.

REAL SOLUTIONS

Ideal systems are formed when chemically similar substances are mixed. These solutions can be dealt with in a simple manner, but, unfortunately, there are not many reasonably ideal mixtures. The behavior of other systems can be determined accurately only from experimental information. Vapor pressure diagrams may be used to represent the degree of variation from ideality, as indicated in Figure 51, A, B, and C. The solid lines in Figure 51, A represent modest positive deviations from the ideal Raoult law (broken lines) for the partial and total vapor pressures. When the substances are less alike chemically, the deviations become greater, as shown in Figure 51, B, where there may be a maximum in the total pressure curve. The upper limit in deviations for systems with maxima occurs when the constituents are so unlike as to cease to be completely miscible. In this instance, in a certain range of composition, two liquid layers will form, the range being greater for substances that are less alike.

Systems with negative deviations from Raoult's law, as in Figure 51, C, are less common than those with positive deviations; however, the mixture of

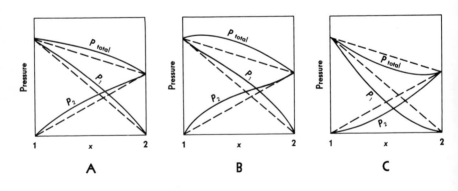

FIGURE 51

Vapor pressure-composition diagrams for real two-component systems. Modest deviations from ideal are indicated in A and greater deviations in B and C. The total vapor pressure curve is depicted as a maximum in B and a minimum in C.

hydrochloric acid and water with its minimum in the total vapor pressure curve is a well-known example of a system having a negative vapor pressure deviation. If this is considered in terms of a boiling point diagram, a maximum occurs in the boiling point curve. Hydrochloric acid of any composition can be distilled continuously until a constant temperature is attained at the maximum point. The remaining solution will distill at a constant ratio of the two constituents; the composition is so constant and reproducible that the solution can be used as a standard acid in analytical procedures.

From an analysis of the diagrams, it might be assumed that the deviations would be expected to be either positive everywhere or negative everywhere. There is controversy, however, concerning the necessity for systems with positive deviations in one concentration range to be positive in all ranges and those with negative deviations to be always negative.[2]

PARTIAL VAPOR PRESSURE CALCULATIONS

The importance of vapor pressure has already been alluded to and partial vapor pressure data are needed, for example, to calculate the number of theoretical plates required for a distillation column to bring about a desired separation of two substances. Satisfactory data for practical applications are comparatively easy to obtain, but, unfortunately, experimental partial pressure determinations are difficult, tedious, and of questionable value when high accuracy is needed.[3] Since total vapor pressures are easier to measure than partial pressures, many methods have been developed for calculating or approximating partial pressures from total values. Most of these methods have as their basis the Gibbs-Duhem equation developed by Gibbs[4] in 1875 and Duhem[5] in 1886. The vapor pressures of the pure components, as well as the total pressures over the entire concentration range, are needed in order to estimate the values of the partial pressures at the desired concentrations. The method proposed by these investigators involves the use of the free energy quantity, G, invented by Gibbs, which is a criterion for the feasibility of a proposed thermodynamic process.

By definition, G, for any system is the difference between the enthalpy, H, and the temperature-entropy product TS:

$$G = H - TS \tag{2}$$

The enthalpy consists of the two energy terms in the defining relation,

$$H = E + PV$$

[2] M. L. McGlashan, *J. Chem. Educ.*, **40**, 516 (1963).

[3] F. Hovorka and D. Dreisbach, *J. Am. Chem. Soc.*, **56**, 1664 (1934).

[4] J. W. Gibbs, *Trans. Conn. Acad.*, **3**, 108 (1875); *Collected Works*, Vol. I (New York: Longmans, Green & Company, Inc., 1931).

[5] C. F. Duhem, *Comptes Rendus*, **102**, 1449 (1886).

and Equation (2) may be written as

$$G = E + PV - TS$$

where E is the internal energy, P is the pressure, and V the volume of the system. For a change in the free energy, then,

$$dG = dE + PdV + VdP - TdS - SdT$$

A change in internal energy is given by the law of conservation of energy:

$$dE = TdS - PdV$$

where TdS is the heat absorbed by the system and PdV is the work done, so that

$$dG = TdS - PdV + PdV + VdP - TdS - SdT$$

or

$$dG = VdP - SdT \tag{3}$$

Thus the total differential of G is expressed in terms of the variables T and P. If the system is more complex, other variables may be involved. For example, with mixtures or solutions the free energy also depends on the composition variable which is expressed in terms of the change in the constituents in the form $\left(\dfrac{\partial G}{\partial n_1}\right) dn_1$. The number of moles of constituent 1 is indicated by n_1, of constituent 2 by n_2, etc. On adding these quantities, Equation (3) becomes

$$dG = VdP - SdT + \left(\frac{\partial G}{\partial n_1}\right) dn_1 + \left(\frac{\partial G}{\partial n_2}\right) dn_2 + \left(\frac{\partial G}{\partial n_3}\right) dn_3 + \cdots \tag{4}$$

The important quantity $\left(\dfrac{\partial G}{\partial n_1}\right)$ represents the way in which the free energy of constituent 1 varies in the solution as the composition changes, and is referred to as the partial molar free energy, $\overline{G}_1$. Gibbs named $\overline{G}_1$ the *chemical potential* and gave it the symbol μ_1. The factor $\overline{G}_1$ represents the effect on the free energy of the solution when some of component 1 is added to such a large quantity of the solution that there is no change in the relative amounts of $n_2, n_3, \ldots$. It is customary to study solutions at constant pressure and temperature in which case the first two terms on the right, VdP and SdT, of Equation (4) become zero, leaving

$$dG = \left(\frac{\partial G}{\partial n_1}\right) dn_1 + \left(\frac{\partial G}{\partial n_2}\right) dn_2 + \left(\frac{\partial G}{\partial n_3}\right) dn_3 + \ldots$$

or

$$dG = \overline{G}_1 dn_1 + \overline{G}_2 dn_2 + \overline{G}_3 dn_3 + \ldots \tag{5}$$

By letting $\overline{G}_i$ be the partial molar free energy of any constituent, i, and the total free energy the sum of all these $\overline{G}_i$ terms, each multiplied by its proper number, n_i,[6] then the total free energy

$$G = n_1\overline{G}_1 + n_2\overline{G}_2 + n_3\overline{G}_3 + \ldots + n_i\overline{G}_i$$

Only two terms are needed for a binary system:

$$G = n_1\overline{G}_1 + n_2\overline{G}_2 \tag{6}$$

On differentiating Equation (6),

$$dG = n_1 d\overline{G}_1 + \overline{G}_1 dn_1 + n_2 d\overline{G}_2 + \overline{G}_2 dn_2 \tag{7}$$

From Equation (5), for a binary system,

$$dG = \overline{G}_1 dn_1 + \overline{G}_2 dn_2$$

and on combining this with Equation (7) we have

$$n_1 d\overline{G}_1 + n_2 d\overline{G}_2 = 0 \tag{8}$$

On dividing Equation (8) by $(n_1 + n_2)$,

$$\frac{n_1}{n_1 + n_2} d\overline{G}_1 + \frac{n_2}{n_1 + n_2} d\overline{G}_2 = 0$$

Since x_1 and x_2 are the mole fractions,

$$x_1 = \frac{n_1}{n_1 + n_2} \quad \text{and} \quad x_2 = \frac{n_2}{n_1 + n_2}$$

On substituting, the following is obtained:

$$x_1 d\overline{G}_1 + x_2 d\overline{G}_2 = 0 \tag{9}$$

Equation (9) is known as the Gibbs-Duhem equation.[7]

The mole fractions may be equated to the vapor pressures if a total of one mole of solution (that is, $n_1 + n_2 = 1$) is taken and the vapors are considered to act as perfect gases. For an ideal gas at constant temperature, Equation (3) becomes $dG = VdP$, and since $V = RT/P$,

$$dG = \frac{RT}{P} dP = RT d \ln P \tag{10}$$

[6] G. N. Lewis, M. Randall, K. S. Pitzer, and L. Brewer, *Thermodynamics* (New York: McGraw-Hill Book Company, Inc., 1961).

[7] This is one of the outstanding equations in the thermodynamic treatment of solutions. An informative discussion of its use in Gibbs's free energy calculations is given by S. D. Christian, *J. Chem. Educ.*, **39**, 521 (1962).

The change in the partial molar free energy of each constituent can be shown to be

$$d\bar{G}_1 = RTd \ln P_1 \quad \text{and} \quad d\bar{G}_2 = RTd \ln P_2$$

and Equation (9) becomes

$$x_1 d \ln P_1 + x_2 d \ln P_2 = 0 \tag{11}$$

where P_1 and P_2 are the partial vapor pressures. (If the vapors deviate from the ideal, a corrective pressure quantity called *fugacity, f,* may be introduced and the relation $d\bar{G} = RTd \ln f$ may be used for any gas, real or ideal.)

The sum of the mole fractions $x_1 + x_2 = 1$, and hence $dx_1 = -dx_2$. Dividing Equation (11) by dx_1 (equal to $-dx_2$) gives

$$\frac{x_1}{dx_1} d \ln P_1 - \frac{x_2}{dx_2} d \ln P_2 = 0$$

and

$$\frac{1}{d \ln x_1} d \ln P_1 = \frac{1}{d \ln x_2} d \ln P_2$$

Rearranging gives

$$\frac{d \ln P_1}{d \ln P_2} = \frac{d \ln x_1}{d \ln x_2} = \frac{d \ln x_1}{d \ln (1 - x_1)} \tag{12}$$

Equation (12) was integrated by Margules in 1895, using an exponential series, to give

$$P_1 = P_1^{\,0} x^{\alpha_0} e^{\alpha_1(1-x)+\frac{\alpha_2}{2}(1-x)^2+\frac{\alpha_3}{3}(1-x)^3+\cdots} \tag{13}$$

and

$$P_2 = P_2^{\,0} x^{\beta_0} e^{\beta_1 x+\frac{\beta_2}{2}x^2+\frac{\beta_3}{3}x^3+\cdots} \tag{14}$$

where $\alpha_0, \alpha_1, \alpha_2, \ldots$ and $\beta_0, \beta_1, \beta_2, \ldots$ are constants. In a binary mixture these constants have the following values: $\alpha_0 = \beta_0 = 1$, $\alpha_1 = \beta_1 = 0$, $\alpha_2 = \beta_2 + \beta_3$, and $\alpha_3 = -\beta_3$. If all but the first two terms of the series are neglected,

$$P_1 = P_1^{\,0} x e^{\frac{\alpha_2}{2}(1-x)^2+\frac{\alpha_3}{3}(1-x)^3} \tag{15}$$

and

$$P_2 = P_2^{\,0}(1 - x)e^{\frac{\beta_2}{2}x^2+\frac{\beta_3}{3}x^3} \tag{16}$$

Zawidski,[8] applying the Duhem-Margules equation to binary mixtures, used the established relationship between the α and β quantities and the first two terms of the series in the equations:

[8] J. von Zawidski, *Z. Physik. Chem.,* **35,** 129 (1900).

$$P_1 = P_1{}^0 x e^{\frac{\alpha_2}{2}(1-x)^2 + \frac{\alpha_3}{3}(1-x)^3}$$

and

$$P_2 = P_2{}^0 (1 - x) e^{\frac{\alpha_2 + \alpha_3}{2} x^2 - \frac{\alpha_3}{3} x^3}$$

Zawidski employed three methods for determining the values of α_2 and α_3. In the first procedure, he chose two points on one of the partial pressure curves and, knowing the values for x_1, P_1, and $P_1{}^0$, obtained two simultaneous equations from which he determined the values of α_2 and α_3. The accuracy of the method could be improved by taking an average of the values for several points. In his second method, Zawidski started with the total pressure and, by a time-consuming trial and error operation, assigned values to α_2 and α_3, then adjusted these values until the sum of P_1 and P_2 equaled the total pressure. By the third method, values of α_2 and α_3 were calculated through the relations:

$$\left(\frac{\alpha_2}{2} + \frac{\alpha_3}{3}\right) \log e = \log\left[\left(\frac{dP}{dx}\right)_0 + P_2{}^0\right] - \log P_1{}^0$$

$$\left(\frac{\alpha_2}{2} + \frac{\alpha_3}{6}\right) \log e = \log\left[P_1{}^0 - \left(\frac{dP}{dx}\right)_1\right] - \log P_2{}^0$$

where $\left(\dfrac{dP}{dx}\right)_0$ is the tangent drawn to the total pressure curve at the point $x = 0$,

and $\left(\dfrac{dP}{dx}\right)_1$ is the value of the tangent drawn to the total pressure curve at the

point $x = 1$. This equation represents the first application of the slope of the total pressure curve, i.e., the first derivative, in solving for partial pressures. This last method, although not too difficult to calculate from available data, has certain drawbacks owing to the uncertainty of the curve in very dilute regions. The first two methods of Zawidski are too tedious for easy manipulation and have not been used to any great extent.

Based on his knowledge of the diagrams of similar systems, Marshall (1906) used the total vapor pressure curve as a guide to sketch approximate partial pressure curves. He used the following three equations for testing specific points from his sketched curves:

(a) $P = P_1 + P_2$

(b) $dP = dP_1 + dP_2$

(c) $\dfrac{dP}{dx} = \dfrac{dP_1}{dx}\left(1 - \dfrac{P_1}{P_2} \cdot \dfrac{1 - x_1}{x_1}\right)$

The curves were then redrawn until they agreed with the equations. This method is especially useful for rapid approximations.

Tinker (1916) developed a rather simple relation using Dieterici's equation of state (page 5) and Raoult's law, as well as the latent heats of vaporization. His equation is easy to use, but the required latent heat information is not always available.

More than a score of methods for evaluating partial pressures have been developed and, except for a few cases, such as those of Marshall and Tinker, all have been modifications of the relations originated by Gibbs, Duhem, and Margules. One of the more recent investigations is that of Gilmont, Zudkevitch, and Othmer who have been able to produce a two-parameter equation which has been applied successfully to approximately 500 binary systems.[9] Perhaps the most encouraging approach is that of Christian, who calculates partial pressures by a digital computer method which is accurate, rapid, and easy to use.[10] We hope that this computer approach will lead to a compilation of superior thermodynamic data.

SOLUBILITY

An inspection of the vapor pressure curves in Figure 51, A–C, shows the relation between vapor pressure, P, and solution composition, x. The vapor pressure of a solution is measured at the point of equilibrium so that a fixed relation between the vapor and liquid composition is established. To illustrate, vapor pressure data show that a liquid solution consisting of 0.70 mole fraction of benzene in acetic acid has a *partial* vapor pressure of benzene of 77.0 mm. Conversely, a benzene-acetic acid mixture yielding a 77.0 mm. partial vapor pressure of benzene must be 0.70 mole fraction in benzene. At this point the solution is saturated with benzene vapor. It is this line of reasoning that permits vapor pressures to be used in predicting solubilities.

Hildebrand made use of this concept in his theory of solubility, which was published in a series of papers starting in 1916. In his first paper HILDEBRAND states:

▼   "There is scarcely anything more important for a chemist than a knowledge of solubilities, but unfortunately he finds it more difficult to predict how soluble a substance will be in a given solvent than it is to predict almost any other important property. . . . Planck has pointed out that the relation between the change in free and total energy in forming a solution, and hence solubilities, could be calculated if we knew, in addition to the heat of solution, the specific heats of solution and pure substances down to absolute zero, the treatment being analogous to the calculation of chemical equilibria by means of the Nernst Heat Theorem. At present our meagre knowledge of

[9] R. Gilmont, D. Zudkevitch, and D. F. Othmer, *Ind. Eng. Chem.*, **53**, 223 (1961).
[10] S. D. Christian, *J. Phys. Chem.*, **64**, 764 (1960).

specific heats of liquids and solutions makes such a treatment impossible. Furthermore to be of real use, the calculation of solubility must be made from the properties of the pure substances only, and not from a property of the solution, such as its specific heat, the experimental determination of which may be more difficult than that of solubility itself. . . ."

"A great deal of the older physical chemistry has had for one of its chief foundation stones the law of van't Hoff $[\pi V = RT]$ for the osmotic pressure of dissolved substances. The fruitful use of this law in dealing with the properties of dilute solutions, and its analogy to the law for perfect gases, have somewhat blinded chemists to its limitations. Nearly all text-books of physical chemistry still use it to derive the ordinary laws for molecular weight determination. . . . It has been pointed out by G. N. Lewis and others that Raoult's Law is a far better fundamental expression, holding for the simplest solutions throughout the entire range of concentration, when the van't Hoff equation leads to absurd values of osmotic pressure."[11]   ▲

The relation between solubility and vapor pressure for a solution obeying Raoult's law is illustrated in Figure 50. The constituents of the mixture are similar in nature and form an ideal solution. In most cases, however, there are differences between the physical and chemical properties of any two substances, and, except for certain isomers and some isotopically different compounds, it is not possible for the two species to be alike in every way. The intermolecular forces described in Chapter 9, as well as molar volume differences, account for many of the deviations from Raoult's law. Generally, the factors that tend to decrease the mutual solubility of liquids cause positive deviations in the vapor pressure curves (Figure 51, A and B).

As a consequence of kinetic activity, the solubility of one liquid in another is increased by a rise in temperature. In Figure 52, A two liquids A and B, at T_1, have only limited solubility as indicated by the region outside the shaded area. As the temperature is raised, B becomes more soluble in A, shown by line cf, and simultaneously the solubility of A in B increases according to line df. The area under cfd represents the region of immiscibility. The two substances are soluble in all proportions about T_2. The temperature at point f is called the *Upper Critical Solution Temperature*. Extreme deviations from Raoult's law exist near the critical solution point as illustrated in Figure 53 for isobutyric acid and water mixtures. The partial and total vapor pressure curves are at 28°C., slightly above the U.C.S.T. of 26°C.

The optical behavior of a solution at the critical solution point is similar to that of a pure gas at its critical point. A critical opalescence is observed, as well as other phenomena, and these effects may be related to the thermodynamic stability of liquid mixtures. There are large fluctuations in concentration be-

[11] J. H. HILDEBRAND, *J. Am. Chem. Soc.*, **38**, 1452 (1916).

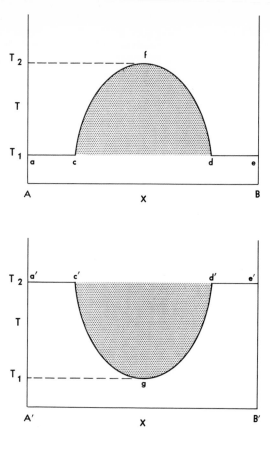

FIGURE 52

In Figure 52, A indicates the increase in solubility with temperature rise for two liquids. Immiscibility exists in the shaded area. B represents the increase in solubility with temperature lowering for a certain group of binary liquid systems. The shaded area represents immiscibility.

tween small elements of volume in these solutions which cause strong scattering of the light. Much information about the nature of solute molecules, such as polymers, may be obtained from scattering measurements. Polystyrene, of approximately 1,000,000 molecular weight, dissolved in cyclohexane has a critical temperature at 29°C. and a critical composition of 2 percent by volume of polymer. Scattering studies in the range 30.0° to 29.1°C., just above the critical point, have been used to determine the range of molecular forces. A newly detected effect is currently being investigated by Debye, one of the pioneers in the study of scattering phenomena.[12] In this effect a change of the

[12] P. J. W. Debye, *Chem. Eng. News*, **41**, 92 (1963); address before the Akron (Ohio) section of the American Chemical Society, Jan. 21, 1965.

scattered intensity may be brought about by the application of an electric field, thus providing a new dimension in the analysis of such solutions.

Several practical applications of critical solution points are described by Francis, who has compiled a list of more than 6,000 observations related to this

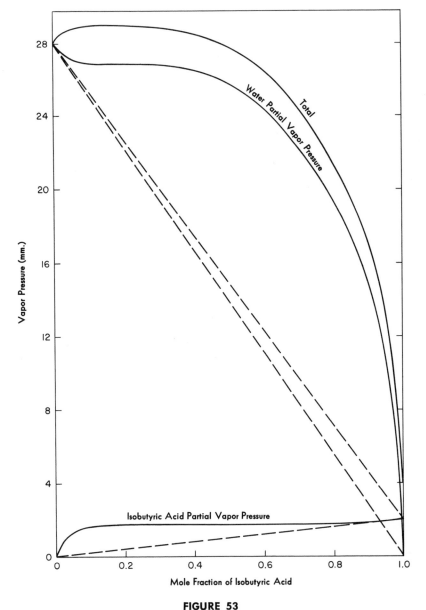

FIGURE 53

Total and partial vapor pressure curves for isobutyric acid and water at 28°C.

phenomenon.[13] The great majority of solutions with critical solution points have the normal increase of solubility with temperature increase and at sufficiently high values an upper critical solution temperature is attained. In a limited number of cases, however, the opposite effect exists where the solubility increases with a decrease in temperature. The vapor pressure curves of such systems may exhibit negative deviations as shown by Figure 51, C. Such solutions usually have constituents in which hydrogen bonding causes a mutual attraction between the different molecular species. The increase in solubility of the two substances due to bonding may be great enough to effect complete mixing of the dissimilar liquids, especially at lower temperatures. The forces of attraction must be sufficient to overcome the dispersing effect of kinetic activity. The constituents A' and B' are only partially miscible at temperature T_2 in Figure 52, B and the solubility increases as the mixture cools along line c'g. At T_1 the two liquids become completely miscible. There is a *lower* critical solution temperature at g, where the kinetic activity has decreased sufficiently for the attractive forces to dominate. However, little practical use has been made of lower critical solution points, and Francis lists only 136 examples of this class of solutions.

A cursory examination of Figures 52 A and B leads to the question of the possibility of joining the two curves to produce a closed solubility curve of the form sketched in Figure 54. Systems of this nature have been reported and Francis cites 31 in his publication. It is not surprising that the number is so small, as several requirements must be met before this phenomenon is realized. The substances need to be dissimilar enough to be only partially miscible at a particular temperature, yet sufficiently alike so that an increase in temperature will bring about complete solubility within the liquid range. Added to such restrictions is the necessity for attractive forces strong enough to cause miscibility on cooling, and this must occur before the solution freezes.

An interesting group of closed solubility systems consists of certain glycol ethers (alkoxy ethanols) mixed with water.[14] Butoxy ethanol (ethylene glycol mono-n-butyl ether) is a commercial solvent marketed under the name of Butyl Cellosolve. Mixtures of this compound with water form a system with an L.C.S.T. (lower critical solution temperature) at 49°C. and a U.C.S.T. at 128°C. The water solution of an isomer, ethylene glycol monoisobutyl ether, has an L.C.S.T. at 24.6°C., which is a convenient temperature for physical property studies. Unfortunately, the U.C.S.T. of 150°C. is too high for the usual applications.

Hydrogen bonding normally results in negative deviations from Raoult's law; however, the total and partial vapor pressure curves for the ethylene glycol isobutyl ether-water system at 24°C., just below the L.C.S.T., show positive deviations. The curves are similar to those for isobutyric acid and water,

[13] A. W. Francis, *Critical Solution Temperatures* (Washington, D.C.: Am. Chem. Soc., 1961).
[14] H. L. Cox and L. H. Cretcher, *J. Am. Chem. Soc.*, **48**, 451 (1926).

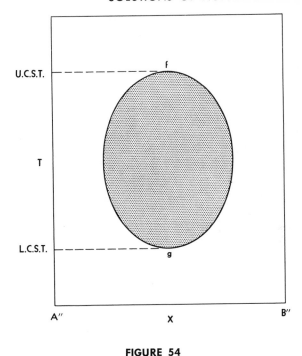

FIGURE 54

A closed solubility curve found in a very limited number of liquid pairs.

Figure 53, although there are minor differences which should be investigated. About the same degree of deviation from Raoult's law exists for both the acid-water and ether-water systems.

Glycerol and guaiacol (*o*-methoxyphenol) form the only reported system with a closed curve in a suitable temperature range (L.C.S.T. at 39.5°C. and U.C.S.T. at 83.5°C.) for which pressures are easy to measure. As with many closed curve systems these two compounds have similar structural units, causing increased solubility at higher temperatures. The ether oxygen in the guaiacol is available for hydrogen bonding with a hydrogen from one of the OH groups of the glycerol molecule, thus increasing the mutual solubility at lower temperatures.[15]

REGULAR SOLUTIONS

Solutions with closed solubility curves represent extremes in the factors causing deviations from the ideal solutions. Existing explanations for the behavior of these mixtures are only qualitative, as might be expected. A reasonable

[15] Commercial grades of these chemicals do not appear to be immiscible, as observed in a preliminary study.

approach to solution theory might involve investigations of systems where only limited or specified deviations occur. Hildebrand proposed such a restricted class, calling them *regular solutions*.[16] He illustrated by experiment and explicitly stated his notions concerning these solutions. Figure 55 shows the solubility of iodine in several solvents as reported by Hildebrand and Jenks (1920).[17] Iodine is violet in the vapor state, and the same violet appearance is found in solutions of certain solvents. The solubility curves of these solutions extrapolate to the melting point of iodine. The curve for benzene (C_6H_6) solutions does not approach the common point, and these solutions are red rather than violet, indicating greater deviation from the ideal. Iodine dissolves in ethanol to form a brown-colored solution.[18] The family having similar curves and violet colors for their iodine solutions are representative of regular

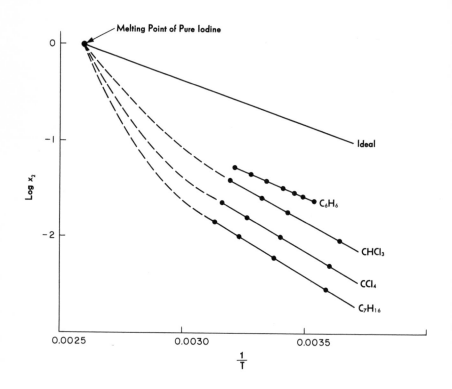

FIGURE 55

The solubility of iodine in various solvents as a function of temperature.

[16] J. H. Hildebrand, *J. Am. Chem. Soc.*, **51**, 66 (1929).
[17] See J. H. Hildebrand and R. L. Scott, *Regular Solutions* (Englewood Cliffs: Prentice-Hall, Inc., 1962), p. 2.
[18] L. R. Summerlin, *J. Chem. Educ.*, **41**, A883 (1964).

solutions. They resemble ideal solutions in their kinetic response to temperature and show complete randomness of distribution at sufficiently high temperatures. Regular solutions have a tendency to unmix as they are cooled and approach their critical solution temperatures. Where complete randomness exists, the entropy of mixing of a regular solution is the same as that for an ideal solution of the same mole fraction. The *excess* entropy change, ΔS^E, is negligible in this class of solutions and the excess free energy, ΔG^E, of mixing equals the excess enthalpy, ΔH^E, as may be seen from the following discussion. By definition $G \equiv H - TS$ and for a constant temperature $\Delta G = \Delta H - T \Delta S$. Since ΔS^E is zero, $\Delta G^E = \Delta H^E$ for the mixing of regular solutions. These excess quantities refer to the difference between the thermodynamic property for the mixing of the actual substances and the value for the formation of an ideal solution of the same composition. Orienting factors and chemical effects are absent in regular solutions and since they are as random in structure as ideal solutions, the two types of solutions should have equal entropies. A correction would be needed for any volume differences that might exist. With the above discussion in mind, Hildebrand gave his definition in this way: "A regular solution is one involving no entropy change when a small amount of one of its components is transferred to it from an ideal solution of the same composition, the total volume remaining unchanged."[19]

It is important to recognize certain aspects of Hildebrand's approach. The ideal solution defined in terms of Raoult's law is taken as the reference state and all deviations are in terms of this state. There are no heat effects when liquids mix to form an ideal solution. The excess heat of mixing, ΔH^E, is a consequence of the nature of regular solutions and represents a deviation from the ideal. Even though no excess entropy of solution, ΔS^E, exists for regular solutions, there is an entropy of formation for all solutions. Those with an entropy change greater than that for ideal solutions deviate too widely to belong to the regular solution class.

Accurate predictions of deviations from ideal solution behavior are not possible at present; therefore, the regular solution concepts are useful for estimating such deviations when experimental information is lacking. Recent studies show that regular solution theory may be applied at rather high temperatures in systems such as fused salts, molten oxides, and metals. The theory has been confirmed by studies of properties of metallic solutions.[20]

Other approaches to methods of studying solutions are being developed and the theorem of corresponding states, as well as the cell model, is being incorporated into these proposals.[21] In his molecular theory of solutions, Prigogine asserts that this treatment of solutions has certain advantages over that for simple substances. For example, predictions on systems of a single substance

[19] Hildebrand and Scott, p. 4.

[20] *Ibid.*, p. 155.

[21] I. Prigogine, *Molecular Theory of Solutions* (Amsterdam: North-Holland Publishing Company, 1957); distributed by Interscience Publishers, Inc., New York.

depend on imperfectly based fundamental relationships, whereas solution calculations are related to the known values of the pure components. There is a wide difference between these two starting points. In either case calculations leave much to be desired and estimations that are sufficiently close to agree with experiment within an order of magnitude are considered triumphs.

FUGACITY AND ACTIVITY

During the past century several methods for dealing with the physical relationships of solutions which rely heavily on experimental information have been developed. Idealized conditions have been set up and deviations from these have been determined. Of the many ways of dealing with these deviations, the most satisfactory system is that of G. N. Lewis, who maintained that, "of all the applications of thermodynamics to chemistry, none has in the past presented greater difficulties, or been the subject of more misunderstanding, than the one involved in the calculation of what has rather loosely been called the free energy of dilution; namely, the difference in the partial molal free energy of a dissolved substance at two concentrations."[22]

One of the postulates used in deriving Equation (10) includes the requirement that the vapor be ideal, although it is recognized that this would seldom be the case. For ideal solutions, the tendency for vapors to escape from the solution is measured by their vapor pressure. While Equation (10) satisfactorily describes this tendency for ideal vapors, it is desirable to define a new function *to preserve the form of this equation* for real solutions and vapors. Lewis introduced such a function and designated it as *fugacity, f.* Fugacity is an empirical quantity that accurately represents the pressure relationships of gases and the escaping tendency of vapors from solutions. According to Lewis, "In the fugacity we are going to define a measure of escaping tendency which bears to the vapor pressure a relation analogous to the relation between the perfect gas thermometer and a thermometer of some actual gas. The fugacity will be equal to the vapor pressure when the vapor is a perfect gas, and in general may be regarded as an 'ideal' or 'corrected' vapor pressure."[23]

To define fugacity further, Equation (10) may be modified by substituting f for P to give

$$dG = RTd \ln f \qquad (17)$$

Between two isothermal states A and B the difference in the free energy is given by

$$G_B - G_A = RT \ln \frac{f_B}{f_A} \qquad (18)$$

[22] G. N. Lewis, *Proc. Am. Acad.*, **37**, 49 (1901); G. N. Lewis, M. Randall, K. S. Pitzer, and L. Brewer, *Thermodynamics* (New York: McGraw-Hill Book Company, Inc., 1961).
[23] *Ibid.*, p. 154.

Since only the ratio of fugacities, not their numerical values, is defined, a standard state is provided by making the fugacity of a perfect gas equal to the pressure of the gas. If G^0 and f^0 are, respectively, the free energy and fugacity in the standard state, the free energy for any state will be

$$G = G^0 + RT \ln \frac{f}{f^0} \tag{19}$$

Since real gases approach ideal behavior at reduced pressure, the fugacity and pressure tend to become the same as the pressure approaches zero; this makes it possible to evaluate the fugacity at any desired higher pressure. The variations of fugacity with pressure for hydrogen, carbon monoxide, and carbon dioxide are shown in Table 8. The tabulated values indicate the degree of

TABLE 8

Fugacity

Gas	Pressure, atmospheres					
	25	50	100	200	500	1000
H_2	25.4	51.5	106	226	690	1900
CO	24.8	49.4	98.0	198	580	1800
CO_2	23.8	43.0	74.5	96.0	230	520

variation between the two quantities and show the need for a quantity such as fugacity to represent the actual behavior of gases.

When a free energy change has been determined, the corresponding value for the ratio of the fugacities is established. This fact is used in the study of mixtures, particularly in the determination of the free energy of the formation or dilution of a solution. If a standard state is arbitrarily chosen, the ratio of fugacities is used as an entity called activity, a, i.e.,

$$\frac{f}{f^0} = a \tag{20}$$

In the standard state the ratio would be unity and $a^0 = 1$. From Equation (19) at any other state, the activity is related to the chemical potential, μ, by the equation

$$\mu - \mu^0 = RT \ln a \tag{21}$$

Activity is especially useful in solution studies where absolute values of fugacities are difficult to determine. Activity, being relative, depends on the choice of the standard state picked by the experimenter for his particular study. This freedom of choice makes it more difficult for the reader, but provides a versatile empirical quantity which gives correct values representative of concentration in free energy equations. Of many possible standard states for solutions, perhaps the most useful is one in which one of the pure liquids at one atmosphere pressure is assigned an activity value of unity when its mole fraction is unity; such liquid is usually designated the *solvent*. The ratio of the activity, a_1, to the mole fraction, x_1, tends to unity as the pure solvent is approached. The ratio is referred to as the *activity coefficient*, $\gamma = \dfrac{a}{x}$. It is desirable to express the deviation from ideal solution behavior by using γ rather than a because the activity varies quite rapidly with composition, whereas the activity coefficient remains almost unity for all but those systems having extensive deviations from the ideal.

From the definition, it is obvious that the activity coefficient is a quantity which may be multiplied by the concentration to provide a value for the active masses of substances in solution, thus making possible correct thermodynamic calculations. These coefficients find application in treating deviations in solutions, particularly solutions of electrolytes. They are useful in solving the problems of ionic equilibria and the kinetics of ionic reactions. Activity coefficients may be obtained from colligative property determinations, such as freezing point lowering, as well as from electrical measurements on ionic solutions.

CHAPTER 13

Solutions of Electrolytes

UNUSUAL PROPERTIES

From Raoult's law, it may be deduced that the lowering of the vapor pressure of the solvent, $P_1^0 - P_1$, is proportional to the mole fraction, x_2, of the *solute* according to the equation $P_1^0 - P_1 = P^0 x_2$. Since

$$x_2 = \frac{\dfrac{g_2}{M_2}}{\dfrac{g_1}{M_1} + \dfrac{g_2}{M_2}}$$

the molecular weight, M_2, of the solute may be calculated from vapor pressure measurements provided the molecular weight, M_1, of the solvent is known, in addition to g_1 and g_2, the number of grams of solvent and solute, respectively. Other colligative properties such as freezing point lowering, boiling point rise, and osmotic pressure may be used for very dilute solutions. Molecular weights obtained from such colligative property studies on non-ideal systems are erratic, being higher than the actual value in some solutions and lower in others, with varying degrees of deviation from system to system. From vapor pressure measurements, the calculated molecular weight of nitrobenzene (mol. wt. 123) dissolved in benzene is about 125 in a 0.1 molar solution, 135 in 0.5 molar, and 150 in 1.0 molar. This system consists of two dissimilar chemical species, with strong interaction between the solute and solvent molecules. On the other hand, benzoic acid dissolved in benzene in varying proportions has an experimental molecular weight of approximately 240, about double the actual value of 122. Here the solute apparently associates into pairs of molecules.

Potassium chloride, with a formula weight of 75, has an experimentally determined molecular weight of about 40 when dissolved in water in dilute solution. Similar results are obtained with water solutions of acids, bases, and salts, whereby their formula weights determined from colligative property measurements are approximately one-half, one-third, etc., the expected figures depending on whether the solute is uni-univalent, uni-divalent, etc., respectively. Acetic acid, ammonium hydroxide, and certain other acids and bases, however, have calculated values only slightly less than their formula weights. Values for electrolytes vary widely, but in practically every case there is a decrease in the apparent formula weight. While not numerous, common widely used substances make up the category of electrolytes, and for this reason special consideration of this class of solutions is justified. In addition to the deviations of their colligative properties, these systems are unique in possessing electrochemical activity. They conduct the electric current, and in the process their constituents may be separated by electrodeposition. Only a few solvents, such as water, can bring about the unique behavior of electrolyte solutions.

ELECTROLYTIC SOLUTIONS

Physical chemistry originated with the physicochemical correlations of Kopp in 1840 and the chemical thermodynamic developments of Horstmann (1869) and J. Willard Gibbs (1875), but this separate division had its early major development in the field of electrochemistry. The first pertinent journal was the *Zeitschrift für Physikalische Chemie*, founded by W. Ostwald in 1887. Van't Hoff, Arrhenius, Kohlrausch, Nernst, Ostwald, Lewis, and other leaders in this field revealed significant contributions through this journal in its first two decades of publication. Some of their important work will be described in the following outline of the long and interesting history of electrochemistry.

The history of electricity extends from ancient man's first rubbing of amber to our present highly specialized electronics technology. The static electric machine was a source of current for the earliest electrochemical experiments. By this means, Bercaria, shortly after 1750, reduced metallic oxides; Van Marum reversed the process and oxidized lead in the presence of air; Joseph Priestly obtained hydrogen from water, and Deimann and Paets van Troostwyk (1789) decomposed water into hydrogen and oxygen. At the turn of the century, Ritter (1801) made the very important discovery that, if electricity is passed through a solution of a silver salt between silver electrodes, silver moves *from the positive to the negative pole*. Valuable results of this nature were obtained by use of the static machine, although such equipment provides high voltage and low amperage and is therefore not especially suitable for electrochemical reactions, which can utilize a higher amperage for most processes.

Electrochemistry came into its own with the invention of the voltaic pile by Volta (1800) as a result of his investigation of Galvani's discovery (1791) of the electrical effects associated with living tissues such as frogs' legs. For the first time, currents of high amperage for extended periods of time were readily available. Many cells were arranged in series to carry out the electrochemical actions; for example, Davy (1807) used over two hundred zinc and copper plates to decompose potash in his discovery of potassium. The electric arc was discovered by Davy, who at one time used as many as two thousand cells to produce an arc ten centimeters long between carbon electrodes.

Many discoveries and hypotheses were made shortly after Volta's publication. Nicholson and Carlisle (1800) decomposed water, and Ritter (1801) gave an explanation for the electrochemical cell and proposed the electromotive series of the metals. In these electrolysis experiments one of the early puzzles revolved around the question of the site of action. When water is decomposed, for example, where does the electrolysis take place? Hydrogen is given off at one electrode and oxygen at the other, even though the two poles may be as much as a meter or two apart. At such distances, how can a molecule of water be involved at both electrodes simultaneously? Von Grotthus (1805) attempted to solve the problem by assuming that a chain of water molecules bridges the gap between the poles. The negative pole would remove a hydrogen from an adjacent water molecule and the remaining oxygen from this molecule would extract a hydrogen from the water molecule next removed and so on to the positive pole. The positive pole would then be able to release the final oxygen of the last water molecule. The electric current provided the energy which was assumed to be needed to bring about dissociation. Davy (1807-8) isolated several alkali and alkaline earth metals and in 1812 proposed an electrochemical theory. He believed the atoms acquired electrical charges by contact and in this way would be able to attract one another. Electrolysis would then simply be a neutralization of the charges on the atom. Berzelius conducted many experiments with the voltaic pile from 1802 to 1819 and published his explanation of electrochemical affinity and electrolysis during this period. He maintained that all atoms had both positive and negative charges of electricity and that the nature of the atom depended on which kind of electricity was in excess. Berzelius' theory, critically discussed and tested, influenced chemical thought for almost a century.

The electrochemical work of Davy was continued and extended by his assistant and successor, Faraday, whose observations led to his now famous laws of electrolysis. As expressed by FARADAY:

▼   "The chemical power of a current of electricity is in direct proportion to the absolute quantity of electricity which passes. . . . The substances into which these [electrolytes] divide, under the influence of the electric current, form an exceedingly important general class. They are combining bodies, are directly associated with the fundamental parts of the doctrine of chemical affinity; and have each a definite proportion, in which they are always evolved during electrolytic action. I have proposed to call these bodies generally *ions*, or particularly *anions* and *cations*, according as they appear at the *anode* or *cathode;* and the numbers representing the proportions in which they are evolved 'electrochemical equivalents.' Thus hydrogen, oxygen, chlorine, iodine, lead, tin, are 'ions'; the three former are 'anions,' and two metals are 'cations,' and 1, 8, 36, 125, 104, 58 are their electrochemical equivalents nearly.

"Electrochemical equivalents coincide, and are the same, with ordinary chemical equivalents. I think I cannot deceive myself in considering the doctrine of definite electrochemical action as of the utmost importance. It touches by its facts more directly and closely than any former fact, or set of facts, have done upon the beautiful idea that ordinary chemical affinity is a mere consequence of the electrical attractions of different kinds of matter."[1]   ▲

─────────────────────

Faraday established beyond doubt that the electrical energy passing through an electrochemical cell caused specific amounts of chemical reaction to take place, and, in modern terminology, one Faraday, 96,500 coulombs, will plate or dissolve 1 gram-equivalent of material at each electrode in an electrochemical cell. Although Faraday did not have a clear picture of ionization and the process of ion transfer within the solution, he explained the reactions occurring at the electrode.

In 1845, Grove developed the forerunner of the present-day fuel cells, an oxygen-hydrogen cell, which obtained its energy from the union of hydrogen gas and oxygen gas. As a result of his experiments, Grove decided that water molecules must be present initially in a state of partial decomposition. Shortly afterward, Williamson (1851) suggested that molecules are not rigid structures and in any chemical system that atoms are moving and shifting continually from one molecule to another in a dynamic equilibrium. Hittorf (1853) investigated the part of electrolytic dissociation neglected by Faraday, namely, the movement of ions in solution. Hittorf showed that the ions were able to move independently through the solution and came to the quite unexpected conclusion that different transporting ion species did *unequal* amounts of electrical work *through* the solution even though equal amounts of work were involved at the electrodes. The ions were assigned *transference numbers* to indicate the relative work done by each one.

Clausius (1857), on considering the above proposals and the published experimental information, interpreted ionization as taking place at the time the solute is dissolved in water, and maintained that the ions from the solute are able to interchange and pick new partners and revert to solute in a dynamic way similar to Williamson's proposed mechanism. Clausius envisioned only a limited

─────────────────────

[1] M. FARADAY, *Phil. Trans. Roy. Soc.*, **124**, 77, 111, 115 (1834).

number of ions as being present in solution at a given time. This was a clear departure from von Grotthus' theory which required that a potential would have to be applied before any ionization could occur and before a current could pass through the solution to decompose the solute molecules. Actually even a small potential will cause some current to flow through a cell if certain ions, such as silver, are available. Kohlrausch (1869) developed a method of measuring the electrical resistance and from that the conductivity of solutions.[2]

Specific conductivity decreases with dilution, but equivalent conductance increases, approaching a limiting value, Λ_∞, at infinite dilution, as indicated in Table 9. Equivalent conductance has the special quality of indicating when all of the solute is able to function as effective or active ions. Kohlrausch discovered the law that at great dilution the equivalent conductance of the solute is the sum of the individual ionic conductances. This law and the earlier discovery of transference numbers by Hittorf were valuable in giving a clearer insight into the arrangement of ions in solution.

TABLE 9

Conductance of Solutions of NaCl

Normality C	Dilution V_{eq} (ml.)	Specific conductance L	Equivalent conductance Λ
1	1,000	0.0742	74.2
0.1	10,000	0.00918	91.8
0.01	100,000	0.001017	101.7
0.001	1,000,000	0.0001063	106.3
0.0001	10,000,000	0.00001079	107.9
—	—	—	—
—	—	—	—
—	—	—	—
—	∞		108.5

Two major contributions to solution theory were published between 1885 and 1887. Van't Hoff (1887) showed that the colligative properties of vapor pressure lowering, etc., depend on the *number* of solute molecules in a given amount of solvent. He also correlated the abnormally high solute effects of

[2] Specific resistance is defined as the resistance of a centimeter cube of any material. A cell fitted with two parallel plates, each 1 sq.cm. in area and 1 cm. apart, could be used for solution studies. The reciprocal of this resistance is the specific conductance, L, and is a measure of the ease of migration of ions. A quantity of greater significance involves a gram equivalent of the ionic substance. The conductivity of such a system is called the equivalent conductance, Λ, where

$$\Lambda = LV_{eq} = \frac{1000L}{C}$$

V_{eq} is the volume needed to hold 1 gram-equivalent of the solute at the given dilution in equivalents per liter, C. A 1-normal solution would require V_{eq} to be 1000 ml. and a cell to hold such a solution would consist of two plates 1000 sq.cm. in area, each arranged 1 cm. apart.

acids, bases, and salts in water with the number of *particles* in solution. The second important contribution was the experimental information about the heat of neutralization of acids and bases by the Danish chemist Thomsen. Prior to this work, investigators could not find a source of energy sufficient to bring about the dissociation of a stable substance, such as a salt crystal. Present-day data indicate that a hundred-fold greater energy is needed to separate the ions of a salt in a vacuum than in water solution.

The results of nearly a century of investigation of the behavior of electrolyte solutions were available to Arrhenius, who published his classic *Electrolytic Dissociation Theory* in 1887. Before discussing this theory it is interesting to reflect that similar concepts were developed from the thermodynamic standpoint by Max Planck, and both he and Arrhenius published their proposals in the first volume of the newly founded *Zeitschrift für Physikalische Chemie*. At the same time Ostwald, too, had come to essentially the same conclusions from his experimental work.

THE ARRHENIUS THEORY

Clausius, one of the chief founders of the theory of molecular motion, maintained that every molecule of a fluid moves in an exceedingly irregular manner, being driven first one way and then another by the impacts of other molecules. This rather violent molecular motion goes on at all times and, except for temperature, is independent of the action of external effects such as electrical potential. The diffusion of one fluid through another is brought about by this molecular agitation. The intensity of the molecular motion increases with rising temperature. It is probable that even at low temperatures some of the encounters are so violent that one or both of the colliding molecules are split up into their constituent units or ions.

Clausius supposed that the electrical potential acted upon the ions during their intervals of freedom, deflecting them slightly from the paths they would otherwise have followed and causing the positive ions to have an over-all tendency to move toward the negative pole and the negative ions toward the positive pole. Nothing is said about the relative proportion of ions and molecules, but, to account for Ohm's law in electrolytic solutions, a very small proportion of ions suffices if the small quantity is always regenerated by the action of the molecules without any interference of the electrical forces. As ions are removed from the solution at the electrodes, new ions are generated by collisions of the undissociated molecules and, hence, the processes of conduction and electrolysis may go on continuously.

In order to put the hypothesis on a quantitative basis, it is necessary to take into account the relative numbers of ions and undissociated molecules. Arrhenius attacked this problem and, in his hypothesis of electrolytic dissociation, explained quantitatively the phenomena exhibited by electrolytic solutions in their ordinary state as well as during electrolysis. He observed that an analogy existed between conductance and chemical behavior. Solutes in solutions that conduct electricity freely would be almost entirely split up into ions, while substances which yield solutions of feeble conductivity would be split up to a very small extent. Only those molecules which are split into ions play any part in the conduction of electricity, the undissociated molecules remaining idle. The conductivity of any given solution depends on the number of ions in solution and the rate at which these ions move. The Hittorf and Kohlrausch experiments provided the information to determine the rate of ionic movement, leaving only the number or proportion of ions to be determined. Kohlrausch had found that the equivalent conductance reached a maximum value characteristic for each different solute. The equivalent conductance is lower at lower dilution and Arrhenius reasoned that the ratio of equivalent conductance, Λ, at any given concentration to the equivalent conductance at infinite dilution, Λ_∞, would be equal to the degree of dissociation, α, i.e.,

$$\alpha = \frac{\Lambda}{\Lambda_\infty} \tag{1}$$

Arrhenius compared these calculated values for α with those which had just been reported by Van't Hoff in his study of osmotic pressure and the other colligative properties of electrolytic solutions.

Van't Hoff had found that

$$\alpha = \frac{\pi - \pi_0}{(n - 1)\pi_0} \tag{2}$$

where π is the osmotic pressure at any given dilution and π_0 is the calculated value on the basis of no dissociation, n is the number of ions that would be obtained from one molecular substance; for example, n would be two for NaCl, three for Na_2SO_4, etc. The same results would hold for other colligative properties, such as vapor pressure lowering. A comparison of the degree of dissociation of KCl from vapor pressure lowering, $P - P_0$, and conductivity measurements is given in Table 10.

Using the data in the table, Arrhenius solved the second part of the problem of determining the conductivity of solutions. The degree of dissociation, α, was being investigated from three different viewpoints. Arrhenius correlated two of them by putting their quantitative relations together in his masterful analysis published when he was only twenty-eight. In the following year (1888), a third equation for α was developed by Ostwald in his dilution law, in which α is related to the ionization constant K_i.

$$K_i = \frac{\alpha^2 C}{1 - \alpha} \tag{3}$$

On ionizing, a simple electrolyte, such as HA, yields the equilibrium, HA = $H^+ + A^-$. From definition, the ionization constant is given by the expression

$$K_i = \frac{C_{H^+} \times C_{A^-}}{C_{HA}}$$

where the concentrations are denoted by C_{HA}, C_{H^+}, and C_{A^-}. From this relation it is therefore possible to calculate K_i for a weak electrolyte, HA, dissociating in water by experimentally determining the concentration values. It is then a simple matter to calculate α using Equation (3).

TABLE 10*

The Degree of Dissociation of KCl from
Vapor Pressure Lowering, P − P$_0$, and from
Conductivity Measurements

Concentration	α	
	From $P - P_0$	From conductivity
0.05	0.885	0.889
0.10	0.846	0.860
0.20	0.814	0.827
0.50	0.790	0.779

* F. H. Getman, *Outlines of Theoretical Chemistry*, 3rd ed. (New York: John Wiley & Sons, Inc., 1922), p. 216.

The theory of the young and unknown Arrhenius met with considerable opposition, largely owing to the difficulty of accounting for the formation and stable existence of the ions. The majority of chemists could not understand how sodium and chlorine, for example, could be contained in a solution of common salt. ARRHENIUS wrote:

▼ "The greatest of the difficulties which this theory has had to overcome can best be explained by an example: If we take one gram of sodium chloride dissolved in 100 grams of water, the majority of the salt — about 81%, is supposed to exist in the solution according to the theory in the form of the individual constituents, positively charged sodium and negatively charged chlorine. But every chemist since Davy's day has known sodium as a very soft metal which floats on water and dissolves in the water with rapid decomposition of the latter. He knows that in such decomposition hydrogen atoms are freed from the water, and that pairs of these atoms combine to form hydrogen gas, H_2, and bubble out into the air, while the sodium combines with the hydroxyl thus set free to form sodium hydrate, NaOH. Chlorine is known to the chemist as a greenish yellow, evil-odored gas, which when it dissolves in water lends to the solution its properties of odor and taste. How then can one claim that this one percent solution of common salt contains a mixture of these two substances? It becomes necessary to postulate that the chlorine in common salt is not ordinary chlorine, but is chlorine carrying a charge of electricity, and that the sodium is not ordinary sodium, but carries a positive charge. Opponents have said that it cannot be that such a slight difference can bring about so great a change in the properties of sodium and chlorine."[3]   ▲

The true significance of these electric charges and their effect on the properties of atoms were not realized until the theories of the electronic constitution of the atom were developed. Fortunately for Arrhenius, both Ostwald and Van't Hoff were enthusiastic supporters of his theory and their application of the theory to coordinate quantitatively the properties of electrolytic solutions soon overcame much of the opposition of the physical chemists. The electrolytic dissociation theory reconciled the osmotic behavior of electrolytic solutions and afforded an explanation of a large and varied range of properties and phenomena. The character of acids and alkalis as determined thermochemically by Thomsen, the density measurements by Ostwald, the catalytic action of acids and alkalis, the color and other physical properties of dilute solutions of salts, Hess's law of thermoneutrality, the heat of neutralization, the strength of acids and alkalis, equilibria in solutions of electrolytes, and reactions in analytical chemistry represent fruitful application of this theory.

W. Nernst was able to show (1888–89) that the production of an electromotive force (E) in galvanic cells could be explained in terms of a solution pressure of the metal electrode tending to throw off charged ions into the solution, this tendency being balanced by the osmotic pressure of the dissolved ions. At this time Nernst also developed his theories of the effects of concentration in voltaic cells (Nernst equation) and the liquid junction potentials at the interface of electrolyte solutions. Nernst (1889) also worked out the important theory of solubility products which helped to explain precipitation reactions. Nernst and J. J. Thomson (1893) independently announced the rule that the ionizing power of a solvent is closely connected with its dielectric constant. Arrhenius' proposals made Faraday's laws of electrolysis more intelligible and explained to some degree practically all the previously known properties of solutions of electrolytes. It is not surprising that a concept which covered such a wide range of laws, relationships, and experimental data should call forth considerable investigation aimed at proving or disproving the various aspects of the theory. Its impetus to research would be sufficient in itself to guarantee a place for this theory in scientific history.

[3] S. Arrhenius, *Chemistry in Modern Life*, trans. by C. Leonard (New York: D. Van Nostrand Company, Inc., 1925), p. 177.

The fate of Arrhenius' all-important theory is indicated by the prophetic statement made in 1923 by H. JERMAIN CREIGHTON to the effect that:

▼   "Arrhenius' Theory of Electrolytic Dissociation has survived 35 years of experimental investigation and criticism, during which period it has stimulated research and has contributed markedly to the progress of chemistry, physics, and other sciences. It has to be admitted however, that it has passed the state of its triumphs, and that the investigator is now faced with the problem of its difficulties and defects."[4]   ▲

Although a vast array of experimental evidence related to Arrhenius' theory is summarized and correlated in Creighton's book, much of which substantiates the theory, a sizable amount of information stands in opposition to Arrhenius' proposals. In a later edition (1935), Creighton states that, "In its original form [Arrhenius' theory] is completely valid only for weak acids and bases and a few salts. In solutions of these electrolytes, ions and undissociated molecules exist in equilibrium."

LIMITATIONS OF THE ARRHENIUS THEORY

The considerable success of the Arrhenius theory in dealing with dilute solutions of weak electrolytes prompted investigators to apply his concepts to more concentrated solutions as well as to strong electrolytes. Considerably less than satisfactory agreement was obtained in these instances. Electrical measurements can be carried out with high precision and the careful conductivity work by Kohlrausch permitted the determination of highly reproducible values of Λ and Λ_{∞}. From such data it is possible to calculate the degree of dissociation by using Arrhenius' relation as shown in Equation (1) on page 157. It may be deduced from Equations (17 to 21) of Chapter 12 that the maximum work of dilution is given by the relation

$$\Delta G = -RT \ln \frac{a_2}{a_1}$$

where $a_2 > a_1$. The free energy of a process can be completely converted into electrical work; i.e., $\Delta G = -n\mathfrak{F}\mathcal{E}$; from these, Nernst obtained the equation bearing his name

$$\mathcal{E} = \frac{RT}{n\mathfrak{F}} \ln \frac{a_2}{a_1} \tag{4}$$

where $\mathcal{E}$ is the voltage, $\mathfrak{F}$ is the Faraday (96,500 coulombs), n is the oxidation number (or valence) change, R is the gas constant, and a_1 and a_2 are the activities of the ions at the two dilutions. According to the definition of activity coefficient, γ, given earlier (page 150),

---

[4] H. J. CREIGHTON, *Electrochemistry* (New York: John Wiley & Sons, Inc., 1924), p. 49.

$$a = m\gamma$$

where m is the molality of the solute. For weak electrolytes γ is approximately equal to α, the degree of dissociation, and

$$a = m\alpha$$

Rewriting Equation (4) as follows,

$$\mathcal{E} = \frac{RT}{n\mathfrak{F}} \ln \frac{m_2\alpha_2}{m_1\alpha_1} \tag{5}$$

it is possible to determine the ratio of $\dfrac{\alpha_2}{\alpha_1}$ by measuring the voltage, $\mathcal{E}$, of a concentration cell at two different molalities, m_1 and m_2. The degree of dissociation, α, may also be obtained from the conductance ratio according to Equation (1). A comparison of the data for $\dfrac{a_2}{a_1}$ by the two methods is given in Table 11.

TABLE 11*

The Ratios of Concentrations Are 10 to 1 for KCl
Solutions in Which Activities Are Compared by
Two Methods

C_2/C_1 (concentration ratio)	a_2/a_1 (conductance)	a_2/a_1 ($\mathcal{E}$ measurements)
0.5 : 0.05	8.85	8.09
0.1 : 0.01	9.16	8.33
0.05 : 0.005	9.30	8.64
0.01 : 0.001	9.62	9.04

* F. H. Getman, *Outlines of Theoretical Chemistry*, 4th ed. (New York: John Wiley & Sons, Inc., 1927), p. 585.

The ratios of concentrations in the first column are 10 to 1. In terms of the possible precision of electrical measurements, it is evident that there is considerable variation between the ratios of the activities in the second and third columns. The discrepancies are beyond reasonable experimental error. It is not possible to measure the activity of a single ionic species, and γ is actually an average value defined in terms of a mean activity of the positive and negative ions,

$$a_+ = (a_+ \cdot a_-)^{\frac{1}{2}}$$

so that

$$\gamma = \frac{a_+}{m} = \left(\frac{a_+ \cdot a_-}{m^2}\right)^{\frac{1}{2}}$$

Arrhenius held that the relative number of ions in solution depended on the concentration and that the ions moved at essentially the same speed regardless of the concentration; he did not take into account any possible interactions of the ions. However, as early as 1900, Jahn questioned the assumption of constant ionic mobility. He expressed surprise that "the effect of dilution on the conductance was attributed, for such a long time, only to the number of ions while the obvious effect on the velocities was entirely neglected."[5]

THE DEBYE-HÜCKEL THEORY

Evidence similar to that briefly mentioned above accumulated to such proportions that many aspects of Arrhenius' theory came under critical scrutiny. Such information, coupled with definite weaknesses of key concepts, e.g. the Ostwald dilution law which held for very dilute solutions but failed at modest and higher concentrations, was sufficient to cause investigators to search for a new approach. J. J. van Laar (1895) and W. Sutherland (1902) proposed that strong electrolytes ionize essentially completely in solution. The fact that colligative property determinations and electrochemical measurements did not show complete ionization was explained by postulating that interionic attractions cause a decrease in the mobilities of the ions. N. Bjerrum (1909) expanded the ideas of complete ionization, and Milner (1912–18) developed a quantitative theory which had considerable merit but which was unwieldy and difficult to test in the laboratory. G. N. Lewis (1913) found experimentally that the activity coefficient depends only on the total number of ions, i.e. the ionic strength, of the solution and not on the nature of the individual ions. The proposal which focused the greatest attention on a new approach was published by J. C. Ghosh in (1918).[6] His work renewed interest in ionic solutions and stimulated arguments pro and con at meetings around the world. In fact, as P. DEBYE states in the introduction to his first paper on electrolytes:

▼ "The present considerations were stimulated by a lecture by E. Bauer on Ghosh's works, held at the Physikalische Gesellschaft. The general viewpoints taken as the basis for the computation of the freezing point depression as well as of the conductivity lead me, among other things, to the limiting law involving the square root of the concentration. I could have reported on this during the winter of 1921 at the 'Kolloquium.' With the active assistance of my assistant, Dr. E. Hückel, a comprehensive discussion of the results and their collection took place during the winter of 1922."[7]   ▲

[5] F. H. Getman and F. Daniels, *Outlines of Theoretical Chemistry*, 5th ed. (New York: John Wiley & Sons, Inc., 1931), p. 381

[6] J. C. Ghosh, *J. Chem. Soc.*, **113,** 449, 627, 707, 790 (1918); *Z. Physik. Chem.*, **98,** 211 (1921).

[7] P. J. W. DEBYE and E. HÜCKEL, *Physik. Z.*, **24,** 185, 305 (1923); *The Collected Papers of Peter J. W. Debye* (New York: Interscience Publishers, Inc., 1954).

The excitement in Debye's eyes can be pictured as he quickly assimilated Ghosh's concepts as they were being developed by Bauer. Considering Debye's training and experience, we can reasonably assume that he left the lecture hall that night, his mind stirring with ideas for the solution of the electrolyte problem.

Debye received his diploma in electrical engineering and his doctorate in theoretical physics, a happy combination which set the direction for the career that evolved. Prior to 1923 he had already published (1912) his two most fundamental works: the theory of polar molecules and the theory of specific heats of solids. Other important areas he investigated were X-ray-scattering forces (1920) and molecular forces and their electrical interpretation (1921).

With this background, and in the atmosphere prevailing in the scientific world at the time, Debye and Hückel[7] developed and published their *interionic attraction theory* thirty-six years after Arrhenius submitted his classic *electrolytic dissociation theory*. Interestingly, about the same number of years have elapsed (forty-two) since the introduction of the Debye-Hückel theory, but it has been received much differently than has Arrhenius' work. A flurry of confirmatory experiments by leading scientists quickly established the essential validity of this theory for dilute solutions of strong (highly or completely ionized) electrolytes. Debye and Hückel reported their developments in several papers. Portions of their first paper is presented below.

▼   "I. Introduction

"It is known that the dissociation hypothesis by Arrhenius explains the abnormally large values of osmotic pressure, freezing point depression, etc., observed for solutions of electrolytes, by the existence of free ions and the associated increase in the number of separate particles. The quantitative theory relies on the extension, introduced by van't Hoff, of the laws for ideal gases to diluted solutions for the computation of their osmotic pressure. Since it is possible to justify this extension on the basis of thermodynamics, there can be no doubt regarding the general validity of these fundamentals.

"However, for finite concentrations we obtain smaller values for freezing point lowering, conductivity, etc., than one would expect on first consideration, in the presence of a complete dissociation of the electrolyte into ions. Let P_k, for instance, be the osmotic pressure resulting from the classical law by van't Hoff for complete dissociation, then the actually observed osmotic pressure will be smaller, so that:

$$P = f_0 P_k$$

where, according to Bjerrum, the 'osmotic coefficient' f_0 thus introduced is intended to measure this deviation independent of any theory — and can be observed as a function of concentration, pressure, and temperature. In fact, these observations do not relate directly to the osmotic pressure but to freezing point lowering, and boiling point rise, respectively, which can both be derived on the basis of thermodynamics, and by means of the same osmotic co-efficient f_0, from their limiting value following from van't Hoff's law for complete dissociation.

"The most evident assumption to explain the presence of the osmotic co-efficient is the classical assumption, according to which not all molecules are dissociated into ions, but which assumes an equilibrium between dissociated and undissociated molecules which depend on the over-all concentration, as well as on pressure and temperature. The number of free, separate particles is thus variable, and would have to be made directly proportional to f_0. The quantitative theory of this dependence, as far as it relates to the concentration, relies on the mass action law of Guldberg-Waage; the dependence on temperature and pressure of the constant of equilibrium appearing in this law can be determined thermodynamically, according to van't Hoff. The complete aggregate of dependencies, including the Guldberg-Waage law, can be proved by thermodynamics, as is shown by Planck.

"Since the electric conductivity is determined exclusively by the ions, and since, according to the classical theory the number of ions follows immediately from f_0, the theory requires the well known relation between the dependence on the concentration of the conductivity on the one hand and of the osmotic pressure on the other hand.

"A large group of electrolytes, the strong acids, bases, and their salts, collectively designated as 'strong' electrolytes, exhibits definite deviations from the dependencies demanded by the classical theory. It is especially noteworthy that these deviations are the more pronounced the more the solutions are diluted.[8] Thus, as was recognized in the course of developments and following the classical theory, it is possible only with a certain degree of approximation to draw a conclusion from f_0 as to the dependence of the conductivity on the concentration. Moreover the dependence of the osmotic coefficient f_0 on the concentration is also represented entirely incorrectly. For strongly diluted solutions, f_0 approaches the value 1; if $1 - f_0$ is plotted as a function of the concentration c, classical theory requires for binary electrolytes, such as KCl, that this curve meets the zero point with a finite tangent (determined by the constant of equilibrium, K). In the general case, provided the molecule of the electrolyte splits into v ions, we obtain from the law of mass action for low concentrations:

$$1 - f_0 = \frac{v - 1}{v} \frac{c^{v-1}}{K}$$

so that in cases where splitting into more than two ions occurs, the curve in question should present even a higher order of contact with the abscissa.

---

[8] A summary presentation of this subject was given by L. Ebert, "Forschungen über die Anomalien starker Elektrolyte," *Jahrb. d. Rad. u. Elektr.*, **18**, 134 (1921).

The complex of these dependencies constitutes Ostwald's dilution law.

"Actually observations on strong electrolytes show an entirely different behavior. The experimental curve starts from the zero point at a right angle ... to the abscissa, independent of the number of ions, v. All proposed, practical interpolation formulas attempt to represent this behavior by assuming $1 - f_0$ to be proportional to a fractional power (smaller than 1, such as $\frac{1}{2}$ or $\frac{1}{3}$) of the concentration. The same remark holds with regard to the extrapolation of the conductivity to infinite dilutions which, according to Kohlrausch, requires the use of the power $\frac{1}{2}$.

"It is clear that under these circumstances the classical theory can not be retained. All experimental material indicates that its fundamental starting point should be abandoned, and that, in particular, an equilibrium calculated on the basis of the mass action law does not correspond to the actual phenomena.

"W. Sutherland, in 1907, intended to build the theory of the electrolytes on the assumption of a complete dissociation. His work contains a number of good ideas. N. Bjerrum (1909) is, however, the first to have arrived at a distinct formulation of the hypothesis. He clearly stated and proved that, for strong electrolytes, no equilibrium at all is noticeable between dissociated and undissociated molecules, and that, rather, convincing evidence exists which shows that such electrolytes are completely dissociated into ions up to high concentrations. Only in considering weak electrolytes, undissociated molecules reappear. Thus the classical explanation as an exclusive basis for the variation of, for instance, the osmotic coefficient, has to be abandoned and the task ensues to search for an effect of the ions, heretofore overlooked, which explains, in the absence of association, a decrease in f_0 with an increase in concentration.

"Recently, under the influence of Bjerrum, the impression gained strength that consideration of the electrostatic forces, exerted by the ions on one another and of considerable importance because of the comparatively enormous size of the elementary electric charge, must supply the desired explanation. Classical theory does not discuss these forces; rather, it treats the ions as entirely independent elements. A new interaction theory has to be analogous in some respects to van der Waals' generalization of the law of ideal gases to the case of real gases. However, it will have to resort to entirely different expedients, since the electrostatic forces between ions decrease only as the square of the distance and thus are essentially different from the intermolecular forces which decline much more rapidly with an increase in distance.

"Milner computed the osmotic coefficient along such lines. His computation cannot be objected to as regards its outline, but it leads to mathematical difficulties which are not entirely overcome, and the final result can only be expressed in the form of a graphically determined curve for the relation between $1 - f_0$ and the concentration. From the following it will further emerge that the comparison with experience, carried through by Milner, supposes the admission of his approximations for concentrations which are much too high and for which, in fact, the individual properties of the ions, not taken into account by Milner, already play an important part. In spite of this, it would be unjust to discard Milner's computation in favor of the more recent computations by Ghosh on the same subject. We shall have to revert, in the following, to the reason why we can not agree to Ghosh's calculations, neither in their application to the conductivity nor in their more straightforward application to the osmotic pressure. We will even have to reject entirely his calculation of the electrostatic energy of an ionized electrolyte, which is the basis for all his further conclusions.

"The circumstances to be considered in the computation of the conductivity are very similar to those for the osmotic coefficient. Here also the new interaction theory has to make an attempt at understanding the mutual electrostatic effect of the ions with regard to its influence on their mobility. An earlier attempt was made in this direction by Hertz. He transcribes the methods of the kinetic theory of gases, and, in fact, finds a mutual interference of the ions. However, the transcription of this classical method, and particularly the use of concepts like that of the free path length of a molecule in a gas for the case of free ions surrounded by the molecules of the solvent, does not seem to be very reliable. The final result obtained by Hertz cannot, in fact, be reconciled with the experimental results.

"In this first note, we shall confine ourselves to the 'osmotic coefficient f_0' and to a similar 'activity coefficient f_a,' used by Bjerrum and stressed in its significance. Even for such (weak) electrolytes, where a noticeable number of undissociated molecules is present, the equilibrium cannot simply be determined by the Guldberg-Waage formula in its classical form:

$$c_1{}^{\mu_1} c_2{}^{\mu_2} \ldots c_n{}^{\mu_n} = K$$

($c_1, c_2, \ldots c_n$, are the concentrations, K the constant of equilibrium). It will be necessary, in view of the mutual electrostatic forces between the ions, to write:

$$f_a K,$$

instead of K, introducing the activity coefficient f_a. This coefficient, just as f_0, will depend on the concentration of the ions. Though, according to Bjerrum, a relation to be proved by thermodynamics exists between f_a and f_0, their dependence on the concentration is different for the two coefficients.

"The detailed treatment of conductivity shall be reserved for a later note. This division seems justified, since the determination of f_0 and f_a requires solely a consideration of reversible processes, whereas the computation of mobilities has to do with essentially irreversible processes for which no direct relation to the fundamental laws of thermodynamics exists."[9]   ▲

The Debye-Hückel equation representing the mutual electrical effects of ions was derived by coupling the equation of Boltzmann with the equation of Poisson. On the basis of an arrangement of ions in solution somewhat similar to the lattice structure of ions in simple crystalline solids, it is possible to describe the behavior of electrolytes in terms of interionic attractions rather than chemical reactions as was done by Arrhenius. The attractions between oppositely charged ions and the repulsions between like ions are coulombic in nature. Each positive ion is surrounded by negative ions and vice versa and, on the average, there are more ions of unlike than of like sign in the immediate vicinity of any given ion. The net effect is that each ion is surrounded by an ionic atmosphere of opposite sign. The separation of ions, as on further diluting a dilute solution, will require internal work against the electrical attraction and thus increase the energy content of the solution. The thermal motion of the solvent molecules prevents the ions from maintaining a fixed structure such as that found in a crystal lattice.

The ratio of the number, n_i, of ions in a given energy state, ϵ_i, to the number, n_0, in the lowest energy state, ϵ_0, is given by the Boltzmann distribution law (p. 21),

$$\frac{n_i}{n_0} = e^{-\epsilon_i/kT} \tag{6}$$

where k is the Boltzmann constant.

Following Dole,[10] for n_+ positive ions per cubic centimeter in a volume element, dV, where the potential energy of the positive ion is $q_+ \psi$ (ψ is the average value of the electrical potential in dV and q_+ is the electric charge on the ion), and n is the average number of positive ions per cubic centimeter, Boltzmann's law provides the relation

$$n_+ dV = n e^{-q_+\psi/kT} dV \tag{7}$$

for the positive ions and a similar equation for the negative ions,

$$n_- dV = n e^{+q_-\psi/kT} dV \tag{8}$$

From the postulated distribution of ions, n_+ will be greater than n in the neighborhood of a negative ion (ψ negative), and smaller than n near a positive

[9] P. J. W. DEBYE and E. HÜCKEL, *Physik. Z.*, **24**, 185 (1923); *The Collected Papers of Peter J. W. Debye* (New York: Interscience Publishers, Inc., 1954), p. 217 ff.

[10] M. Dole, *Introduction to Statistical Thermodynamics* (New York: Prentice-Hall, Inc., 1954), p. 57 ff.

ion (ψ positive). For a salt consisting of univalent ions the *excess* electric charge in dV will be (letting ϵ represent the absolute value of the charge, i.e., disregarding the sign)

$$(n_+\epsilon - n_-\epsilon)dV \qquad (9)$$

The electrical density, ρ, is the charge per unit volume, and

$$\rho = \frac{(n_+\epsilon - n_-\epsilon)dV}{dV} = \epsilon(n_+ - n_-) \qquad (10)$$

From Equations (7), (8), and (10)

$$\rho = n\epsilon(e^{-\epsilon\psi/kT} - e^{+\epsilon\psi/kT}) \qquad (11)$$

Since

$$e^x = 1 + x + \frac{x^2}{2!} + \cdots$$

and

$$e^{-x} = 1 - x + \frac{x^2}{2!} - \cdots$$

the equation for ρ may be written in terms of these relations. The resulting equation is considerably simplified if only the first term in x is retained as is justified when x is small. Debye and Hückel assumed $\epsilon\psi \ll kT$ for univalent ions of low concentration in a solvent with a high dielectric constant, such as water. With the above simplification and under these assumptions, Equation (11) becomes

$$\rho = n\epsilon[(1 - \epsilon\psi/kT) - (1 + \epsilon\psi/kT)] = -2n\epsilon^2\psi/kT \qquad (12)$$

It is important to note the restriction to *very* dilute solutions in the derivation of this charge density equation relating the electric density to the potential.

According to Coulomb's inverse square law, the force between two charged particles q_+ and q_-, separated by a distance, r, and in a medium of dielectric constant, D, is

$$f = \frac{1}{D} \cdot \frac{q_+ q_-}{r^2}$$

Expressed in terms of the electrical potential, ψ_I, due to a charge, q_i, this becomes

$$\psi_I = \frac{1}{D} \cdot \frac{q_i}{r} \qquad (13)$$

i.e., the potential varies inversely with the distance, r, from a charge. This is the basis for the Poisson equation for a volume symmetrically filled with electricity of density ρ. Poisson's equation is

$$\frac{\partial^2\psi}{\partial x^2} + \frac{\partial^2\psi}{\partial y^2} + \frac{\partial^2\psi}{\partial z^2} = -\frac{4\pi\rho}{6D}$$

or

$$\nabla^2\psi = -\frac{4\pi\rho}{D} \tag{14}$$

where $\nabla^2\psi$ is the divergence of the gradient of the potential.[11] Stated in terms of force, the total outward force at any point in a medium is proportional to the charge density at the point.

Both the Boltzmann distribution law and the Poisson equation of electrostatics relate the electric density, ρ, to the potential, ψ, at any given point in the solution. Debye and Hückel pictured the arrangement of ions in a solution as reasonably fulfilling the requirements of a Poisson distribution, which is spherically symmetrical.

If we substitute Equation (12), relating ρ to ψ, into Equation (14), we obtain

$$\nabla^2\psi = \frac{8\pi\epsilon^2 n}{DkT}\psi \tag{15}$$

This is the fundamental differential equation of the Debye-Hückel theory. The factor on the right has the dimension of the inverse of the length squared. If we let K be the reciprocal of the length, then

$$K^2 = \frac{8\pi\epsilon^2 n}{DkT}$$

and if we substitute this value for K in Equation (15), we get

$$\nabla^2\psi = K^2\psi \tag{16}$$

According to Debye and Hückel, "The length, $\left(\dfrac{1}{K}\right)$, introduced in this way

$$\frac{1}{K} = \sqrt{\frac{DkT}{8\pi\epsilon^2 n}} \tag{17}$$

is the essential quantity in our theory and replaces the average distance between ions in Ghosh's consideration." It is customary to refer to K^{-1} as the **Debye radius,** a quantity which represents the mean thickness of the ion atmosphere. If we substitute values for water as the solvent at 0°C. and at concentration C in moles per liter into Equation (17), we get

$$K^{-1} = \frac{3.06}{\sqrt{C}} \times 10^{-8} \text{ cm.}$$

For a one-molar concentration the characteristic length is of the order of a molecular diameter, i.e., 3Å.

[11] The Laplacian operator ∇^2, sometimes represented by Δ, is $\dfrac{\partial^2}{\partial x^2} + \dfrac{\partial^2}{\partial y^2} + \dfrac{\partial^2}{\partial z^2}$ in rectangular coordinates.

On recalling the earlier discussion on pages 136 and 148, the partial molal free energy of an electrolyte can be expressed by the relation

$$\mu = \mu^0 + RT \ln \gamma_\pm N_\pm$$

and μ may be divided into two parts μ_N and μ_γ:

(a) $\mu_N = \mu^0 + RT \ln N_\pm$

(b) $\mu_\gamma = RT \ln \gamma_\pm$

where (a) applies to an ideal solution in which there are no interactions between particles and (b) to completely ionized electrolytes in dilute solution for which Debye and Hückel assumed the deviation from ideality to be the sole result of electrical interactions between the ions. For an ion, j, the electrical free energy was shown by Debye and Hückel, and in a different way by Güntelberg, to be equal to

$$-\frac{1}{2}\frac{\epsilon^2 K}{D}$$

and hence

$$kT \ln \gamma_j = -\frac{1}{2}\frac{\epsilon^2 K}{D} \tag{18}$$

G. N. Lewis (1913) showed empirically that the activity coefficient, γ_j, depends on the *total* ionic strength, I, of a solution:

$$I = \tfrac{1}{2}(C_1 Z_1{}^2 + C_2 Z_2{}^2 + \cdots + C_r Z_r{}^2) = \frac{1}{2}\sum_{j=1}^{r} C_j Z_j{}^2$$

and not on the specific ions present. The concentration of the ion, j, is denoted by C_j and its charge number by Z_j, whereas the total number of different ionic species in the solution is indicated by r. The ionic strength for a uni-univalent electrolyte then equals its concentration, C, and for a 1–2 electrolyte I is $3C$, for a 2–2 electrolyte I is $4C$, etc.

The ionic strength may be incorporated into the quantity, K, in the following form[12]

$$K^2 = \frac{8\pi\epsilon^2}{DkT} \cdot \frac{1}{2}\sum C_j Z_j{}^2$$

For the concentration in terms of moles per liter, c, this becomes

$$K^2 = \frac{4\pi\epsilon^2}{DkT} \cdot \frac{N}{1000}\sum c_j Z_j{}^2 \tag{19}$$

[12] *The Collected Papers of Peter J. W. Debye* (New York: Interscience Publishers, Inc., 1954); E. Güntelberg, *Z. Physik. Chem.*, **123**, 199 (1926).

where N is the Avogadro number. Substituting in Equation (18) and solving for $\ln \gamma_{\pm}$ (where $\gamma_{\pm}$ is the mean ionic activity coefficient[13]) we obtain the following relation:

$$\ln \gamma_{\pm} = -Z_{+}Z_{-} \left[\frac{\pi \epsilon^6 N}{1000(DkT)^3}\right]^{\frac{1}{2}} \sqrt{\sum c_j Z_j^2} \qquad (20)$$

The valence of the ion is indicated by a Z.

This is the Debye-Hückel *limiting law* for the mean activity coefficient of the ions in solution. On substituting values for the various terms as applied to a uni-univalent electrolyte in water at 25°C., the equation becomes

$$\ln \gamma_{\pm} = -0.509\sqrt{I} \qquad (21)$$

The following relations have been found for very dilute solutions: the coefficient of $-\sqrt{I}$ is essentially 0.5 for 1–1 electrolytes and increases to 1.0 for 1–2 electrolytes, to 1.5 for 1–3 electrolytes, to 2.0 for 2–2 electrolytes, 2.5 for 2–3 electrolytes, etc. It is evident that the proportionality of $\log \gamma_{\pm}$ to $\sqrt{c}$ is a successful result of the Debye-Hückel theory.

The actual size of the ion was neglected in the simplified development of the theory outlined above. The ionic diameter is indicated by the distance of closest approach, a, and Equation (18) may be modified to the following form in order to allow for the actual ion:

$$\ln \gamma_{\pm} = -\frac{Z_{+}Z_{-}\epsilon^2}{2DkT} \cdot \frac{K}{1 + Ka} \qquad (22)$$

Equation (22) was among those used to test the Debye-Hückel theory. From the freezing point data of Hovorka and Rodebush,[14] it was possible for Fowler and Guggenheim[15] to obtain concordance to 0.0001°C. for all values of the ionic strength up to 0.01. The value of a is different for each electrolyte and is determined by adjustment within the range of 2 to 4Å for most substances. C. W. Davies made further adjustments to obtain a more satisfactory relation, as shown in Figure 56.[16]

Since its inception, the Debye-Hückel theory has been subjected to intensive investigation and has been found to give acceptable results from the lowest

---

[13] The activity coefficient of a salt is defined in terms of the separate activity coefficients so that $\gamma_{\pm} = (\gamma_{+}\gamma_{-})^{\frac{1}{2}}$ for a 1–1 salt. The general definition is $\gamma_{\pm} = (\gamma_{+}{}^{\nu+}\gamma_{-}{}^{\nu-})$ for a salt yielding ν_{+} positive ions and ν_{-} negative ions, and also $\nu = \nu_{+} + \nu_{-}$.

[14] F. Hovorka and W. H. Rodebush, *J. Am. Chem. Soc.*, **47**, 1614 (1925).

[15] R. H. Fowler and E. A. Guggenheim, *Statistical Thermodynamics* (Cambridge: Cambridge University Press, 1939), p. 401.

[16] See J. N. Butler, *Ionic Equilibrium* (Reading: Addison-Wesley Publishing Company, Inc., 1964), p. 437.

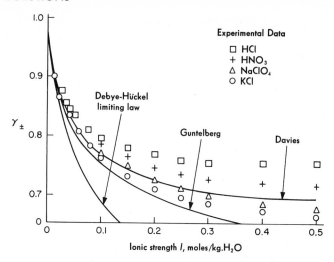

FIGURE 56

*Comparison of various empirical activity coefficient expressions with ex-
perimental data for HCl, HNO₃, NaClO₄, and KCl. The Debye-Hückel
limiting law fits the data very poorly; the Guntelberg equation falls below
all the experimental results; but the Davies equation represents the experimental results as accurately as can be expected. Adapted from J. N. Butler,
Ionic Equilibrium (Reading: Addison-Wesley Publishing Company, 1964).*

(limiting) values of concentration up to 0.001 molal or higher. Accurate experimental determinations are possible above 0.001 molal, and, while it is desirable
to have a theory that can apply to all concentrations, it is clear that the Debye-
Hückel theory provides information when experimentation is not possible.

The concluding remarks to the first DEBYE-HÜCKEL paper on electrolytes
indicate the validity of the theory and also point to the need for investigation
of other factors, such as conductivity.

▼   "X. General Remarks

"From the preceding discussion it may be concluded that it is inadmissible
from a theoretical as well as from an experimental point of view to consider
the electric energy of an ionic solution to be essentially determined by the
average mutual distance of the ions. Rather, a quantity which measures the
thickness of the ion atmosphere or, to connect with something known better,
the thickness of a Helmholtz double-layer proves to be a characteristic
length. In view of the fact that this thickness depends on the concentration
of the electrolyte, the electric energy of the solution also becomes a function
of this quantity. The fact that this thickness is inversely proportional to the

square root of the concentration is responsible for the characteristic appearance of the limiting laws for highly diluted solutions. . . .

"The computations and comparison with experience were carried out by taking the conventional dielectric constant for the surrounding solvent. The success justifies this assumption. Though this procedure is justifiable for low concentrations, it should cause mistakes for higher concentrations. . . .

"In another respect concentrated solutions should show a special behavior. If many ions are present in the surroundings of each single ion, this can be regarded as a change of the surrounding medium with respect to its electrical properties, an effect which has not been taken into account in the preceding theory. . . . In conventional language, it is said that a predominant hydration of the ions occurs, and that this is to be regarded as an exothermic process. Obviously the above considerations intend an explanation of this so-called hydration on a purely electric basis. . . . These considerations have some bearing on the freezing point observations inasmuch as they suggest the possibility of computing why and to what extent the curves found for the percentage deviation . . . bend downward for higher concentrations and may even cross the abscissa provided the concentration is high enough. In this instance, the freezing point depression exceeds the one expected from classical theory (also, as may be stated explicitly, if the classical theory is used in its unabbreviated form). . . .

"However, before conditions for concentrated solutions can be investigated, it must be shown that the irreversible process of electric conduction in strong electrolytes can also be understood quantitatively from our point of view. . . . If an ion moving in a liquid is subjected to the influence of an external field, the surrounding ions will have to move constantly in order to form the ion atmosphere. If we now assume for a moment that a charge is suddenly generated in the electrolyte, an ion atmosphere will have to appear which requires a certain time of relaxation for its formation. Similarly, for a moving ion, the surrounding atmosphere will not attain its equilibrium distribution and thus cannot be computed on the basis of the Boltzmann-Maxwell principle. However, the determination of its charge distribution can be carried through on the basis of an obvious interpretation of the equations for the Brownian movement. It can be estimated qualitatively in which direction this effect, caused by the presence of a finite relaxation time, will be operative. At a point in front of the moving ion (i.e., a point toward which it moves) the electric density of the ion atmosphere must increase with time; it must decrease for a point behind the ion. As a consequence of the relaxation time, the density in front of the ion will be slightly smaller than its value at equilibrium; behind it, however, it will not yet have decreased to its equilibrium value. Consequently, during the movement there always exists a slightly larger electrical density of the ion atmosphere behind the ion than in front of it. Since charge density in the atmosphere and charge of the central ion always carry opposite signs, a force braking the ion movement will occur, independent of its sign, and obviously this force will increase with increasing concentration.

"This is one effect which operates in the same sense as a decrease in dissociation calculated on the basis of Ostwald's dilution law. However, still another effect is present which must be taken into consideration. In the vicinity of an ion are predominantly ions of the opposite sign, which under the influence of the external field will, of course, move in the opposite direction. These ions will, to a certain degree, drag along the surrounding solvent, thus causing the considered single ion not to move relative to a stationary solvent but relative to a solvent moving in the opposite direction. Since, apparently, this effect increases with increasing concentration, we have a second effect operating in the same sense as a decrease in dissociation. The effect can be calculated quantitatively according to the principles used by Helmholtz for the treatment of electrophoresis.

"The common factor of the two effects just mentioned consists . . . in the fact that both are closely related to the thickness of the ion atmosphere, and that, therefore, the generated forces are proportional to the square root of the concentration of the electrolyte, at least in the limit for very low concentrations. Thus we obtain a law, found by Kohlrausch, according to which for low concentrations the percentage deviation of the molecular conductivity from its limiting value at infinite dilution is proportional to the square root of the concentration. Also the proportionality factor thus finds a molecular interpretation.

"Anticipating the detailed representation of electrolytic conductivity in prospect for a following article, we can state as an over-all result that the view, according to which strong electrolytes are completely dissociated, is entirely supported."[17]

▲

This monumental publication of Debye and Hückel was followed immediately by another in which they applied their concepts to the conductivity of electrolytic solutions. The stage was now set for a new surge of investigation of solutions of electrolytes, and publications mushroomed overnight.

THE DEBYE-HÜCKEL ERA

The theory of Debye and Hückel was the first statistical theory of electrolytic solutions, and it proved to be especially successful when applied to very dilute solutions as a limiting law. The natural desire is to extend this theory to solutions of greater concentration and of less ideal conditions in general.

Whenever ions are forced to move, frictional resistance must be accounted for, and electrophoretic and relaxation effects come into play. These phe-

---

[17] P. J. W. DEBYE and E. HÜCKEL, *Collected Papers*, pp. 259–262.

nomena were investigated by Debye and Hückel[18] and also by Onsager,[19] who incorporated a more detailed analysis of the various effects, such as viscosity and the Brownian movement of the ions, into the theory. For a 1–1 electrolyte, Onsager obtained an equation for the equivalent conductance as follows:

$$\Lambda = \Lambda_\infty - \left[\frac{82.4}{(DT)^{\frac{1}{2}}\eta} + \frac{8.20 \times 10^5}{(DT)^{\frac{2}{3}}} \Lambda_\infty \right] \sqrt{C}$$

The constants are given numerical values, η is the viscosity of the medium with a dielectric constant of D, and the concentration of ionized electrolyte in moles per liter is C.[20] Onsager's equation may be simplified to

$$\Lambda = \Lambda_\infty - (A + B\Lambda_\infty)\sqrt{C}$$

where A, B, and Λ_∞ are constant quantities. For water at 25°C., A is 60.2 and B is 0.229. The variation of conductivity with the square root of concentration is in agreement with the empirical discovery of Kohlrausch in 1885, namely, that

$$\Lambda = \Lambda_\infty - k\sqrt{C}$$

While it is necessary that the equivalent conductance bear a relation to the square root of the concentration, the slope of the line calculated from A and B is of greater significance. A comparison of the experimental to the calculated values from the Onsager equation is quite good as shown in Figure 57.[20] Deviations appear with more concentrated solutions, however, because of restricting assumptions.

Experimental information about conducting solutions confirms the basic concepts of the ionic atmosphere proposed by Debye and Hückel. Ordinary conductance experiments are carried out at modest voltages and at frequencies of 1000 cycles per second or less. Above 20,000 c.p.s. stray capacity effects cause anomalous conductivity readings. At very high frequencies, above 2×10^6 c.p.s., the *Debye-Falkenhagen effect* (1928) becomes significant. In this frequency range the ionic atmosphere is not able to keep up with the rapidly changing field, and the ions are not subjected to the drag effect of the surrounding ionic atmosphere. The equivalent conductivity is then able to increase with the frequency. If the frequency becomes too high, however, the motion of the ions may be erratic, with a consequent reduction in mobility.

Wien (1927) discovered an increase in the equivalent conductance when a high potential of the order of 40,000 volts was applied to a solution of electrolytes. In this case the velocity of the ions literally outstrips the ionic atmosphere, which is hampered by its relatively slow relaxation time. The concepts of the

[18] P. J. W. Debye and E. Hückel, *Physik. Z.*, **24**, 305 (1923).
[19] L. Onsager, *Physik. Z.*, **27**, 388 (1926).
[20] S. Glasstone, *Textbook of Physical Chemistry* (New York: D. Van Nostrand Company, Inc., 1946), p. 905.

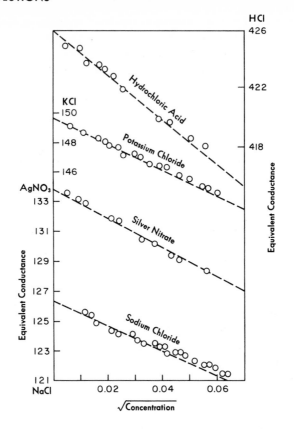

FIGURE 57

Comparison of experimental conductivities of solutions of electrolytes with values calculated by means of the Onsager equation. Adapted from S. Glasstone, Textbook of Physical Chemistry (New York: D. Van Nostrand Company, Inc., 1946).

Debye-Hückel theory are confirmed by the experiments with high frequency currents and high voltages.

In attempting to extend the useful range of the Debye-Hückel theory, Gronwall, LaMer, and Sandved (1928) dropped the restriction of $\epsilon\psi \ll kT$ (page 168) imposed by Debye and Hückel, solved the Poisson-Boltzmann equation, and thus obtained acceptable calculated values at slightly higher concentrations. In 1926 Bjerrum, and also Fuoss and Kraus developed an ion association theory for more concentrated solutions. With the ions in close contact, it is reasonable to suspect that oppositely charged ions are sufficiently near each other to behave as ion pairs for a short time. These pairs would resemble molecular units and would not contribute to the conductivity of the solution during the brief period of their existence. Deviations caused by the association effect were determined and the resulting data were superior to those derived from the theory of Debye and Hückel.

Agar[21] stated in his review of the literature on solutions of electrolytes for the year 1963, that "Progress is steady rather than spectacular and I do not think that 1963 will rank with 1923 as a vintage year." Onsager, among many others, has remained active in this field. Fuoss and Onsager have recently published a series of articles, beginning in 1962, on an extensively revised treatment of conductance.[22] Although their expressions fit the data for salts, there are discrepancies with solutions of HCl which are not explained. Agar comments that, "Rather surprisingly, Pitts' equation fits them [HCl solutions] very well,[23] although there are some unsatisfactory features in its derivation, and there is no obvious reason why it should be better than the Fuoss-Onsager expressions." Such dilemmas do not appear to daunt investigators and interest remains high in the fields of solutions of electrolytes and non-electrolytes.

A basic difference between electrolytes and non-electrolytes exists because of the nature of the forces of attraction and interaction in the two classes of solutions. In both cases a strong and rapidly decaying repulsive force is encountered when the dissolved particles are close enough for electron cloud overlap. The force of attraction between two non-ionic molecules, however, varies inversely as the seventh power of the distance of separation, in contrast to ionic molecules with their inverse square relation. Interionic forces are long range in nature, whereas the forces in non-ionic systems are effective only when the molecules are close together and behave as non-interacting clusters.

Mayer initiated a cluster theory approach which may be applied to ionic and non-ionic solutions and gives promise of further extension into higher concentration ranges. A detailed discussion of the concept is given by Friedman.[24]

Among the early proposals of liquid structure theory was the cluster-expansion development of Mayer (page 11). Extensions of this concept have occurred in recent years as shown in Rice and Gray's supplement to Fisher's book on liquid theory.[25] Rice and Gray feel that even though "interest in the theory of liquids has grown steadily . . . no completely satisfactory solution of the several problems exists at present."

Although improvements of the solution theory take place slowly, Figure 56 illustrates the contention that progress is being made. New problems are generated in solving old ones. Like the general theory of liquids, the treatment of more concentrated solutions of electrolytes remains one of the major unsolved problems of physical chemistry and of chemical physics.

[21] J. Agar, *Annual Review of Physical Chemistry* (Palo Alto: Annual Reviews, Inc., 1964), p. 469.

[22] R. Fuoss and L. Onsager, *J. Phys. Chem.*, **66,** 1722 (1962).

[23] E. Pitts, *Proc. Roy. Soc., London*, **A217,** 43 (1953).

[24] H. L. Friedman, *Ionic Solution Theory* (New York: Interscience Publishers, Inc., 1962).

[25] I. Z. Fisher, *Statistical Theory of Liquids*, trans. by T. Switz (Chicago: University of Chicago Press, 1964); supplement by S. A. Rice and P. Gray; also S. A. Rice and P. Gray, *The Statistical Mechanics of Simple Liquids* (New York: Interscience Publishers, Inc., 1965).

APPENDIX

The Radial Distribution Function in Liquids

One of the significant papers on liquid structure theory was published by Kirkwood and Boggs on the radial distribution function in liquids. Use is made of the superposition approximation introduced by Kirkwood as an assumption to facilitate the solution of an otherwise almost insoluble family of equations.* There are limitations to the use of this approximation and the results leave considerable room for improvement, but no better method exists at present.

The Radial Distribution Function in Liquids

JOHN G. KIRKWOOD AND ELIZABETH MONROE BOGGS

In accordance with the general methods of an earlier paper (reference 1) an integral equation is evolved for the radial distribution function for pairs in a liquid, and an approximate solution is effected for a system of "hard spheres." The form of the function depends on a single parameter, λ, which can be related to certain observed physical properties of the liquid and to the diameter of closest approach. The theoretical function has been calculated for a value of λ appropriate to liquid argon at 90°K, and compared to experimental radial distribution functions derived from x-ray scattering data.

In an earlier article, a general method[1] of study of molecular distribution functions in liquids has been proposed by one of us. In a later article,[2] the formulation of an integral equation for the radial distribution function in liquids was given, and an

---

* See also J. G. Kirkwood, *J. Chem. Phys.*, **3**, 300 (1935); J. Yvon, *Actualités Scientifiques et Industriel* (Paris: Hermann et Cie, 1935); M. Born and H. S. Green, *Proc. Roy. Soc. London*, **188**, 10 (1946); I. Z. Fisher, *Statistical Theory of Liquids* (Chicago: University of Chicago Press, 1964), Chapter 5.

[1] J. G. Kirkwood, J. Chem. Phys. **3**, 300 (1935), hereafter referred to as SMF, Statistical Mechanics of Fluid Mixtures.

[2] J. G. Kirkwood, J. Chem. Phys. **7**, 919 (1939).

attempt at the solution of the equation was presented. In the present article, we shall employ the methods earlier developed to obtain a more complete solution to the problem of the radial distribution function in a system of spherical molecules with no attractive forces, subject to certain well-defined approximations. Comparison of the theoretical radial distribution function with recently determined experimental distribution curves for argon indicates that attractive forces probably play a secondary role in determining the radial distribution. This is physically plausible, since the fluctuations in the potential of intermolecular attraction at liquid densities are doubtless small.

Recently other methods of calculation of the radial distribution function have been proposed by Wall,[3] Rushbrooke and Coulson,[4,5] and Corner and Lennard-Jones.[6] Although intermolecular attractive forces are taken into account in the latter two papers, the distribution function is referred to an assumed lattice, and the positions of the maxima are not predicted by the theory. While these methods may be regarded as useful alternatives to our own, we believe that liquid structure cannot be adequately described in terms of a lattice blurred by thermal motion, but that the local order in liquids manifested in the radial distribution function is of an essentially different nature from the long range order in crystals.

Before proceeding to the details of the theory, we shall state certain of the fundamental properties of the radial distribution function, which we shall denote by $g(R)$. The function $g(R)$ is so defined that $(N/v)g(R)$ specifies the local molecular density at a distance R from any specified molecule in a system of N molecules occupying a volume v. At large distances $g(R)$ tends to unity and at small intermolecular distances tends to zero, due to intermolecular repulsive forces opposing interpenetration.

$$\lim_{R\to\infty} g(R) = 1 + 0(1/N),$$
$$\lim_{R\to 0} g(R) = 0. \tag{1}$$

The normalization condition is

$$\frac{1}{v} \int^v g(R)dv = 1. \tag{2}$$

In the development of the theory to follow, it is convenient to define a function $\varphi(R)/R$, vanishing at infinity, by the relation

$$g(R) = 1 + \varphi(R)/R + \epsilon, \tag{3}$$

where ϵ is of the order $1/N$. Because the volume is proportional to N, the integral $\rho_0 \int \dfrac{\varphi(R)}{R}\, dv$ fails to vanish even in the infinite fluid. It has previously been shown[7]

[3] C. N. Wall, Phys. Rev. **58**, 307 (1940).
[4] G. S. Rushbrooke, Proc. Roy. Soc. Edinburgh **60**, 182 (1940).
[5] G. S. Rushbrooke and C. A. Coulson, Phys. Rev. **56**, 1216 (1939).
[6] J. Corner and J. E. Lennard-Jones, Proc. Roy. Soc. London **A178**, 401 (1941).
[7] L. S. Orstein and F. Zernicke, Physik. Zeits. **27**, 261 (1926); J. Yvon, Thesis (Paris, 1937).

that

$$\rho_0 \int^v \frac{\varphi(R)}{R} \, dv = kT\kappa\rho_0 - 1, \tag{3a}$$

where ρ_0 is average density (N/v), κ the compressibility, and k Boltzmann's constant. The term $kT\kappa\rho_0$ is the relative density fluctuation of the fluid, which is of importance in the theory of light scattering.[7]

The radial distribution function, although only one of many types of molecular distribution which characterize liquid structure, is of particular interest since it determines the angular distribution of x-ray scattering and can be calculated by a Fourier integral transformation from the experimentally determined x-ray scattering curve.[8]

The Integral Equation for the Radial Distribution Function

The distribution functions for sets of molecules in a fluid may be expressed in terms of local free energies $W_n(\mathbf{R}_1, \cdots \mathbf{R}_n)$, defined in the following manner,

$$\exp\left(-W_n(\mathbf{R}_1, \cdots \mathbf{R}_n)/kT\right) = v^n \int^v \cdots \int^v \exp\left(-V_N/kT\right) dv_1 \cdots dv_{N-n}, \tag{4}$$

where V_N is the potential of intermolecular force and the integration extends over the coordinates of all N molecules of the fluid in the volume v, except a fixed set n situated at positions $\mathbf{R}_1, \cdots \mathbf{R}_n$. We shall be concerned here only with distribution functions for sets of one, two, and three molecules;

$$\begin{aligned}
\rho_1(\mathbf{R}_1) &= \exp\{-[W_1(\mathbf{R}_1) - W_0]/kT\}, \\
\rho_2(\mathbf{R}_1, \mathbf{R}_2) &= \exp\{-[W_2(\mathbf{R}_1, \mathbf{R}_2) - W_0]/kT\}, \\
{}^1\rho_2(\mathbf{R}_1, \mathbf{R}_2) &= \exp\{-[W_2(\mathbf{R}_1, \mathbf{R}_2) - W_1(\mathbf{R}_1)]/kT\}, \\
{}^{12}\rho_3(\mathbf{R}_1, \mathbf{R}_2, \mathbf{R}_3) &= \exp\{-[W_3(\mathbf{R}_1, \mathbf{R}_2, \mathbf{R}_3) - W_2(\mathbf{R}_1, \mathbf{R}_2)]/kT\},
\end{aligned} \tag{5}$$

where $(N/v)\rho_1(\mathbf{R}_1)$ is the local density of molecules at the point $\mathbf{R}_1$, $(N/v)^2\rho_2(\mathbf{R}_1, \mathbf{R}_2)$ the density of molecules in the six-dimensional space of pairs, $(N/v) {}^1\rho_2(\mathbf{R}_1, \mathbf{R}_2)$ the local density of molecules at a point $\mathbf{R}_2$ in the neighborhood of a molecule fixed at a point $\mathbf{R}_1$, and $(N/v) {}^{12}\rho_3(\mathbf{R}_1, \mathbf{R}_2, \mathbf{R}_3)$ the density of molecules at a point $\mathbf{R}_3$ in the neighborhood of a fixed pair of molecules situated at the point $\mathbf{R}_1$ and $\mathbf{R}_2$. In a fluid system,[9] the distribution function $\rho_1(\mathbf{R})$ has the constant value unity, and the distribution functions $\rho_2(\mathbf{R}_1, \mathbf{R}_2)$ and ${}^1\rho_2(\mathbf{R}_1, \mathbf{R}_2)$ become identical and depend only on R_{12}, the distance between the points $\mathbf{R}_1$ and $\mathbf{R}_2$.

$$\rho_2(\mathbf{R}_1, \mathbf{R}_2) = {}^1\rho_2(\mathbf{R}_1, \mathbf{R}_2) = g(R_{12}), \tag{6}$$

where $g(R)$ is the radial distribution function, which we wish to investigate here. In studying the radial distribution function, we shall need to consider the distribution

---

[8] F. Zernicke and J. A. Prins, Zeits. f. Physik **41**, 184 (1927); P. Debye and H. Mencke, Physik. Zeits. **31**, 797 (1930); B. E. Warren, J. App. Phys. **8**, 645 (1937).

[9] J. G. Kirkwood and E. Monroe, J. Chem. Phys. **9**, 514 (1941).

function $^{12}\rho_3(\mathbf{R}_1, \mathbf{R}_2, \mathbf{R}_3)$ related to the radial distribution function itself in the following manner,

$$^{12}\rho_3(\mathbf{R}_1, \mathbf{R}_2, \mathbf{R}_3) = g(R_{13})g(R_{23}) \exp{(-w_3/kT)},$$
$$w_3 = W_3(\mathbf{R}_1, \mathbf{R}_2, \mathbf{R}_3) - W_2(\mathbf{R}_1, \mathbf{R}_2) \tag{7}$$
$$- W_2(\mathbf{R}_1, \mathbf{R}_3) - W_2(\mathbf{R}_2, \mathbf{R}_3) + 2W_0,$$

where the local free energy w_3 determines the correlation in the statistical density distributions around two fixed molecules at the points $\mathbf{R}_1$ and $\mathbf{R}_2$. In the approximation of vanishing w_3, the average force acting on a molecule at point $\mathbf{R}_3$ in the vicinity two molecules at points $\mathbf{R}_1$ and $\mathbf{R}_2$ is the sum of the forces which would act on the molecule at $\mathbf{R}_3$ if each of the fixed molecules at points $\mathbf{R}_1$ and $\mathbf{R}_2$ was present alone. This we shall call the superposition approximation.

We now proceed to set up an integral equation for the radial distribution function according to the methods of SMF. We suppose the potential of intermolecular force to have the form

$$V_N = \sum_{k<l} V(R_{kl}), \tag{8}$$

where $V(R_{kl})$ is the potential of the force between the molecular pair k, l situated a distance R_{kl} from each other. We introduce a coupling parameter ξ for an arbitrarily selected molecule and write

$$V_N(\xi) = V_{N-1} + \xi V_1,$$
$$V_1 = \sum_{k=2}^{N} V(R_{1k}). \tag{9}$$

By allowing ξ to assume values in the interval zero to unity, we can continuously vary the force acting between molecule 1 and the other molecules of the system from zero to its full value in the actual fluid. If we differentiate the distribution function $^1\rho_2(\mathbf{R}_1, \mathbf{R}_2, \xi)$ with respect to ξ, we obtain from Eqs. (4), (5), and (9),

$$\frac{\partial \log {}^1\rho_2(\mathbf{R}_1, \mathbf{R}_2, \xi)}{\partial \xi} = -\frac{1}{kT}[{}^{12}\langle V_1 \rangle_{\mathrm{Av}} - {}^1\langle V_1 \rangle_{\mathrm{Av}}], \tag{10}$$

where $^{12}\langle V_1 \rangle_{\mathrm{Av}}$ is the mean potential energy of molecule 1 fixed at point $\mathbf{R}_1$ in the neighborhood of a second molecule fixed at point $\mathbf{R}_2$, and $^1\langle V_1 \rangle_{\mathrm{Av}}$ is the mean potential energy of molecule 1, averaged over the configurations of all molecules. The mean potential energies $^{12}\langle V_1 \rangle_{\mathrm{Av}}$ and $^1\langle V_1 \rangle_{\mathrm{Av}}$ may be expressed in terms of the distribution functions in the following manner,

$$^{12}\langle V_1 \rangle_{\mathrm{Av}} = V(R_{12}) + \frac{N}{v} \int^v V(R_{13}) {}^{12}\rho_3(\mathbf{R}_1, \mathbf{R}_2, \mathbf{R}_3, \xi) \, dv_3,$$
$$^1\langle V_1 \rangle_{\mathrm{Av}} = (N/v) \int^v V(R_{13}) {}^1\rho_2(\mathbf{R}_1, \mathbf{R}_3, \xi) \, dv_3. \tag{11}$$

If we restrict ourselves to a fluid system, for which Eq. (6) is valid, we obtain from Eqs. (10) and (11) after integration with respect to the coupling parameter ξ, and use of the fact that $^1\rho_2(\mathbf{R}_1, \mathbf{R}_2, 0)$ is equal to unity,

$$\log g(R) = \chi(R) - \int^v \psi(R, r, r')[g(r) - 1] \, dv,$$

$$\chi(R) = -\frac{1}{kT}\left\{V(R) + \frac{N}{v}\int_0^v \int_0^1 V(r')g(r', \xi)\right.$$

$$\left. \times [\exp(-w_3/kT) - 1] \, d\xi \, dv\right\}, \tag{12}$$

$$\psi(R, r', r) = \frac{N}{vkT} V(r') \int_0^1 g(r', \xi) \exp(-w_3/kT) \, d\xi,$$

where for convenience in notation the symbols R, r, r', replace R_{12}, R_{23}, R_{13}, respectively. We shall now introduce the approximation of superposition of average force between pairs. In this approximation Eq. (12) becomes

$$\log g(R) = \chi_0(R) - \int^v \psi_0(r')[g(r) - 1] \, dv,$$

$$\chi_0(R) = -V(R)/kT, \tag{13}$$

$$\psi_0(r') = \frac{N}{vkT} V(r') \int_0^1 g(r', \xi) \, d\xi.$$

Solution of the non-linear integral Eq. (13) with an appropriate potential of intermolecular force, for example one of the Lennard-Jones type, should yield an approximation to the radial distribution function consistent with the superposition assumption, which has been discussed in SMF.

Solution of the Integral Equation for Rigid Spherical Molecules with No Attractive Forces

In a liquid composed of rigid spherical molecules of diameter a_0, the potential of intermolecular force $V(R)$ has the form,

$$V(R) = 0, \quad R > a_0,$$
$$V(R) = \infty, \quad R < a_0, \tag{14}$$

and the radial distribution function has the property,

$$g(R, \xi) = 0; \quad \xi > 0; \quad R < a_0$$
$$\frac{NV(R)}{kT} g(R, \xi) = \psi_0(R) \delta(\xi); \quad R < a_0 \tag{15}$$

where $\delta(\xi)$ is the Dirac delta function. We shall denote by $\langle \psi_0 \rangle_{Av}$ the integral,

$$\langle\psi_0\rangle_{Av} = \frac{4\pi}{\omega_0} \int_0^{a_0} r^2 \psi_0(r) \, dr,$$

$$\lambda = 3\langle\psi_0\rangle_{Av}\omega_0, \tag{16}$$

$$\omega_0 = \frac{4\pi a_0^3}{3},$$

where λ is a constant we shall presently use.

. . . .

It is now possible to proceed with calculations provided a value can be assigned to the single parameter λ, which is characteristic of the physical system to which the calculated radial distribution function applies. By Eq. (18) of SMF, the chemical potential of the liquid is given by

$$\frac{\mu}{kT} = \log\frac{N}{v} + \frac{N}{vkT} \int_0^v \int_0^1 V(r)g(r, \xi) \, d\xi \, dv + \mu^*(T)/kT, \tag{30}$$

where $\mu^*(T)$ is a function of temperature alone. From Eqs. (13) and (16), we observe that

$$\frac{N}{vkT} \int_0^v \int_0^1 V(r)g(r, \xi) \, d\xi = \frac{\lambda}{3} + \frac{N}{vkT} \int_{\omega_0}^v \int_0^1 V(r)g(r, \xi) \, d\xi \, dv, \tag{31}$$

where the second integral extends over the region exterior to ω_0 and is confined to the region of intermolecular attraction. If, as we have supposed in the present treatment, $g(r, \xi)$ is determined by repulsive forces alone, we may write

$$g(r, \xi) = g(r); \quad \xi > 0, \quad r > 0;$$
$$\int_0^1 g(r, \xi) \, d\xi = g(r); \quad r > a_0, \tag{32}$$

where $g(r)$ denotes the radial distribution function $g(r, 1)$ for full intermolecular coupling. Thus

$$\frac{N}{vkT} \int_{\omega_0}^v \int_0^1 V(r)g(r, \xi) \, d\xi \, dv = \frac{N}{vkT} \int_{\omega_0}^v V(r)g(r) \, dv = N\langle V\rangle_{Av}/vkT, \tag{33}$$

where $\langle V\rangle_{Av}$ is the mean potential energy of a molecular pair. The energy of vaporization of the liquid to vapor at zero density is

$$\Delta E_v = N^2\langle V\rangle_{Av}/2,$$
$$N\langle V\rangle_{Av}/vkT = 2\,\Delta E_v/NkT. \tag{34}$$

Thus in the approximation that the radial distribution is determined by repulsive forces exclusively, we have

$$\mu/kT = \log(N/v_l) + \frac{\lambda}{3} - \frac{2\,\Delta E_v}{NkT} + \mu^*(T)/kT,$$

TABLE III.

(a) Theoretical		(b) Experimental		
λ	$\Phi(\lambda)$	a_0	$\Phi(T = 83.4°)$	$\Phi(T = 90°)$
13.3	0.074	3.35	0.240	0.238
20	.225	3.6	.258	.257
25	.298	3.72	.265	.264
34.8	.272	3.8	.269	.268

where $\lambda/3$ may also be interpreted as the work of formation of a cavity of volume ω_0 in the liquid. Let us consider equilibrium between the liquid and its own vapor. At low vapor pressures, the chemical potential in the vapor is

$$\mu_g/kT = \log(N/v_g) + \mu^*(T)/kT, \tag{35}$$

where v_g is the molal volume of the vapor. Equating μ and μ_g and solving for λ, we obtain

$$\lambda = 3\left\{\frac{2\Delta E_v}{NkT} - \log v_g/v_l\right\}, \tag{36}$$

a formula which may be used for the determination of λ from the energy of vaporization, the volume of the liquid and the volume of the vapor in equilibrium with the liquid at the vapor pressure.

Another relation between λ and certain experimental quantities can be obtained through the normalization condition mentioned earlier. From Eq. (3) we find:

$$\int_1^\infty x\varphi(x)\,dx \equiv \Phi(\lambda) = \frac{1}{3}\left[1 - \frac{1}{\rho_0\omega_0}(kT\kappa\rho_0 - 1)\right]. \tag{37}$$

The left-hand side can be evaluated analytically, as has been done for φ in the approximate form (26), yielding the results listed in Table III(a). Table III(b) shows the values computed for the right-hand side of Eq. (37) using known values for the density and compressibility of liquid argon[12] and various assumed values for the diameter of closest approach a_0. It may be remarked that the term involving the compressibility is negligible for condensed liquids and that in effect $\Phi(\lambda)$ depends only on the "expansion," i.e., the ratio of the total to the excluded volume, which indeed must be the only intensive property affecting the radial distribution function for a system of hard spheres. Nevertheless, the method of the preceding section is probably the more reliable in the assignation of λ, and that has been used in the application which follows.

Application to Liquid Argon

As already suggested, the indications are that the attractive van der Waals forces in a system of neutral molecules of spherical symmetry play a role subordinate to that

---

[12] For physical data on argon see reference 9.

of the repulsive forces in determining the radial distribution function. We may therefore anticipate that the results of the foregoing theory will be applicable to the rare
gases in the liquid state. Among these argon has been most studied experimentally,
and recent determinations[13, 14] of its radial distribution function at 90°K from x-ray
scattering data invite comparison.

The expression (36), appropriately evaluated,[12] gives us $\lambda = 27.4$. Calculation of
the corresponding $\varphi(x)$ to [an] ... approximation ... yields the function $g(x)$ shown
as curve B in Fig. 2.

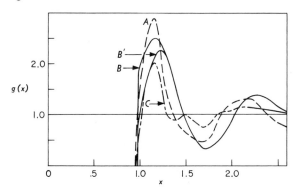

FIGURE 2

*Theoretical and experimental radial distribution functions for liquid argon
at 90°K. Curve A is from Lark-Horovitz and Miller; Curves B and B′ are
theoretical; Curve C is from Eisenstein and Gingrich. g(x) gives ratio
of local to average density. x in diameters, r/a₀.*

. . . .

In order to compare the theoretical with the experimental results it is necessary to
assign a value to a_0; this may be taken as the solution $r = a_0$, of the equation
$V(r) = kT/2$ where $V(r)$ is the usual intermolecular potential function for argon,
which, for this purpose, we assume to have the analytic form due to Buckingham.[15]
We thus obtain the value $a_0 = 3.35A$. Curves A^{14} and C^{13} represent experimentally
determined radial distribution functions reduced to the scale $x = r/a_0$. The former is
from recent (1941) unpublished data. It may be remarked that the deviations of the
theoretical curve from A are in the direction that one would anticipate as a result of
the neglect of attractive forces. The interatomic potential for argon shows a minimum
in the neighborhood of $x = 1.15$, and we would expect a sharpening of the first peak
about this point and with it a shift to the left of the second peak, when these additional
forces are introduced. Nevertheless, our contention that the principal characteristics
of the radial distribution function are determined by repulsive forces seems to be
borne out.

[13] A. Einsenstein and N. S. Gingrich, Phys. Rev. **58**, 307 (1940).
[14] K. Lark-Horovitz and E. P. Miller, Nature **146**, 459 (1940) and unpublished data. We
are indebted to Professors Gingrich and Lark-Horovitz for private communications concerning
these data.
[15] R. A. Buckingham, Proc. Roy. Soc. **A168**, 264 (1938).

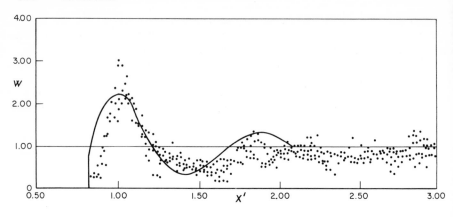

FIGURE 3

Theoretical radial distribution function (W) for expansion 1.81 (argon) compared with distribution in macroscopic systems of expansions 1.86, 1.92 (superimposed) from Morrell and Hildebrand. Abscissa, X', in units of the first maximum. Scale of theoretical curve chosen to give coincidence of first maximum.

The observations of Morrell and Hildebrand[16] offer another opportunity for comparison, this time with a macroscopic model of a system of hard spheres. The parameter here is the expansion, expressed as the ratio of the molar volume to that of a mole of close packed spheres. This ratio for argon is 1.81 which is comparable with expansions used by Morrell and Hildebrand in two sets of their observations. In Fig. 3 we compare the theoretical curve B' for $\lambda = 27.4$ with the macroscopic distribution (dots) for expansions of 1.86 and 1.92 (superimposed). We note that, *ceteris paribus*, λ is inversely proportional to the expansion, and ... we see that increasing expansion is therefore associated with smaller amplitude A, greater damping and a longer period, as would be anticipated, and as is indicated by the observations of Hildebrand and Morrell.

[16] W. E. Morrell and J. Hildebrand, J. Chem. Phys. **4**, 224 (1936).

Biographical Sketches

The following are biographical sketches of some of the important contributors to the knowledge of liquids and solutions.

SVANTE ARRHENIUS (1859–1927): Professor of Physics at Stockholm and later Director of the Nobel Institute. As a comparatively unknown scientist, he published the electrolytic dissociation theory which focused attention on this new field of chemistry. His theory was not accepted universally and much persuasion was necessary to convince the leading physical chemists of its merits. This monumental work was followed in two years by his explanation of the effect of temperature on reaction rates, another outstanding achievement for this versatile scientist who was awarded the Nobel prize in chemistry in 1903.

J. D. BERNAL (1901–   ): Professor at Birkbeck College, University of London. In collaboration with R. H. Fowler, he developed a concept of the structures of water and ice near the melting point that provided a successful explanation of the anomalous behavior of water. A quarter of a century later, in 1959, he published a general theory of the structure of liquids in which he incorporates the idea of five-fold symmetry. Such symmetry does not exist in crystalline solids.

JÖNS JAKOB BERZELIUS (1779–1848): He was born in Väfersunda, Sweden, the son of a teacher. He studied medicine, took up hospital work in Stockholm, and carried out chemical experiments in his spare time. These investigations eventually led to his becoming Professor of Chemistry at Stockholm. Among his many achievements, his explanation of electrolysis helped to organize thinking in this field and some of his concepts prevailed for almost a century.

MAX BORN (1882–   ): Fellow of the Royal Society. In collaboration with H. S. Green while at the University of Edinburgh, he published a series of papers in the *Proceedings of the Royal Society* in 1946 and 1947. These were reproduced and bound as *A General Kinetic Theory of Liquids*, one of the classic works in the field of liquid structure. Professor Born has been in the forefront of many of the outstanding developments in science and was associated with Heisenberg and others at Göttingen during the fruitful 1920's. Born shared the Nobel prize in physics in 1954.

RUDOLF J. E. CLAUSIUS (1822–1888): Professor of Physics at the University of Zurich. He redeveloped the Clapeyron equation and extended its range, was instrumental in organizing the second law of thermodynamics, introduced the concept of entropy, and was the first to consider electrolytes as dissociating into ions prior to electrolysis.

JOHN DALTON (1766–1844): Professor of Mathematics and Natural Philosophy in New College, Manchester, from 1793 until 1799. He resigned from New College and gave private lessons to support himself. In 1801, he discovered the law of partial pressures of gases as a result of his meticulous meteorological records and investigations. He also found that the solubilities of gases are proportional to their partial pressures and that gases expand equally for a given rise in temperature. These investigations about the nature of gases eventually led to his outstanding atomic theory.

PETER J. W. DEBYE (1884–   ): He was born in Maastricht in 1884, studied electrical engineering, and was awarded his doctorate in theoretical physics. He held professorships at a number of the leading universities in Europe and is Professor Emeritus at Cornell University where he is actively pursuing X-ray studies of solutions of macromolecules. He was a pioneer in the application of X-rays in the determination of the structure of matter. His study of liquids set the stage for greater emphasis on liquid investigations. Debye's publication with Hückel in 1923 of the interionic attraction theory was the first statistical approach to the behavior of electrolyte solutions and has remained one of the outstanding contributions to the field. Professor Debye has received many awards, among which was the Nobel prize in chemistry in 1936.

HENRY EYRING (1901–   ): Professor of Chemistry at the University of Utah. He has been a recognized authority in chemical kinetics for over a quarter of a century. His interest in liquids parallels that in kinetics and he published one of the earliest theories of liquids on the basis of a cell model. He has been able to utilize kinetic concepts in his description of the behavior of liquids. In a recent publication, he has shown that his theory of liquid structure gives more practical results of acceptable quality than any other theory.

MICHAEL FARADAY (1791–1867): Director of the Laboratory of the Royal Institution and later Professor of Chemistry. He spent his early years in London where he received only meager training at a common day school. His scientific education began while he was an apprentice to a bookbinder and read books after work. He furthered his knowledge by buying material for experiments from his limited earnings. Although he grew up in such poverty that a "loaf of bread had to last a week," he never lost his perspective when the opportunity came to earn large sums by consulting for commercial firms. He decided in favor of his scientific investigations even though it meant that he would always be a relatively poor man. His contributions in chemistry and electricity laid the foundations for the modern ionic solution theory, for the electromagnetic concepts developed later by Maxwell, and for present-day electrical technology.

J. I. FRENKEL (1894–1952): He was the first to consider the similarity between liquids and solids on the basis of holes or vacancies, following the proposal of the existence of interstices by Joffé. He developed a one-dimensional statistical theory to describe the behavior of liquids and pointed out that the thermal motion of liquid molecules consists of irregular vibrations with frequencies close to those of the particles of crystalline solids. Added to these vibrations would be an occasional jump of a molecule from one position to another in a self-diffusion process. His book on the kinetic theory of liquids was published in 1945 and describes a number of his original concepts concerning the structure of liquids.

JOSIAH WILLARD GIBBS (1839–1903): Professor of Mathematical Physics at Yale University. He was a leader in the fields of thermodynamics and vector analysis. His mathematical ideas were so advanced that few American scientists understood his work. His original studies of heterogeneous equilibria, including the phase rule, won world-wide recognition for him. However, it did not appear to be uppermost in his mind to seek much acclaim as his work was published in obscure journals.

WILLIAM HENRY (1775–1836): He received a degree in medicine but ill health prevented him from continuing in this field. He turned to scientific research and in 1803 discovered one of the first laws of solutions, namely, that the amount of gas absorbed by a liquid is proportional to the pressure of the gas above the liquid. This discovery was extended to mixtures of gases by Dalton.

JOEL H. HILDEBRAND (1881–   ): Professor Emeritus of Chemistry, University of California at Berkeley. He has spent more than fifty years in physical chemistry at Berkeley and has made many contributions to liquid theory and to solutions of nonelectrolytes. His first paper on solubility was published in 1916; this and many subsequent papers in the J. H. Hildebrand 80th Birthday Symposium were published in 1962. A special group of "Regular Solutions" were set aside by Professor Hildebrand as an aid to organization in the complex field of solutions. In his contributions to liquid structure theory he has been steadfast in opposition to any concept that implies a model similar to that of crystals.

JOHN G. KIRKWOOD (1907–1959): Professor at Cornell University. He was a leader in studying the problems of liquid structure from the standpoint of the radial distribution function. The idea of a superposition approximation was introduced by him in order to make calculations based on the interactions of only two molecules at a time. His approximation approach has been widely criticized, but, after a quarter of a century, it still holds the greatest promise for the solution to the problem of liquid structure.

GILBERT NEWTON LEWIS (1875–1946): Professor of Chemistry at the University of California at Berkeley. His elementary school training was rather poor, but this did not appear to be a handicap as it put him in the same company of many distinguished men with similar experiences. He proposed an atomic model in which electrons could form a non-ionic linkage by sharing in pairs. Using this concept, he developed a widely used acid-base system. His method of treating the problems of solutions through the use of activities and fugacities is the major system in use today. His classic book with M. Randall on thermodynamics was adopted extensively and was not in need of revision for many years. (Published in 1923, it was finally revised by others in 1961.)

WALTHER HERRMANN NERNST (1864–1941): Professor of Physical Chemistry in Göttingen and later in Berlin. Using the idea of a solution pressure of metals, he gave the first explanation of electrochemical action at the electrodes of a cell. He derived a relation showing the effect of solute concentration on the voltage of a cell and also determined the effect of ionic transference on the potential. Nernst studied the specific heat of solids at very low temperatures and developed a successful relation for calculating this quantity. He was the first to explain chemical chain reactions such as occur when hydrogen and chlorine unite, and his heat theorem or third law of thermodynamics is one of his chief contributions to science. He was awarded the Nobel prize in chemistry in 1920.

WILHELM FRIEDRICH OSTWALD (1853–1932): Professor at Riga and at Leipzig. His chief contributions are in the field of solutions of electrolytes where he studied the partition of a base between two acids, the rates of hydrolysis of esters, the conductivity of solutions, and the affinity constants of electrolytes. The Ostwald dilution law resulted from these investigations. His writing and teaching did much to further the field of physical chemistry.

MAX PLANCK (1858–1947): Professor of Physics at Berlin. His early interest in thermodynamics led him to consider solutions of electrolytes and to develop a theory involving dissociation of electrolytes which was published at the same time as that of Arrhenius. Planck's rare understanding of entropy paved the way for his quantum theory which marked the beginning of the new way of approaching the problems of physics. He received the Nobel prize in physics in 1918.

FRANÇOIS MARIE RAOULT (1830–1901): Professor of Chemistry at the University of Grenoble. He discovered experimentally that it is possible to determine the molecular weights of many solutes by the freezing point depression method. Three years before the dissociation theory was disclosed by Arrhenius, Raoult noticed that certain substances, such as salts, act the same as a solution of the radicals making up the salts. Raoult's chief contribution came from the study of vapor pressure lowering which led to his formulation of the law bearing his name.

JACOBUS HENDRICUS VAN'T HOFF (1852–1911): Professor of Chemistry in Amsterdam and later in Berlin. He developed a theory of the asymmetric carbon atom in 1874. Work with the problem of mass action led to his famous reaction isotherm relation. His analysis of the behavior of dilute solutions resulted in his theory of osmotic pressure. He was considered one of the leading physical chemists of his time. He received the first Nobel prize in chemistry in 1901.

INDEX

ABCDEFGHIJ–M–7543210/698/0